The word "nigger" is one of t…
dehumanizing, and offensiv…
However, I will use the tern…
when appropriate. To remo…
would present an inaccurat…
account of the past, but it is…
should remain. Rev.…

To Gizelle Noel
very beautiful young
lady
[illegible]
04/24/08

VICTORY AFTER THE FALL

VICTORY AFTER THE FALL

Memories of a Civil Rights Activist

H. K. MATTHEWS

WITH

J. MICHAEL BUTLER

NEWSOUTH BOOKS
Montgomery | Louisville

NewSouth Books
P.O. Box 1588
Montgomery, AL 36102

Copyright © 2007 by J. Michael Butler
All rights reserved under International and Pan-American Copyright Conventions.
Published in the United States by NewSouth Books, a division of NewSouth, Inc.,
Montgomery, Alabama.

Library of Congress Cataloging-in-Publication Data
Matthews, H. K. (Hawthorne Konrad), 1928-
Victory after the fall : the memories of a civil rights activist / H.K. Matthews
with J. Michael Butler.
p. cm.
Includes bibliographical references and index.
ISBN-13: 978-1-60306-000-4
ISBN-10: 1-60306-000-6
1. Matthews, H. K. (Hawthorne Konrad), 1928- 2. African American civil rights
workers—Florida—Biography. 3. Civil rights workers—Florida—Biography. 4.
African American political activists—Florida—Biography. 5. African Americans—
Civil rights—Florida—History—20th century. 6. Civil rights movements—Florida—History—20th century. 7. Florida—Race relations—History—20th century.
8. Escambia County (Fla.)—Race relations—History—20th century. 9. Pensacola
(Fla.)—Race relations—History—20th century. I. Butler, J. Michael. II. Title.
F316.23.M38A3 2005
323'.092'396073—dc22
2005004974

Design by Randall Williams
Printed in the United States of America

To Lucy Purifoy Johnson

To Karen

Contents

Preface

H. K. Matthews

The writing of *Victory After the Fall* has been a three decades-long odyssey. I began to seriously consider documenting my life experiences after I moved to southern Alabama in 1978. It seemed that everyone I encountered was familiar with my civil rights activities in Pensacola because of the press coverage they received. I felt famous, or infamous, depending on the individual I encountered, because my story was well known. In the early 1960s, I helped organize a sit-in movement in downtown Pensacola. I participated in the first attempted Selma to Montgomery march on March 7, 1965, which later became known as "Bloody Sunday." I served as president of both the youth and adult branches of the Pensacola NAACP. I brought the SCLC to northwest Florida and served as its first president. I exposed the misuse of Confederate imagery at Escambia High School during its earliest stage of integration. I organized black Pensacolans in protest of a police shooting of a young, unarmed black man. And I was imprisoned for a crime that I did not commit. Nearly everyone I met after my relocation to Brewton, then, asked the same question: "H. K., when are you going to write a book?" *Victory After the Fall* is the answer to those many inquiries.

The completion of this book, though, was never a forgone conclusion. I once possessed two scrapbooks of newspaper clippings, both of which recorded my struggle for racial justice, and I hoped to use them as the basis of a future autobiography. However, during my first trip to the Florida state penitentiary, some correctional officers at the prison tore one to pieces in front of me. It was as if the sacrifices that I made on the behalf of human dignity had been destroyed; a personal history of the civil rights movement in Northwest Florida ripped apart. As the years passed, I asked a few individuals if authoring my memoirs interested them. All said yes, but I had very little documentation to use for the project and heard nothing else from them. I had almost given up hope of ever recording my story until I received a call in the autumn of 2000. A young man named J. Michael Butler contacted me and requested an interview for his history dissertation from the University of Mississippi. I had no idea what to expect and cautiously scheduled a thirty-minute interview for October 27, 2000. We talked for well over three hours.

As it turned out, a significant part of Mike's dissertation concerned the Pensacola movement. My phone number and address are not listed in the telephone directory, so he called a list of individuals he had accumulated who were involved in the local struggle, interviewed them, and eventually found someone who had my contact information. Simply put, meeting Mike was a God-send. He possessed a plethora of newspaper articles and numerous other research materials concerning my ordeal that I had not seen in years. He was also very insightful and quite familiar with the time line and events concerning the Pensacola movement, as I realized during our first interview. We talked several more times in the coming weeks and I asked if he would be interested in writing my story. He assured me that he was and seemed genuinely excited about the opportunity. After he completed his dissertation in May 2001, we began our long journey together. Several interviews and countless hours later, *Victory After the Fall* has become a reality.

The title of the work summarizes my life journey. I worked hard for a cause that is just, hit the lowest point in my life as a consequence of my activism, and experienced redemption and true victory as time elapsed. I was the only individual in the entire Pensacola struggle sent to prison, and it was for a nonexistent felony. After my release from the Florida state penitentiary, I lost everything. I had no job, no money, and no friends. The only person I believed was on my side was God Himself, but I was beginning to wonder if He too had forsaken me. People that I had nearly given my life for refused to speak to me, or give me a minimum wage job for fear of how it would make them look to those who hated me. People that I had nearly given my life for enjoyed their rights because of the protests I organized, but they treated me as a social leper. I became bitter and angry. I pledged to never again fight for the rights of others. I left Pensacola a broken man. But that is only half of my story.

After I moved to Brewton, I started a new family with a wonderful woman. I became pastor of a church that was aware of my past and proud of the sacrifices that I made on behalf of God's children. I made new friends, earned their respect, and gained their trust. And I regained my desire to help those in need, which is why God put me on this earth. My love for and trust in humanity was reborn in Brewton, Alabama. As the years transpired, individuals and organizations have recognized what I have done for the citizens of Escambia County, Florida. Among the numerous accolades I have received, I have been called "the Martin Luther King" of Pensacola, given a key to the city, and had a day proclaimed in my honor. The awards and recognition continue to come in, and they further validate what I now fully realize: I have experienced victory after the fall.

Yet this book is about more than my personal redemption. It is also an inside account of the Pensacola civil rights movement. I have heard too many rumors and untruths concerning black activism in the 1960s and 1970s in northwest Florida, and I want to provide an African-American perspective concerning the long struggle. My experiences reveal a much more complex movement than most realize. The story of the black struggle for racial justice has no clearly defined groups of heroes and villains. Simply put, not all white people were bad and not all black people were good. Some whites silently supported our movement while some blacks conspired to undermine our demands for human equality. Social class also played an important role in the local struggle. Some upper-class blacks proved to be some of my harshest critics because they had the most to lose from our so-called "rabble rousing," while wealthy whites frequently granted our demands because black protests hurt their businesses. In addition, the national branches of the NAACP and SCLC intervened in the Pensacola movement only to a limited degree. When local leaders, particularly me, most needed their help, the help was not there. *Victory After the Fall*, therefore, is a much-needed narrative of the

Pensacola movement and all of its intricacies.

I also wrote this book to leave an account of the social, political, and economic difficulties blacks encountered in decades past. I want young African-Americans, in particular, to know where they came from so they can fully appreciate the rights they currently enjoy and often take for granted. For instance, most people do not know what it is like to be denied service at a restaurant because of the color of their skin. They do not know how it feels to pass restrooms labeled "whites only" while they search for one that accommodates blacks. They do not know how it feels to be bussed to schools where they are an unwanted minority. Thank God that those days are in the past. However, it is important to understand that individuals of previous generations did endure those indignities and fought to have them permanently changed. The youth of today can not fully appreciate the freedoms they possess unless they understand the sacrifices others made to secure those liberties.

It would be impossible to name all of those to whom I am indebted for their spiritual and intellectual support throughout the course of my trials and tribulations. There are simply too many who offered encouragement throughout the years to name individually. Each person who has contributed to this work has my heartfelt gratitude. There are some individuals, though, who merit special consideration. I am deeply indebted to the writer of this work, Dr. J. Michael Butler, for his dedication and untiring commitment in pulling the book together. It is because of his desire to preserve history that *Victory After the Fall* has finally become a reality. My wife, Bobbie, and our children, Chris and Drayon, provided the love and support that sustained me along the way when I became discouraged and believed that this project was an exercise in futility. They will never fully understand how much they have influenced the completion of these memoirs.

I would be remiss if I did not mention two former co-workers from Jefferson Davis Community College, Connie Branch and Kathleen Hall, who constantly encouraged me to press forward with the writing of *Victory After the Fall*. Janice Thomas, an employee at Regent's Bank in Brewton, also demonstrated a remarkable amount of interest in this project and never failed to ask about its progress. Several members of the African Methodist Episcopal Zion connection supported me from the time I accepted a position in the Brewton District, but Bishop John Henry Miller and Bishop Cecil Bishop never failed to provide encouragement for both my religious and secular activities. My current bishop, James E. McCoy, has also supported me in every possible way. Others in the religious community who stuck with me through thick and thin are the late Rev. William "Bill" Marshall, Bishop Nathaniel Jarrett, Bishop Marshall Strickland, the late Bishop Milton Williams, Rev. James French, and Rev. Ezekiel Washington. Rev. Claude Shuford was the individual most responsible for two honors I received from the International Ministerial Association, including the Paul Robeson Award. I am tremendously thankful for the efforts he made on my behalf.

There are also many people who supported me during the height of my activism in Pensacola that I must mention. In particular, three people stood by my side when I most needed them without giving a single thought to the consequences that could have accompanied such decisions. During a time when many black public officials disparaged civil rights activism, Elmer Jenkins exhibited no fear. He was a former member of the Escambia County School Board and worked at Pensacola Junior College as a Biology professor, but he never missed an organized demonstration or planned march. When someone fired a shotgun through my home, Michael Jackson sat up night after night with a shotgun in his lap to ensure that I received adequate rest. LeRoy Boyd was one of my closest associates from the time that I organized the Pensacola NAACP Youth Chapter and was a consistent presence in the local movement. I will never forget any of their unselfish actions.

There was a time when the *Pensacola News Journal* did all it could to criticize or undermine public support for the Pensacola civil rights movement in general and me in particular. Thankfully, those days are long gone because of individuals like Reggie Dogan and Troy Moon. They have addressed the area's past racial history and the current state of local race relations in a very honest manner. I have nothing but the utmost respect for their bravery and journalistic integrity.

Another individual who deserves my utmost gratitude is Dan Benboe, the owner of Benboe Funeral Home in Pensacola. In 1998, he paid the entire cost for a bronze bust of my likeness that the Kwanzaa Committee of Pensacola presented in my honor. It is now located at the Leigh Library on the Jefferson Davis campus in Brewton. The former president of JDCC holds a special place in my memories. George McCormick took a chance and hired me to work at the institution in a position where I could help others and retire comfortably, in spite of the protests of some influential Brewton residents. His successor, Dr. Sandra McLeod, also supported my activities on and off of the college campus. Mrs. Dorothy Tillman, an alderman for City of Chicago, has always been a staunch supporter of my civil rights work and issued a formal proclamation from the city that recognized my contributions to the national movement. Ellison Bennett and Edward Broughton, former presidents of the Escambia County branches of the SCLC and NAACP, respectively, always included me in events that occurred in Pensacola long after I left the state. Again, those named in this acknowledgment are by no means all who inspired me during the course of comprising this book. God bless them all.

Of all the people who have inspired me, the one who had the most impact on my life was Lucy Purifoy Johnson, my grandmother. Words can not begin to describe what she taught me and how she influences me to this very day. It was my grandmother who instilled in me, as a child, a spirit of perseverance that is a consistent feature of my life's work. Without her, there would be no *Victory After the Fall*. It is to her, then, that this book is dedicated.

Introduction

J. Michael Butler

On February 24, 1975, approximately five hundred blacks gathered at the Escambia County, Florida, sheriff's department in Pensacola to demonstrate against what they considered a grave injustice. Two months earlier, Deputy Douglas Raines shot and killed a young black named Wendel Blackwell from a three-foot distance. Despite the existence of significant evidence that suggested foul play, a local grand jury quickly declared the incident "justifiable homicide" and the local sheriff, Royal Untreiner, refused to take any disciplinary action against Raines.[1] The incident represented the latest in a series of conflicts between the local white power structure and black residents, who had grown increasingly frustrated with their social and economic marginalization in northwest Florida. Rev. H. K. Matthews, president of the county Southern Christian Leadership Conference (SCLC) and the individual area blacks recognized as their primary leader and spokesperson, organized a series of nonviolent demonstrations that reminded many of the previous decade's civil rights campaigns. Blacks routinely gathered on the county sheriff's department's front lawn, carried protest signs, sang familiar spirituals, chanted popular slogans, and prayed. The demonstrations that Matthews coordinated had occurred nearly every evening for the previous two months, and the February 24 protest did not deviate from earlier patterns. Matthews knew that the sheriff's department's patience with the demonstrations had grown thin, but he did not anticipate the severity of their retribution.

The crowd that formed on the twenty-fourth was in jovial spirits. They conversed with deputies, joked with each other, and sang uplifting religious choruses. As he had done numerous times on previous evenings,

Rev. Matthews addressed the crowd through a bullhorn. He repeated black grievances through the amplifier—they demanded the termination of Raines, for starters—and led the assembly in prayer. Another minister then took the horn from Matthews and led the crowd in the same mantra that he had conducted at earlier demonstrations: "Two, four, six, eight, who shall we incarcerate? Untreiner, Raines, the whole damn bunch!" Soon after the chant ended, seventy nightstick-wielding deputies moved into the crowd. They arrested forty-seven blacks on misdemeanor charges, including Rev. Matthews, but three days later added felony extortion counts to the charges against him and another individual. The case went to trial four months later and an all-white jury found the two men guilty of the felony counts. Deputies testified that Matthews threatened to "assassinate," not "incarcerate," the county sheriff and deputy, which explained the extortion charges. While his accomplice received probation, a judge sentenced Matthews to five years of hard labor in the Florida State Penitentiary.[2] The controversial sentence crippled the once-vigorous civil rights movement in northwest Florida.

Despite its far-reaching ramifications, the felony extortion trial is just one episode in the eventful life of Rev. Hawthorne Konrad Matthews that deserves attention. The African Methodist Episcopal (AME) Zion minister dedicated the majority of his adult life fighting for the equal treatment of blacks in Florida, Alabama, and Mississippi. Matthews became involved with the Escambia County black direct action protest movement since its early 1960s origins. By the middle of the decade, Matthews had become the primary organizer and unquestioned leader of the local civil rights struggle. He endured thirty-five arrests for his activities and suffered considerable personal, professional, and financial loss because of his commitment. In addition, most of his activities occurred during the 1970s, a decade that many civil rights historians have previously ignored. The Matthews story, therefore, is a historically important and inspirational tale of sacrifice, suffering, and moral courage during a watershed period in American race relations. Yet it is also much more. For scholars, Matthews's life reveals several elements that contribute to a more complete understanding of the era. Three themes, in particular, stand out in a detailed account of Matthews's role as a local civil rights leader.

First, his activities as spokesman for blacks in northwest Florida expose much about the development of other local movements throughout the South during the same period. For instance, Matthews organized local demonstrations within the framework of national civil rights organizations such as the National Association for the Advancement of Colored People (NAACP) and the SCLC. Yet he utilized elements from each organization that best suited the struggle in northwest Florida, and often conflicted with executive leaders from each group concerning his tactics. In short, Matthews used each organization for their usefulness on a local level rather than joining them for a broader, national purpose. The leadership role H. K. Matthews held also magnifies the tensions that existed within the black community during the height of local civil rights activism. Matthews repeatedly states that although Pensacola blacks faced tremendous resistance to their demands from the white community, their most daunting challenges came from local upper-class blacks that both directly and indirectly opposed their activities. In addition, Matthews faced difficulty persuading many adults to join the local protest movement due to their economic dependence upon white employers. The reluctance of adults to join the emerging freedom struggle encouraged Matthews to lead the Pensacola County NAACP Youth Chapter in the early 1960s. Consequently, the minister relied heavily upon young people for the duration of his civil rights work in northwest Florida. The experiences of H. K. Matthews, then, reveal interesting details concerning the civil rights movement in Florida's panhandle that historians can use to understand the national black freedom struggle more completely. The importance of the local movement in comprehending a greater campaign, though, is only one reason Matthews's story is historically significant.

Another crucial detail that the life of H. K. Matthews exhibits is the centrality of Christianity in area freedom movements. Religious faith is inseparable from the Escambia County civil rights movement. Historians have noted the importance of the black church in many local freedom struggles. As Aldon Morris states, "The black church functioned as the

institutional center of the modern civil rights movement." Yet scholars
rarely go beyond the importance of the institution as an organizing
mechanism for the black community.[3] In Pensacola, to be sure, several
churches provided local leaders, participants, and gathering places to the
area movement. But the importance of the church goes much farther
in understanding the Escambia County struggle. The Christian faith
provided Matthews with the ultimate goal of his activities, which was for
local whites to recognize the dignity of all human beings. To Matthews
and his supporters, racial hatred violated the basic humanity of every
citizen because God created all individuals as equals. Discrimination,
Matthews reiterated repeatedly, violated both God's will and the United
States Constitution, in that order. He intentionally characterized the
movement he led as one for every disenfranchised citizen in northwest
Florida, and not just black residents. Matthews and his supporters reached
out to the poor and oppressed of all races and described their grand
purpose as redistributing political and economic power to the social "un-
derdogs." Local demonstrations possessed a tone of moral righteousness
and resembled religious services more than political gatherings. Divine
principles, therefore, inspired H. K. Matthews, guided the civil rights
movement in Escambia County, and underscored the indispensable role
Christianity played in one local struggle.

Finally, and perhaps most importantly, Matthews's activities reveal
several interesting aspects of the black freedom struggle after the 1960s
ended. Historians have begun to trace the civil rights movement to its
pre-twentieth century origins, but seldom examine its development after
the 1968 death of Rev. Martin Luther King, Jr. Although King represented the most visible national spokesman for racial justice, he by no
means represented the most important activist in many Southern locales.
Likewise, the fight for black equality continued after King died. In fact,
the 1970s is a crucial period in understanding the accomplishments
and shortcomings of the previous decade's struggle. The experiences of
H. K. Matthews illuminate many elements of the 1970s movement.
Combating *de facto* segregation and economic injustices proved the most
daunting challenges the Pensacola movement faced after the 1960s ended.

Matthews's campaigns helped to effectively end *de jure* segregation in the area during the 1960s, but racial injustice still plagued the Florida panhandle into the subsequent decade. The divide that separated whites and blacks surfaced in 1973 during disputes concerning the Confederate imagery a local high school utilized, and resurfaced a year later when a white sheriff's deputy shot and killed a young black motorist. Racial hostilities culminated in the February 24, 1975 arrest of Matthews and several of his followers. The leaders' imprisonment on fraudulent felony charges rendered the local movement impotent and resulted in his eventual relocation to southern Alabama. Yet the Pensacola ordeal is of greater importance in understanding the limitations black leaders faced in the era following Dr. Martin Luther King's death. Blacks and whites remained divided when the 1960s ended; racism continued to exist into the new decade and increased as it progressed. Whites in northwest Florida, in particular, resented the legal gains civil rights activists had achieved in the 1960s and despised individuals who openly questioned the racial status quo. H. K. Matthews continued to protest white supremacy in the 1970s, which infuriated white leaders who believed they had done enough over the past years to accommodate area blacks. Matthews continued to utilize the protest techniques he and countless other civil rights leaders had used during the previous decade to bring attention to black grievances, including nonviolent direct action protest demonstrations, organizing mass meetings at local churches, selective buying campaigns, downtown marches, and requesting assistance from national civil rights organizations. White leaders, however, reacted to the activities much differently than they did in the 1960s.

The white power structure in Escambia County did not condone the use of violence against the demonstrators or encourage whites to take their frustrations out on black protestors. In fact, they openly opposed the emergence of a Ku Klux Klan chapter in the panhandle. Yet the repudiation of vigilante tactics to combat black dissent did not mean that white resistance to racial equality had abated. On the contrary, resistance to civil rights demands grew as intense as ever during the 1970s. White leaders just developed alternative ways of silencing black leaders during the decade. White public officials used numerous legal methods, including court injunctions, arrests, and imprisonment, to crush black activism. Matthews requested legal aid from both the NAACP and SCLC, but each group either avoided or withdrew from the local movement at critical junctures due to the degree of white legal pressures in the area. After Matthews's arrest and five-year sentence in Raiford State Penitentiary, many blacks abandoned the local movement for their own protection. The example had been set; local whites would do whatever they could to silence black protest in the 1970s. The black community in northwest Florida either disengaged from local civil rights activity entirely or remained completely silent concerning racial discrimination in the area. The arrests, trials, and imprisonment of H. K. Matthews provides valuable insight into the challenges civil rights leaders faced after the movement lost King. Indeed, a new period in the continuing struggle for racial equality had began. Matthews's story, therefore, is historically important because of the grand themes it reflects about the American civil rights movement. Yet the life of H. K. Matthews reveals many intriguing details about the twentieth century Southern black experience, and his memoir is divided into ten chapters that accentuate a number of fascinating themes.

The first chapter, "Origins and Inspirations," covers the activist's early years. H. K. Matthews was born on February 7, 1928 in Snow Hill, Alabama. Snow Hill, located in Wilcox County, was an interesting community during the era because most of its black residents worked as self-sufficient farmers who had relatively limited contact with whites. One of the most fascinating aspects of the initial chapter is Matthews's recollections of the thriving black social, religious, and cultural environment in Snow Hill. Of particular interest is his description of Snow Hill Institute, a secondary school that his granduncle, Rev. W. J. Edwards, began in the late nineteenth century. Edwards wanted the Institute to resemble Tuskegee Institute but focused the school curriculum on liberal arts, as well as technical instruction. Matthews's four years at Snow Hill Institute profoundly effected his later life and provides historians with an interesting account of a thriving black learning institution during the pre-World War II era. Another important aspect of the first chapter is that Matthews identifies his grandmother as the most influential person in his young life. Lucy Johnson, a teacher in the county's segregated schools, raised H. K. from a young child and taught him the values that he later applied in his civil rights activism. Matthews states that his earliest encounter with racism involved his grandmother and a segregated bus in nearby Camden, Alabama. He, like many later black leaders, never forgot the humiliation Jim Crow brought upon a respected loved one.

The second chapter, "Awaking a Sleeping Giant," traces the evolution of Matthews's social consciousness. He traces much of his personal growth to the time he spent in the United States Army, which he joined in 1950 while still enrolled at Alabama A&M University. Matthews later served in the Korean War. The experience of serving in an integrated unit represented a crucial period in Matthews's young life. The Korean War marked the first time that American soldiers served in integrated units and the conflict inspired many blacks to question the existence of Jim Crow after their release and return to the American South. Yet the war also marked the first time that Matthews had significant exposure to people of different races and separate cultural backgrounds. He soon realized that a person's race proved irrelevant while fighting a common enemy, and his combat experience further convinced him of the equality of all individuals. After leaving Korea, Matthews experienced integrated life at Fort Devins, Massachusetts. He returned to Snow Hill in 1954, but possessed few ambitions and drifted aimlessly between jobs and relative's homes in Snow Hill and Escambia County, Florida. He also developed a drinking habit that he placed above all concerns. In 1959, though, Matthews experienced a life-changing religious conversion and, soon thereafter, became a minister in the AME church.

One of the first individuals to mentor the new minister was Rev. William Curtis Dobbins, a man who had moved to Pensacola in 1959 and used his faith to question the subordinate social position of blacks in northwest Florida. Matthews, who noticed the discrepancy between fighting for his nation overseas and being treated as a second-class citizen in his own hometown, joined a local organization Rev. Dobbins formed to combat segregation called the Pensacola Council of Ministers (PCM). From the beginning of his public life, Matthews linked the secular and the sacred in his fight for social justice. His religious conversion and membership in an organization that consisted entirely of ministers combined social activism with concepts of divine appointment. During the same period, Matthews also joined the NAACP and became president of its Youth Council.

Chapter three, "Building Momentum: The Sit-ins, Selma, and Youthful Enthusiasm," begins with a description of the 1961 Pensacola sit-ins and downtown boycotts, the most important activities the PCM organized during its existence. The PCM and NAACP Youth Council worked together to stage a series of sit-ins and boycotts in downtown stores that depended heavily upon black customers but retained segregated dining areas, water fountains, and restrooms. The protestors encountered tremendous resistance from area whites, particularly law enforcement officials. Matthews's account of the planning, development, and resolution of the sit-ins provides a wonderfully detailed account of how one Southern protest movement succeeded from the perspective of one who organized the campaigns. Soon after the struggle to integrate public facilities in Pensacola ended, Dobbins left the city and Matthews became president of both the PCM and local NAACP.

The third chapter also discusses a crucial milestone for both the national civil rights struggle and in the evolution of H. K. Matthews's social consciousness. In 1965, Matthews responded to the call of Rev. Martin Luther King, Jr., for activists to descend upon Selma, Alabama and participate in a march to support a voting rights bill. Matthews traveled to Selma, in part, because of his new role as a spokesman for the black community in Pensacola. He wanted to lead his people by example, yet had no idea what he would encounter in Selma. On March 7, 1965, Rev. H. K. Matthews crossed the Edmund Pettus Bridge when Alabama State Troopers and Dallas County sheriff's deputies attacked the peaceful crowd. Matthews provides a riveting account of the terror he and approximately three hundred others faced near the bridge as troopers mounted on horseback rode through clouds of tear gas to beat protestors with their clubs. Most importantly, Matthews relates how the experience inspired him to fight even more doggedly for civil rights in northwest Florida. How he chose to combat the remaining pillars of Jim Crow in Escambia County is the focus of chapter four.

In "The SCLC Comes to Northwest Florida," Matthews recalls how and why he began a chapter of the national organization in Escambia County. He remained a member of the local NAACP and served the group in several official capacities, but Matthews felt that the organization's bureaucratic structure frustrated its members and stifled direct action on the local level. Therefore, he joined the SCLC and became the association's first coordinator in northwest Florida. His recollections concerning the decision offer historians an interesting perspective on the two groups and their tactics from an individual who used each for different reasons. Matthews used both the NAACP and SCLC in the Pensacola civil rights struggle to integrate local public accommodations and obtain greater employment opportunities for local blacks. With the NAACP, Matthews relied primarily upon the enthusiasm of young members who belonged to the Youth Council. The SCLC, though, organized adults and ministers who previously belonged to the Council of Ministers, which dissolved after Dobbins left the area. In addition, Matthews used the SCLC to champion racial justice throughout the entire Florida panhandle. The SCLC proved less bureaucratic and more supportive of Matthews's activities for a variety of reasons, so he relied upon its assistance more than the NAACP in mobilizing civil rights crusades throughout northwest Florida. He traveled from Pensacola to Tallahassee in support of civil rights and worked in rural, isolated areas that remained strongholds of white supremacy. The confrontational tactics Matthews used to demand racial equality in the panhandle as leader of both the NAACP Youth Council and SCLC contributed to his growing reputation as a "trouble maker" and "rabble rouser" among area whites, while enhancing his standing as leader of the black community. On one such occasion, Matthews led several blacks into a segregated laundry and they placed one article of white clothing in each washing machine and dryer. The tactic had immediate financial effects upon the owners, who chose to close their business rather than integrate. Matthews told officers called to the scene that his group merely followed the instructions of a conspicuous sign that stated, "Whites only." Similar incidents solidified his popularity with local blacks while simultaneously infuriating whites.

Chapter five, "'Rebels,' Riots, and Freedom Schools: A Community Divided," summarizes the gains Pensacola civil rights activists made in several areas and introduces a new challenge Matthews and his followers faced as the 1970s began: the intimidation of black students at recently desegregated schools. This is an extremely intriguing issue because it provides insight into what happened in public schools after they integrated, an issue that historians often overlook. Although Matthews had to campaign against white harassment in schools throughout the county, his greatest challenge occurred at Escambia High School due to the inflammatory use of their school's Confederate nickname, symbols, and iconography. Matthews continuously maintains that blacks were not against the use of the symbols, but rather their misuse. Tensions surrounding the symbols peaked in 1973, as Matthews orchestrated a county-wide boycott of public schools by black students. During their protest, the SCLC established several Freedom Schools throughout Pensacola to educate participating students. The use of Freedom Schools beyond the 1960s is an issue that adds to local uniqueness in the northwest Florida civil rights struggle. The tactic proved successful and the county school board promised to examine their complaints if blacks returned to school. Upon their return, however, white students at Escambia High responded with violence and a riot engulfed the campus. School administrators called Matthews to the scene, where they told him that there would be no arrests. When he announced "No one is going to jail" to the nervous students through a bullhorn, deputies arrested Matthews on a felony charge of inciting a riot. Although an all-white jury acquitted Matthews of the charge, the arrest was the first serious effort of the local power structure to silence him. It would not be the last such attempt.

The Escambia High School symbols controversy produced another interesting aspect historians have previously neglected. In 1973, Matthews and several other black parents filed suit against the county school board seeking to ban usage of the Confederate flag, the "Rebel" nickname, and the Johnny Rebel symbol at the school. Circuit court judge Winston Arnow ruled the symbols "racial irritants" and ordered the local school system to abandon them. It set a legal precedent that subsequent controversies surrounding similar symbols rarely acknowledge. The chapter ends as racial tensions build in Pensacola during the following year. In chapter six, Matthews thoroughly explains the two incidents that brought blacks into direct conflict with the local power structure. It is appropriately titled, "December 1974: The Showdown Begins." The month represented the most pivotal four weeks in Pensacola's civil rights history. Matthews, the SCLC, and the NAACP had grown frustrated with white officials throughout their perpetual struggle against racial inequities in Pensacola. Whites, on the other hand, had tired of Matthews's constant criticism. In December 1974, each of these sentiments peaked. The first incident involved the drownings of five black male Atlanta natives in Pensacola's Santa Rosa Sound. The deceased's families contacted national SCLC president Ralph Abernathy with suspicions that local whites murdered their loved ones. Matthews initiated a local investigation of the incident for the organization and concluded that the men were murdered. National media attention focused on Pensacola while Abernathy and Matthews charged the local sheriff's department for, at the very least, withholding evidence concerning the drownings. Nightly mass meetings began at black churches throughout the area and their discontent mounted with each inflammatory discovery. Black attention soon focused on another incident concerning county law enforcement agencies. On December 20, a white sheriff shot and killed a young black male in Pensacola from a three-foot distance. The event increased local blacks support of Matthews, who organized nightly mass meetings and demanded the agency fire their deputy. Two separate grand juries ruled the drownings an accident and deemed the shooting "justifiable homicide." The decisions angered blacks and initiated a new stage in both the local civil rights movement and the life of H. K. Matthews.

Chapter seven, "The Arrests and Their Effects," discusses the protest activities Matthews organized following the December 1974 shooting and details his felony arrest and its immediate aftermath. Matthews increased SCLC organization of the local black community as 1975 began. Area blacks met on a nightly basis for over two months. In scenes reminiscent of protests that occurred throughout the region ten years earlier, blacks marched in front of the county sheriff's department and initiated a boycott of all stores in downtown Pensacola to bring attention to their grievances. Matthews and several supporters even traveled to Tallahassee and met with Governor Reuben Askew concerning the situation. On February 24, 1975, white restraint concerning the growing movement ended. Police moved into a peaceful gathering outside of the sheriff's department and dispensed it with force. Officers arrested Matthews and another man on felony extortion charges stemming from the "Two, four six, eight" chant. Although a third man, whom officers did not arrest, led the chant and used the word "incarcerate," deputies claimed that Matthews tried to extort the sheriff to dismiss an officer by threatening to "assassinate" the official. After the arrest of H. K. Matthews, civil rights activities in Pensacola slowly dissipated. Chapter eight details the subsequent trial and nadir of the Pensacola movement.

In "A Legal Lynching," Matthews describes his felony trial. The proceedings began on an ominous note. One prospective juror admitted seeing Matthews on television creating "a lot of agitation" in Pensacola. The man was later selected to serve on the body. Only two people testified on behalf of the defense, while eight deputies testified against Matthews. Although several of their comments contradicted each other and some openly perjured themselves on the stand in an attempt to condemn Matthews, the all-white jury found him and another black guilty of the two felony counts. Days later, a judge revoked Matthews's bond because the minister told a Pensacola reporter he would continue his fight for racial equality. The NAACP and SCLC national offices refused to support Matthews due to his controversial reputation, and area blacks abandoned the movement in fear. According to Matthews, local white leaders had finally fulfilled their promise to silence him. The available evidence substantiates Matthews's claim that a vindictive local justice system crushed the local civil rights movement. For instance, while the presiding judge sentenced the controversial Matthews to five years of hard labor in Raiford Penitentiary, the other man arrested on the same felony charges and tried simultaneously with Matthews received probation. The episode is of extreme importance in understanding the post-1960s Southern civil rights struggle. Matthews's tribulations demonstrate that blacks were not satisfied with the few gains they earned in the 1960s and that racism continued to exist in several forms. Most importantly, the trial, conviction, and imprisonment reveal that civil rights leaders often faced the retribution of angry whites when the media attention of, public interest in, and the federal government's concern for the Southern black plight eroded throughout the 1970s.

In chapter nine, Matthews recounts the costs he paid due to his activities. "The Fall" chronicles his prison stay and the reaction of the local black community to his incarceration. After the Florida Supreme Court ordered that Matthews be released on bail from the state custody, the disheartened minister experienced several setbacks upon his return to Pensacola. No one in the city hired him and many of the people he considered friends and supporters publicly repudiated him. The AME Zion Church eventually transferred him to Evergreen, Alabama, so he could pastor more churches. The decision to leave Pensacola devastated Matthews, yet his disappointments continued. The SCLC and NAACP refused to assist with Matthews's legal expenses, despite the fact that the SCLC declared him their "number one political prisoner in America" in 1978 and initiated a national fund-raising campaign in his name. Later the same year, Matthews applied for a second trial based on newly discovered evidence that exonerated him of the felony charges, but it was denied. He also appealed his conviction to the Florida Supreme Court, but it also denied his request. In 1978, Matthews spent another thirty-three days in state custody before Governor Reuben Askew commuted his sentence. During his incarceration, Matthews fully realized the sacrifice his efforts to gain black equality required when he learned that his wife had filed for divorce. The chapter ends on a note of uncertainty, as Matthews tells a gripping story of his personal and spiritual conditions after his release from prison. "The Fall" clearly establishes that H. K. Matthews paid a heavy price for blacks who expressed their dissatisfaction with the racial status quo in northwest Florida.

The final chapter begins on a morose note but ends triumphantly. "Victory" concludes the story of H. K. Matthews as one of perseverance, redemption, and the continued struggle for racial equality in the South. In 1979, the AME Zion Church once again transferred Matthews to a new congregation. He moved to Brewton, Alabama as pastor of the Zion Fountain AME Zion Church. The move represented a homecoming of sorts, as Matthews returned to and resumed civil rights activities in his home state. In the same year, Florida governor Bob Graham formally pardoned Matthews of all charges after the U.S. Supreme Court refused to hear his case on a technicality. Most importantly, though, Matthews remarried and started a new family in Brewton. He also began a new career as administrator at Jeff Davis Junior College and earned a promotion as superintendent of his AME Zion district. Matthews continued to work for racial equality in the 1980s and 1990s in southern Alabama and Pensacola, a city that Matthews considered home even after residing for over twenty-five years in Brewton. In his latter years, a new generation of Southerners recognized and honored the sacrifices and achievements of H. K. Matthews. He received numerous accolades in the late twentieth and early twenty-first centuries, including several Lifetime Achievement Awards from various organizations throughout the nation because of his civil rights activism. He was listed in the first edition of "Who's Who Among Black Americans" in 1975-76, received a city key from Pensacola in 1986, and witnessed the celebration of "H. K. Matthews Day" in Alabama, to name just a few of his honors. The Pensacola Kwanzaa Committee even preserved his likeness in a bronze bust. The life of H. K. Matthews, therefore, is one of "victory after the fall."

Matthews's memoirs are also important for historical purposes. There are many reasons why his experiences demand the interest of scholars, but three stand out as most significant. First, his role as what one journalist described as "Pensacola's Martin Luther King" contributes to the growing knowledge of local civil rights leaders and their activities that are unknown outside of their immediate regions of influence. Second,

Matthews's long fight for racial equality emphasizes the importance of Christianity in local movements. The faith, in other words, proved more important in the development of area civil rights struggles than the church itself and should be analyzed as such. Finally, the life and legacy of Rev. H. K. Matthews serves as a point of comparison for those interested in the post-1960s civil rights movement on the regional and local levels. On a more practical note, however, H. K. Matthews's life account reveals the importance of recording the stories of civil rights pioneers.

I first encountered the civil rights contributions of Rev. Matthews while conducting research for my dissertation at the University of Mississippi. In the school's federal documents collection I located a 1981 study by the United States Commission on Civil Rights study titled, "The Administration of Justice in Pensacola and Escambia County." Six paragraphs in the nineteen-page report sparked my curiosity. They summarized the February arrest and conviction of H. K. Matthews and concluded that his ordeal demonstrated to the community "that law enforcement officers could treat blacks as they wished and anyone who objected was inviting persecution by the authorities."[4] The conclusion intrigued me and I investigated the Pensacola movement more thoroughly. I rapidly discovered that racial tensions in Escambia County transcended the February 1975 incident. Blacks in northwest Florida panhandle had successfully protested Jim Crow laws in the 1960s using nonviolent direct action demonstrations and had continued their struggle against racism into the 1970s. The name that continuously appeared in the accounts as the leader of the local black freedom struggle was Rev. H. K. Matthews.

Initially, the *Pensacola News, Pensacola Journal,* and *Pensacola News Journal* served as my only sources of information. No one had written about the Pensacola movement and no archive or library possessed significant materials concerning the struggle, so my research was entirely original. It was an exciting yet daunting challenge, so I started my investigation with the local papers. The newspaper reports that I discovered, however, were tainted by the reporters' critical accounts of black activities. The articles clearly sympathized with white leaders, particularly law enforcement

officials. In short, I realized that journalistic accounts of the local civil
rights movement would not suffice as my primary source of evidence. I
decided that the oral histories of those involved in the struggle should also
serve as a pillar of my burgeoning study, and the person whose account
seemed most crucial in forging a more complete understanding of the
period was H. K. Matthews. Yet I knew very little about the man. I had
become familiar with his activities and ordeal through the newspapers,
and knew from the articles that he had left Pensacola in 1978 to pastor
a church in Evergreen, Alabama. I was not even sure that he still lived.
I contacted others involved in the local struggle during the 1970s and
listened to their account of events, which often differed dramatically
from contemporary reports of the same occurrences. I also pieced together the whereabouts of Rev. Matthews. I learned that he had moved
to Brewton, Alabama, after serving in Evergreen and remained an active
civil rights leader. His address and telephone number, though, did not
appear in area phone books or computer databases. I finally received
his contact information from LeRoy Boyd, the leader of a Pensacola
civil rights group called Movement for Change. Boyd belonged to the
Escambia County NAACP Youth Council when Matthews served as its
president and remained in close contact with his mentor. I nervously
telephoned Matthews and explained my project. I had relatives who lived
approximately eighty miles from Brewton, so I asked if I could interview
him in person. He agreed, and we selected a day, time, and place for the
interview to take place.

We finally met on October 27, 2000. The Reverend told me that the
interview could only last thirty minutes, as he had a meeting to attend.
As our conversation progressed, Matthews canceled the appointment and
we talked for over three hours. He wanted to read my finished study of
the Pensacola movement, and I happily obliged. Days after reading the
requested parts of my dissertation, Matthews telephoned me and asked
if I would write his memoirs. I was both humbled and honored for Matthews to choose me for a project that he had been contemplating for a
number of years. Yet I knew that it would require even more research
and hours of interviews. The fact that we lived about three hundred

miles apart provided an additional challenge. Yet from 2000 through 2003, I recorded nearly thirty hours of interviews with Rev. Matthews. We conducted the proceedings in person both in Brewton and Douglas, Georgia over a two-plus year period. In addition, I often discussed details with Matthews over the telephone and recorded all conversations in numerous pages of notes. I used newspaper articles, court records, police files, and his collection of personal papers to supplement and support his recollections of events that happened years ago. In addition to his own clippings and correspondences, Matthews also possessed approximately twenty hours of audio recordings of meetings and conversations related to his civil rights work during the 1970s. He provided me with access to the invaluable materials during the course of our joint project. The tapes verified much of the information he recounted, refreshed his memory in many instances, and presented a rare opportunity to listen as a community created history. Matthews read each chapter as I completed it, which often led to him remembering even more valuable details.

Throughout the course of this project, I have painstakingly researched every part of Rev. Matthews's story. I verified facts, clarified names, dates, and events, prepared thoughtful interview questions, and probed Rev. Matthews for more information when needed. I badgered the Reverend for thoughtful reflection and analysis when he believed his opinions and interpretations mattered little. Finally, I constructed a narrative from thousands of pages of primary documents and secondary sources. In other words, the shortcomings of this volume are all mine. Furthermore, this story is H. K. Matthews's recollection of his own life, and not a historical interpretation of his experiences. I have been fortunate enough to serve as the vessel through which he recalled his experiences, but Matthews represented the final authority on all items included in these pages. *Victory After the Fall*, therefore, is a story of moral courage that resonates with historical importance. Yet it also demonstrates the importance of collecting the stories of civil rights leaders before it is too late. A critical element of the civil rights movement in numerous locations is missing without the first-person accounts of those who led, organized, and participated in the struggles. Because he decided to share his experiences, therefore, the life of H. K. Matthews can now be placed in the pantheon of local leaders who dedicated their lives to fighting for the rights of others.

Victory After The Fall

Lucy Purifoy Johnson

I

Origins and Inspirations

I was born on February 7, 1928. My parents named me Hawthorne Konrad Matthews, but I have always gone by H. K. I do not know why they hung that long name on me, but I have lived with it. I was born in a little town in Wilcox County, Alabama called Snow Hill. Wilcox County is in the southern central part of the state, called Alabama's "Black Belt" because of its rich soil, and it is about seventy miles southwest of Montgomery. Dallas County borders Wilcox County to the north and Snow Hill is forty miles south of its largest city, Selma. My mother, Louveenia Johnson Matthews, passed away of tuberculosis when I was six weeks old. During that time, we were not aware of the treatments available for the sickness. My grandmother, Lucy Purifoy Johnson, began to rear me as her own son as soon as my mother died. She is the only mother that I ever knew anything about and remains my greatest inspiration to this day. I know nothing about my grandfather, who died before I was born. Grandmother always said he was a good man and a good provider.

My own father, John Henry Matthews, lived about twenty-five miles west of Snow Hill near Camden, Alabama. He was born and reared there, as were most of his relatives. He and my mother lived near Camden until she became ill. My grandmother took care of her until the disease took its toll. After mother passed away, my father remained in Camden. Years later he remarried and had three more children. As a child, I only saw my father a few times each year. He was a land-owning farmer who was always good to me when we were together. He always shared his produce with us, especially his watermelons and sweet potatoes. My granddaddy,

35

Charlie Matthews, was also a farmer who owned his own land. Most of my paternal relatives lived in a place five miles outside of Camden called Whisky Run. It got its name because the local residents had a lot of moonshine stills and did a lot of bootlegging. I have always loved my father but we have never been that close because of the physical distance. I was pretty close, though, to my grandmother's family. She had four boys and two girls, including my mother. I never knew Aunt Herma because she, too, died of tuberculosis when I was young. But I remained close to my uncles through their lives.

My uncles were named Thomas Edison Johnson, Clayton Johnson, Roscoe F. Johnson, and Albott Sidney Johnson. Uncle Sidney worked both as a Church of God pastor and carpenter until he passed away at ninety-three years old. All of my uncles graduated from Tuskegee except for Uncle Edison, who graduated from Alabama State in Montgomery. He became a teacher and was the first black pharmacist to serve in the Navy. Most of my uncles lived in Pensacola, Florida, except for my Uncle Clayton. He lived in Birmingham, Alabama. My grandmother lived in Snow Hill since her birth on January 7, 1878. That was home for her and she reared all of her children there. So I, too, grew up in Wilcox County.

Lucy P. Johnson made her living as a country school teacher. The Wilcox County Board of Trustees assigned her to teach in many different areas near Snow Hill. I attended elementary school wherever my grandmother taught for the year. Classes were usually held in older houses or churches. Before school started, the male students had to cut wood and start the fire in a potbelly stove that heated the building. During that time, blacks were not allowed to attend classes with whites. There were no buses available for to us ride, and at one point, my grandmother and I walked thirteen miles a day one way to go to school. Sometimes, if the weather was too cold or it was raining, we could catch a ride on the back of a wagon. White kids often passed us in buses while we walked to school. Grandmother told me we could not ride the bus or attend their schools, which were closer in distance to our home, because we were not the right color. I guess it never really hit me until later why this custom was so wrong.

The town I grew up in, Snow Hill, was a little village nestled between Camden and Montgomery, Alabama. A lot of people have asked me how the name Snow Hill came to be, and wondered if it snowed a lot. Well, it never snowed, but it was a hilly area where a lot of cotton grew. It was named Snow Hill because of the way the town looked when the cotton bloomed. The area, as far as African-Americans were concerned, was basically known for Snow Hill Institute. The Institute was an all-black boarding school that accommodated students from everywhere. As a matter of fact, Snow Hill Institute was founded by my grand-uncle, William J. Edwards, in 1893. The school was nicknamed "Little Tuskegee" because my grand-uncle was a very good friend of Booker T. Washington, and many Snow Hill graduates later attended college at Tuskegee. Mr. Edwards moved the school from a little wooden shack to two thousand acres in 1918 after he raised the necessary money from northern philanthropists. Snow Hill initially offered courses in fourteen different trades and Uncle W. J., as I called him, prepared young men and women to enter their community as productive workers. He wanted to end tenancy for local blacks and was pretty successful in doing so in the area around the school. He even started the "Black Belt Improvement Society" to uplift local African-Americans. Uncle W. J. retired in 1925 and died in 1950. Snow Hill Institute closed in 1973 due to a state desegregation order but reopened in 1980 as a performing arts center. The Springtree/Snow Hill Institute for the Performing Arts offers educational and cultural programs for children and adults throughout central Alabama.

Snow Hill possessed a substantial majority of black citizens when I lived there, most of whom taught or farmed for a living. They were pretty independent people who did not rely too much on any outside help, so Snow Hill was a pretty self-sustaining community. Most blacks made a living off the land that they personally owned. Very few rented from whites, which was quite unusual for that time. The black folks who worked for whites were employed at a local sawmill. They often found that when it came time for payday, they had very little money. That was because the mill had a commissary where their workers traded, and the man who owned the store would tell them that they only "broke even" for the week. The white man kept the books, so no black could ever prove him wrong. What he said went. I guess that is one of the instances where the pen is mightier that the sword. But the locals we associated with did not depend on whites for their livelihoods. They did not have to borrow from whites or buy on credit, either. Local blacks farmed, produced their own goods, sold them, and reaped the full benefits of their labor. There was no middle man to steal from them.

I personally did no farming and never even learned to plow. The only thing that my grandmother had was an average-sized garden. She planted snap beans, Irish potatoes, and things of that nature. I tried picking cotton once, but that did not work out at all. I was tremendously blessed because I was never exposed to any real hard work and my grandmother

Tattered and faded, this is the first known picture of H. K. Matthews. It was taken on his grandmother's farm in Snow Hill, circa 1936.

provided well for us. We lived in a big house with four bedrooms, a dining room, a living room, and a kitchen. We had outdoor premises because there was no running water inside our home. But I slept in my own room as I grew up. We had one great big piano in the living room, and a large hallway that was about six feet wide. I can remember the hallway because I used to ride my tricycle up and down it as a young child. We also had a big swing on the front porch. I would get in that swing or ride my tricycle and tell everyone who listened, "I am going to New York." My grandmother owned the house and quite a bit of land around it. We kept the land cleared off and had several fruit trees in the back yard. I spent much time as a child exploring Snow Hill on foot.

There was a community spring in Snow Hill where everyone would gather and wash their dirty clothes. Adults washed the laundry in big black iron pots on the grounds and hung their clothes on a community clothesline. The spring was located at the bottom of a steep hill near my house. It was not very far away, but it looked like it was. My grandmother did not wash there too often, but I loved going. I used to pray for rain, because they often washed in rainwater. A lot of times, though, grandmother would send me to the spring with big heavy buckets for me to fill up with water and carry up the hill to her. She used the water to fill up her washtub. That was an experience during the so-called "good ole days" that I never want to relive.

Local residents called downtown Snow Hill "the Station," because trains stopped there on their way through town. For recreation, my cousins and I, one of whom is the father of movie director Spike Lee, used to visit other relatives at the Station. We would all walk there to see them, and when we had to leave, they walked halfway back with us. Then we would turn around and walk halfway back with them. That was so dumb, but it was the kind of fun that we had. Most white people in the area lived close to downtown, but there were still a couple of black-owned businesses near the Station. One of my distant cousin's grandfathers, Isadore Lott, had his own grocery store. He sold vegetables, raised cows, and butchered his own beef. Isadore's store was the primary grocery for blacks at that time, but whites even traded with him. What we could not get at Isadore's store, we bought at another downtown black businesses. For the most part, there was little interaction between my family and whites in Snow Hill. If we went into a store where whites were present, we got what we needed and left. We were real respectful and used courtesy terms like "yes, sir," and "no, sir," because we knew we must. They were in control near the Station, but they were not in charge of the countryside near the academy. That was our turf.

When my grandmother and I went to the Station, we had to walk. We did not have any rural transportation, taxi cabs, or buses, and had no access to an automobile. It is amusing now, I guess, but I used to tote home our groceries in old fifty-pound flour bags my grandmother saved for such occasions. Uncle Isadore, as we called him, would fill up the bag, throw it across my shoulder, and we would go marching home. I can remember that when we got close to Snow Hill Institute, which was less than a mile from our house, I would sit on an old wooden bench under an oak tree. I was so tired from carrying those groceries that I would tell my grandmother, "I want to turn around and go back to the Station." She would say to me, "Baby, you are almost home now. There is no sense in turning around." This is what I tell people in the religious community; when you are going through so much and you feel like giving up and turning around, I quote my grandmother to them. I learned a lot during those days from her, including how wrong segregation really was.

My first experience with direct racism came on a bus that we boarded at the Station. My grandmother took me to see my father twice a year when school was not in session, and we rode a public bus to Camden for each visit. The roads then were rough and unpaved. We had to stand in the aisle if the segregated back area was filled when we boarded, and it often was, for people caught the same bus from Montgomery to Snow Hill. My grandmother and I often stood, even though there were empty seats at the front of the bus and the back seats were packed. We could not sit there because we were just the wrong color. Blacks were not allowed to occupy seats in the front of the bus. They were reserved for whites. Segregation on that particular bus was driver-enforced. There were no signs posted. I do not think there was a marked boundary or anything separating the sections. There were just so many rows of seats from the front to the back that were reserved for whites, and blacks were not allowed to sit in them.

So grandmother and I had to stand in the bus aisle, and she held onto a strap to keep us balanced. During that time, the bus had a strap that came down from the top railing for standing passengers to hold. My grandmother held the strap with one hand to keep from falling while holding a little nap-sack under her arm and clutching me with her other hand. The bus bobbed and weaved, and grandmother nearly fell several times. I then first thought, "We are human beings but can not sit down on this bus because of the color of our skin?" I looked up to my grandmother as tears formed in my eyes that day and asked, "Why is it, mother, that they treat us like they do?" My grandmother looked down at me and repeated one of her favorite sayings: "That's all right baby. Life is like a revolving wheel. Those who are on top today will be on the bottom tomorrow." On that day, the indignity of segregation really worked on me for the first time. I think it bothered me more to see my grandmother have to experience that than it was to have it happen to me, because I dearly loved my grandmother. She was my protector, she was my mentor, she was my everything. To see her standing there, holding on as the bus bobbed and weaved while seats were open was just too much to bear. I also recall that when the mailman came during the summer, my grandmother and I would sit around an old tree where all the mailboxes were located and wait on his delivery. The mailman always referred to her as "Auntie." To him, it meant "little girl," or something even more degrading. It was like whites never viewed blacks as mature adults. The injustice hit me when I saw racism directed toward my grandmother, but I never knew what to do about it. I just grew up with it, and lived with it.

When I reached the seventh grade I finally got to attend Snow Hill Institute. Although it was a boarding school, I lived at home with my grandmother until graduation because we were within walking distance of campus. Snow Hill was, like many of the area's African-Americans, self sufficient. The school owned a big farm and grew whatever was needed to feed the students who lived on the campus. The school even had livestock on the grounds. The students who lived in the dormitories, both male and female, came from places like Mobile, New Orleans, and other large Southern cities. They came because it was a good school with a great reputation. There were about six hundred students there when I attended. The Institute had several dormitories, a big administration building, a kitchen, a dining area, and a huge laundry on campus. Students tended the crops and washed their own clothes. There were some people that the school hired to farm the land, but most of the labor came from the male students. I learned one valuable lesson on the "Snow Hill farm."

During that time when I was in school, students could not smoke on campus. When anyone violated any rule, they were put to work on the farm. I have a large scar on my forehead that came from one of my transgressions. I was in the bathroom smoking with other boys, and a coach named Mr. Rhodes caught us. When I heard him coming I cuffed the cigarette and put it in my pocket. He asked, "Konrad, are you smoking?" I said, "No sir." He replied, "But your pocket is on fire." I received five days on the farm and had to dig a six-by-six ditch with the other boys. We had to line the ditch with big boulders and passed them down the line from one male to the next. I turned and passed the boulder to the young man that was standing next to me, and when I turned back to the right, the next rock caught me right on the forehead. The guy who tossed the boulder did not realize that I had not turned around to catch it earlier. Right now, I can hit that spot and it is still sore because it was never properly taken care of. This is what I mention when I tell people about forgiveness. People often say, "I'll forgive you but I can not forget." That is fine, as long as you do not remember with vengeance. I will always remember what happened to me and how it happened, but there is nothing to forgive because it was not done intentionally. And I don't remember the incident with a vengeance. That is the type of work we had to do on the farm if we were caught doing anything that we had no business doing. If the girls were caught doing something wrong, they had to work in the laundry. Boys had the fun tasks.

Snow Hill Institute offered a variety of different courses for its students. Male and female teachers instructed general studies classes such as English, Math, Chemistry, and History. We had an Agriculture instructor, but trades were rarely taught at Snow Hill. They had Home Economics classes where they taught sewing and cooking, but mostly girls took that class. Our Agriculture instructor was from Tuskegee, and his name was Mr. Brooks. I will never forget him. He used to eat garlic and belch all the time. We would say, "Excuse me," but he would reply, "There is no use saying it because I am going to do it again." I remember one day, toward the end of the term, I was sitting there watching Mr. Brooks work on his report. They did not have the technology that we have and he wrote it all out by hand. He had been working on the report and left the classroom for something. While he was gone, another boy and I began horse playing. We started wrestling and turned over a bottle of ink on Mr. Brooks's report. He came back to the classroom, saw the paper, and asked who did it. He had a leather strap that was attached to a wooden handle. The strap had five slits in its end that Mr. Brooks used for troublemakers. We called it "Five Finger Jim." He kept asking who did it and nobody would say anything. He said, "I'll tell you what. If nobody in here admits who did it, I'm going to assume that everybody did it and whip everybody." When he said that I thought, "Oh Lord, that's it. He's going to get us now." Sure enough, those other boys and girls pointed us out. Mr. Brooks got me and the other boy and whipped us with Five Finger Jim until we could nearly not sit down. He sent us back to our seats, looked at his ruined report, and whipped us again! I bet he whipped us three times that day. He is the one teacher at Snow Hill Institute that stands out in my mind because he did not play games. To show you the difference of the times, I was seventeen then. Try whipping a seventeen-year-old now in high school and either the student will kill you or the Department of Human Resources will end your career. After the whipping, I thought, "What is going to happen when I get home and my grandmother finds out about this?" I was scared to tell her, but I could not help it because she noticed that I was sore and moved slowly. When I told her what I had done, I got another whipping. Mr. Brooks was responsible for four whippings for me! Needless to say, no one had any more problems with me wrestling in class.

In 1947, I graduated from Snow Hill Institute at the age of nineteen. I should have graduated a year earlier, but my grandmother held me back a year because she did not think I learned enough that particular term. She wanted me to understand that I had to be serious about what I was doing. Because of her support, I was a good student. The school was a great place, a wonderful experience. It showed blacks how to provide for themselves and provided a stepping stone for many to Tuskegee Institute, due to the connections that my granduncle made between Snow Hill and Tuskegee. Everything that I was taught at Snow Hill Institute helped me later in life. I may not have agreed with the punishments at that time, but they were lessons like those I learned from my grandmother. I can remember her saying to me, "You may think that I am mean, but one of these days you will thank me for it. " She was not mean, and I never thought that she was. I never sassed my grandmother or talked back to her. I knew better. I knew what I would get. I remember that I once got to the point that I was not going to cry when my grandmother whipped me. She picked a switch off of a hedge bush, stripped leaves off of the switch until the ends were keen, and whipped me good. She would not whip my clothes either; she whipped all skin. I remember that I said to myself one day, "I'm gonna show her. She can whip me today if she wants to but I am not going to cry." She began whipping me and I refused to break down. She said, "You're not going to cry? Then I'll keep going." I said, "AAAAHHHHHHHHH!" and the tears started flowing. If that would stop her from whipping me, I thought, then I am going to cry right now! I learned a lot from her, even though I strayed from it later in life. Yet the Bible says to train a child the way it should go and when he's old, he will not depart from it. I strayed, but I did not depart from those values because grandmother taught them to me when I was young.

One of the things my grandmother stressed to me at an early age was the importance of church. I had complete and total exposure to the church as a child. I actually used the fact that I attended church so much as a child as an excuse for not attending while I was in the military. That was a stupid thought. My grandmother did not send me to church like parents do sometimes today. We went together and she was a good Christian. We attended a little Baptist church in Snow Hill called Brooks Chapel because it was located close to our home. My grandmother, I, and just about the entire community were members. The pastor's name was Rev. Davis, and it was one of the first churches I regularly attended. When we did not go to Brooks Chapel, we shared our time with a local Holiness church. The Holiness pastor's name was Rev. Dan House. I think Rev. House was the cause of me of not going to church for a certain time because when we went there, we would stay all day. At about one o'clock he would literally lock the doors and we stayed inside the church until about three o'clock in the afternoon.

The Holiness Church was more charismatic than the Baptist Church. It was more emotionally charged and the people there did a lot of expressive things. The people at Brooks Chapel became involved in the service and got caught up in the spirit, but never to the extent of the Holiness Church. The Holiness members did a lot of speaking in tongues and other charismatic stuff that my grandmother and I really did not understand. I think I might say this at the risk of sounding awful, but when some people speak in tongues they are just "playing church." I think that worship is serious business, and you do not go to church to see how emotional you can cause other people to become. You go to worship God; that is bottom line. If the service causes you to react in a certain way, fine, as long as it is real. I remained a member of the Baptist Church until I moved to Pensacola later in life.

I also attended the Methodist Church as a young man. Most of the churches at the Station were Methodist. It really did not matter to my grandmother and I. We just went to church. If they were not having church here, we would go to church there. We did not miss a week of church because one was open somewhere every Sunday. Sometimes at Brooks Chapel services were held twice a month, while the Holiness Church opened every Sunday. On the off-Sundays at Brooks Chapel, we might go to Rev. House's church. We might go for both Sundays in a given month. Then in some months, we would go out to the Methodists churches. Just wherever my grandmother decided she wanted to go, we went. We were going to be in somebody's church on Sunday morning. She emphasized that God was too good for us to stay home on the Sabbath. Going to church does not save you, but at least you fellowship with other Christians and express thanks to God for taking care of us. He has provided for us, so we should always give Him our time and a portion of our earnings.

It was not a drudgery for me to go to church. I enjoyed going. I did not like getting locked in until two or three o'clock, but I enjoyed the services. Grandmother and I also went to the revivals, which were called the "big meetings." I always recall the dinner on the first Sundays of those meetings. The food stretched from here to yonder, and most of the community attended. All of the food was put outside. During revival week, the church was packed each night. Those events influenced me to begin preaching as a young boy. I would stand on a crate under a big apple tree and deliver a sermon to my "congregation." Those in the community began calling me "the little preacher." On big occasions, I would speak to my friends at Snow Hill Institute from the steps that connected the administration and agriculture buildings on campus. I really preached the Gospel then. I went Holy on those folks! I guess I have been a preacher all of my life. I may not have acted like it as a young adult, but public speaking and leadership are gifts that have always been with me.

Everything that I have become that is positive, I attribute to my grandmother. She directed me in the right way. She reared me properly. I thought she was hard on me sometimes, but I never thought she was mean. I always thought that she was a loving grandmother. She made me the person I am today. Even though I strayed away when I went into the military, even though I did not want to go to anybody's church and did not go to anyone's church, and even though I loved the bottle, in the recesses of my mind, I could visualize her telling me that my life was not right. And I eventually came back to the values I learned as a boy in Snow Hill.

After I graduated from Snow Hill Institute in 1947, I decided to attend Alabama State University. Actually, my grandmother made those plans for me. I wanted to go to a college somewhere, and she suggested

Alabama State. I enrolled there in the fall of 1947 but did not stay long. My uncle, Chester Johnson, Sr., and his wife, Zenobia, ran the dining room at Alabama State. He was my grandfather's brother, but I did not want to be at any place where my kinfolk were. I was going through a wild phase in my life and did not want to be where people knew too much about me. I wanted to do only what I wanted to do, which was follow the crowd. I am not going to blame any of my actions on other people, though, because I was just as bad as they were. I did not want to do my schoolwork, but I still maintained passing grades. The problem was that Uncle Chester and Aunt Zenobia saw what I was doing and told me that I could do better. They constantly reminded me that I did not come to college to play. However, I had reached the age where I felt like they were interfering in my business. I had escaped the strict rules of my grandmother, which I appreciated, but I did not want anyone else telling me what to do. So I thought, "I'll show them. I'll leave this school." My grandmother was not really aware of why I wanted to leave Alabama State. I was lying to get away from my relatives and told her that I was running into some problems with other students. She was again my protector and tried to take care of me. She said, "If you are having problems and there is trouble, transfer to another school." Uncle Chester never told her about my actions, and I never told them why I transferred to Alabama A&M.

I went to A&M with the intention of doing what I did at Alabama State: partying. I was not enrolled even a year when I found out that one of my cousins taught at Alabama A&M. I felt lost and messed up, but realized that I could not run away from my problems. I thought, "If I go to Timbuktu I will find kinfolks there, so I might as well do what I came here to do." So I spent the remainder of my college career at A&M. I was still wild and did some stupid things, but I buckled down for my lessons. I probably would have eventually done the same if I would have stayed at Alabama State, because I liked school and never wanted to do anything to hurt my grandmother. That remained the most important thing to me: making her proud. My not wanting to hurt her kept me out of a lot more trouble than I found.

My major in college was English and my minor was History. I loved
those classes. I was always kind of dumb in Math, but I loved English
and History. My grades also improved after I enrolled at A&M. I had
some good educational experiences at the university, and nothing profoundly good or bad happened while I was there. I merely went to class
and received my education. I do have a few regrets, though, related to
college. As I look back over my life now, I just wish that I had gone to
law school. When I think about all of the court cases that I have fought,
both for myself and other people, I believe that I could have made a fine
lawyer. Another regret is that I never graduated because I instead enlisted
in the Army. After two years at A&M, I became restless and wanted to
go into the military. A lot of friends of mine joined, and I just knew
that during that Korean Conflict there was going to be a draft. The
military recruiters at the college also said that it would be easier on me
in the service if I volunteered, and they promised that I would be able to
decide where I would be stationed. That did not prove to be true. Still,
in 1951 a busload of students from A&M traveled to the Army recruitment center in Gadsden, Alabama, and we all joined. I signed up for a
two-year term of service and entered the Army on August 23, 1951.[5] I
had left school to be a soldier.

My first duty station was in Fort Chaffee, Arkansas. Fort Chaffee
was close to Little Rock, and I did my basic training there. When I
finished basic training at Fort Chaffee, I went to Fort Sill in Oklahoma.
I was deployed to Korea from Fort Sill. It was 1951 when I arrived in
Korea, and I stayed over there for one year. I saw a little bit of combat
in the conflict, but not a lot. The action I saw was limited because my
company was stationed toward the rear. I belonged to an artillery unit
and also served some time in the infantry. Even in the rear, though, I
saw some bad stuff happen. Land mines exploded, people got shot and
died. I even got hit by some shrapnel from a mortar round in my back
while I worked in the artillery unit. It was not a terrible injury, but it
did take me out of the field for a few days. I saw the most terrible things
from those who returned from the front lines. The ones that went above
the thirty-eighth parallel really caught it, but I never made it that far

Matthews in Korea, second from left, circa 1952. This is one of his favorite pictures because it includes white, African-American and South Korean soldiers he befriended during the conflict.

north. The Korean Conflict was not a good experience for me, but it was not as bad as what some of the other people had to go through. The interesting thing about that war was it was the first time the American military fought as an integrated force.

I basically had my first experience in interacting with the white race when I was in the military. I had contact with whites in Snow Hill, but my first real interaction with whites occurred in the Army while I served in a desegregated unit. I felt like black and white soldiers pretty much approached each other as equals because we were all in the same fix. Maybe we did not have a choice when it came to getting along because we had similar fears and had a job to do. There was some racial separation, but we were not dogmatically segregated. In fact, we slept in the same barracks and ate in the same halls. One of my favorite pictures is of me and three other fellow soldiers in Korea. One of us was black, one was South Korean, and two were white fellows. That picture shows what life there was like for soldiers, as far as interacting with each other. My impression of whites after dealing with them in the Army was that they were the same as me. It was something that I had felt all along, and my military experience confirmed it. The whites that I came in contact with in the military did not treat me any different from the way that they treated each other. We were in the same predicament, were in the same place, and were after the same results. Whether it was genuine or it was only on the surface, we just got along. So I really cannot say that I encountered any racism or much discrimination in the Army. A lot of subtle stuff happened, but that happens daily in every walk of life. I can not say that anybody who was white went out of their way to let me know that I was black.

After I left Korea, I came back to the states and was stationed in Fort Devins, Massachusetts. It is close to Ayers, Massachusetts, which is about thirty-five miles from Boston. Most of the soldiers on the base went to Boston every weekend, and I was among them. Boston was a big city that differed from Snow Hill in many ways. There was a seafood restaurant in Ayers, for example, where soldiers often ate, called the Chatterbox. I ate my first clams there. There was a lot to do in Boston and Ayers, while where I came from there was nothing to do. I learned there were things to do and different places to go when I went to Alabama A&M and Alabama State. I went to theaters and things of that nature in Huntsville while I was at college. It was a relief from the back woods of Snow Hill, but the bright lights I got accustomed to in Huntsville were not on the scale that I experienced in Massachusetts. We attended movies on base most of the time, but went to city theaters on the weekend. I noticed pretty fast that the restaurants and other public facilities in Boston were open to all races. In those areas, everything was integrated. Even though it may have been an uneasy integration, it was there. Black soldiers went any and everywhere we wanted to go. I could not help but notice that it was a more open society than in the South. Even Huntsville, which I thought was a big city and was very different from Snow Hill, was not integrated at that point. The racial differences of the North definitely had an impact on me. I could not help but allow it to open my eyes concerning the injustices and racial prejudice that existed in my home region.

After my initial two-year term in the Army expired, I re-enlisted for three more years. I finally got out of the army in 1955. After my stay at Fort Devins, I went to Yokohama, Japan and worked as a processor. I also spent some time in Virginia after my time in Japan ended, and processed a soldier named Elvis Presley. When my second enlistment term ended, I was ready to get out of the Army. I was discharged at the rank of Private on June 24, 1955.[6] I had served my time well but was glad to be free! I was discharged from Fort Jackson, South Carolina. I had no big plans when I got out of the military. I had no goals, no real purpose for my life; I was just ready to be a civilian again. I decided to go back to Snow Hill, live with my grandmother, and wait on something to happen. So that is what I did. I got out of the Army and returned to Alabama with my pride showing and my chest stuck out. It was like I was saying, "Look world, I am back." It did not take long for me to discover that the world did not even know that I had been gone. People were trying to get me to go back to college, but I did not listen to anyone. I did not do much of anything, including work full-time. I left Snow Hill only a few months after I came back because there was simply nothing for me to do there. I still had no idea what I wanted to do with my life, but I knew I needed to get out of Snow Hill. It was then that I decided to move to Pensacola, Florida.

2

AWAKING A SLEEPING GIANT

Pensacola has always been the largest city in Escambia County, which is in the panhandle in the northwest part of Florida. Escambia is bordered on the west and north by Alabama, on the east by Santa Rosa County, and on the south by the Gulf of Mexico. Pensacola is 225 miles east of New Orleans, Louisiana, and two hundred miles west of Tallahassee, Florida. The closest big city is Mobile, Alabama, about sixty miles to the northwest. When I was growing up, people in Wilcox County considered Pensacola a "big city." It was like the melting pot for Snow Hill, probably because it was a port city in a different state. All of my uncles but one lived there. They frequently visited my grandmother after they moved and I would be so thrilled because they had new cars. I did not see many of those where I grew up. I wanted to move to Pensacola one day, and did so not long after I got out of the Army. I needed to work and there was little available in Snow Hill. I left for Pensacola to work with my Uncle Sidney. He owned a grocery store and let me work and live with him and his family. I helped him in the store and drew unemployment compensation from the military. I had to travel to Camden, the county seat of Wilcox, once a month to pick up my pension. Although I lived in Escambia County, Florida, I remained listed as a Wilcox County resident for some time. My unemployment was called "twenty-six, twenty-six" because we got twenty-six dollars a week for twenty-six weeks.

Working with my uncle was not steady employment, because I only worked when he needed me. He also closed the grocery store not long after I moved in with him, so I started working with a moving and storage company called Ferris Warehouse. I called it a "work-a-day job." Every day I reported to the warehouse and asked if they had anything for me to do. If they did, I would work and leave the warehouse when I completed the task, sometimes after only one hour. I would work one day and hope I could do the same the following morning. I had no real aim in life then. It was a tough period because I was searching for myself. You see, I had also picked up a habit by the time I left Snow Hill. When I began college, I started to live a faster life. I was scared of the strap in high school and I respected my grandmother enough to obey her rules. I was a little hard-headed as a teenager, but the respect for and fear I had of my grandmother kept me in line. I could not be defiant at home, so I started doing my own thing when I went to Alabama State. I was not terribly defiant, but I did rebel by drinking and partying. I smoked and drank all through my college and army career, but began drinking even more heavily when I moved to Pensacola.

By the time I started working at Ferris Warehouse, I was only concerned with my next bottle. In fact, I was working just enough to buy more liquor. In retrospect, I was nothing but a drunk. I just loved it because it seemed good to me. I reported to work at the warehouse full of liquor, and kept my job just so I could keep drinking. I even worked outside of my day job if I had to. Then I would wake up and do it all over again. I drank every night and every day, and I was not picky about what I consumed. I drank anything that I could get my hands on. My bare minimum was a pint of liquor and a quart of beer every day, and it did not matter if I had to beg, borrow, or steal to get it. My life simply revolved around the bottle. I eventually moved out of my uncle's house because I did not want to cause him grief because of my actions. Uncle Sidney was a Church of Christ minister and I did not want to hurt his reputation. I guess I still had some sense, despite the drinking. But I did not want to stop my activities, so I rented a room at a Pensacola boarding house. The folks that I lived with were living the same way I did; they drank all of the time, too. By 1956, I had left the boarding house and moved in with a friend who was in the Navy. He let me live with him and his wife for free if I baby-sat his children during the day.

I took the job because my other work was so slow. I kept my warehouse job, though, to supplement my drinking money. The couple I lived with did not care. They were drinking. I was drinking. We were all drunks together. I stayed there until I married Mary Lee Posey in 1957, with whom I had a son in 1950.

After my marriage, I still worked day-to-day jobs. Sadly enough, my drinking did not slow down at all. For two years, even with a new family, I just worked enough to support my habit and continued to hang out at the local bars. Mary and I lived with my mother-in-law, Josephine Posey, in Pensacola. She was a good woman and always treated me like a son. She died in 1970, but my family lived at that house until I left the city in the late 1970s. I did take a job at Baldwin Dairy in Pensacola after I married. I needed the extra income because we added a room to our home and had a monthly fifty-dollar mortgage for the addition. I also began attending school to collect eighty dollars a month under the G.I. Bill, which paid my rent. I took business classes at Washington Vocational School at night. I was interested in business because of my clerical experiences in the Army and knew I needed a career in something. The remaining cash, and anything left over from my dairy check after family expenses were covered, was all mine and I spent it on liquor. My wife never said much about my lifestyle. She would drink a beer every now and then, but she never went to the bars with me. That was my time, my activity, and she never asked me to quit. The drinking did, though, affect one member of my family.

I used to pass a ball field down the road from my house when I came home from the bars, usually drunk. One day I came home in my usual state, making one step forward and two steps backwards, and my son and his friends were playing ball in the vacant lot. One of the boys told Joe, "There goes your old drunk daddy." He got into a fight over the comment, which was not the first time he did so because someone made fun of me. It was sad, but I never paid any attention to what was going on around me in those days. It did not matter what my family thought about the drinking. I knew that my son was getting into fights and such, but the ridicule and humiliation he experienced simply did not register. That was not going to stop me from drinking. I had to decide on my own that the alcohol had to go. I finally made that decision on November 20, 1959.

My G.I. Bill check always came on the twentieth. In November, 1959, though, the twentieth came on Sunday and I received my check on the previous Friday, the eighteenth. I had already paid the mortgage with my Baldwin Dairy check, so the entire eighty dollars was mine to spend. I was determined to enjoy every cent. I started drinking that Friday night and drank all day Saturday. I was the type of person who, when I started drinking, I was just happy. I thought I had a lot of true friends, but I found out that everyone is your buddy as long as you have money and are willing to throw it away on them. By Sunday afternoon, I had seventeen dollars left. I had drunk sixty-three dollars worth of liquor. I then realized that I wasted all of that money. That Sunday night, the twentieth of November, 1959, I got in the bed and had a quart of Spearman beer sitting by me on the floor. I poured another glass of beer, held it up, and just stared at it. I did not say anything to my wife but thought, "When I drink this, I am not drinking any more." The next morning, I was back in the bar. I usually went to the same place every morning to refresh myself after drinking the entire night, but this time I only drank a 7-Up. From November 21, 1959, until this very day, I have not had a drink. I am not exactly sure why I decided to quit, but that was the end of my habit. People found out that I had quit drinking and they doubted I would stay sober. Someone told my wife, "Just give him until Thanksgiving and he will drink." On Thanksgiving Day I went to the bar, but did not drink. Another person said, "Oh, just give H. K. until Christmas. He will drink then." But I proved them wrong. I never even wanted to drink since then.

The only thing my wife ever asked me to do with her was to go to church. She and my mother-in-law were members of Allen Chapel African Methodist Episcopal Church in Pensacola. Mary pestered me about attending services but my mother-in-law always told her, "Leave him alone. When he gets ready to go to church he'll go." On Sunday mornings when they prepared for church, I encouraged them to hurry and leave so I could fix a drink. I did not think that I had time for church and did not want to be bothered with it for some time. One Sunday morning, though, before I quit drinking, I decided to go to church with my family. I have been going ever since. I am not sure why I went to services that particular morning. It was similar to my drinking; I just made the decision to do it. At the time, I did only what I wanted to do. I thought that I was a happy person, but looking back, I realize that I was not. I thought that I was really enjoying life, but I was not living. I was merely existing. I did not have a life of my own because I was a slave to the bottle. Drinking was the only thing that brought what I thought was happiness. When I look back over my life and I see people that are drunks, staggering up and down the streets, I look at them and say in my mind, "But for the grace of God." I remind people all of the time to be careful in condemning those they see in that condition. Maybe if they had an escape or a way out they would not drink. They may not realize the grief they cause to their family and the others around them. They may think that they are happy, like I did. Maybe they do not realize that they are not living. They are just existing, just like I was.

Despite the changes I made, I never deserted my true friends. Even after I began preaching, I still visited and hung out at the bar with my old friends. I continued to meet, mix, and mingle with them. I decided that those who were my friends when I was drinking would continue to be my friends after I quit. We still talked and joked, and they still drank. I would, too: a 7-Up. Some of my friends from the bar later ended up in my congregation when I started preaching. Not drinking alcohol was not as difficult as I thought it would be. I enjoyed my 7-Up and friends as much as I thought I was enjoying the liquor I once consumed. Smoking, though, was a different story. Cigarettes were tougher to give up, and I did not quit smoking until 1962. Even now when I smell somebody smoking a cigarette, it does not make me sick. It makes me want one. But it was easy to stop drinking.

I began going to church on a much more regular basis when I stopped drinking. I even began to teach a Sunday School class at Allen Chapel AME Church. It was a complete transformation for me; a happy transformation. As I got more involved in church, God began to speak to me about my life. My conscience has always told me that preaching was my calling. From the time I was a little boy, people told me I would be a preacher. I kept hearing the call to preach but I tried to ignore it. A voice kept pushing me, but I still turned away. The more I ran, the more it was there. Things started happening to me and I thought it was because I resisted God. One time I went out on the town with a pretty new straw hat, and somebody sat on it. Another night, I wore a fine silk shirt out and ruined it with hot cigarette ashes. Every time something like that happened I heard a voice in my mind say, "Remember when you were a child and you preached? You are supposed to preach. You need to preach." I heard this message when I was a young man in college until the time I moved to Pensacola. It was a statement that I would hear periodically. When I drank, the alcohol must have clouded my mind because I did not hear the command for some time. Then it got to a point, especially after I quit drinking, where it became a persistent message. I kept saying, "But God, it is not what I want for my life." He kept saying, "But it is what you are going to do. If you do not answer My call, you are going to wind up in a bad way." I thought that I had already been in a bad way and did not want to go down that road again, so I figured I needed to listen to what God told me. Finally, I yielded to His will. I talked to my pastor at Allen Chapel AME Church, Rev. Yale Benjamin Bruce, and told him I wanted to obey God's call. The need to preach came directly from God because my subconscious could not have equipped me to do the job. Only God could have equipped me to speak on His behalf and serve Him. My subconscious could, and did, speak to me but God gave me the gifts I needed to successfully spread His message. He has given everyone gifts. The most dominant talents in my life are communication and leadership. I decided to use them for God's work and now people can not make me shut up! Before I entered the ministry completely, though, I lost my biggest supporter.

On July 6, 1959, my grandmother passed away. She was eighty-one years old and died of natural causes in her sleep. The news was devastating to me. I felt as if I lost my heart. She was the only mother

I had ever known, and it was the most hurtful experience I have ever
had up to that time in my life. She was buried in Rose Hill Cemetery in
Pensacola because most of her relatives were either living or laid to rest
in the area. I never got over her death, and I miss her still to this very
day. Her memory and inspiration, though, kept me going. Everything I
became is due to her positive influence. She contributed to my decision
to begin preaching, and she inspired me to fight racial injustice in our
part of the world. Every time that I grew frustrated or weary with the
later struggle, I remembered the indignities she dealt with from whites
when I was a child. Those memories encouraged me to keep fighting,
even in my darkest hours. Nothing that occurred in Pensacola which I
was involved with would have turned out like it did without her influence. Because I did not commit to God's call until over a year after my
grandmother died, she never heard me preach.

On a Tuesday night in October 1960, I delivered my first sermon.
I gave it at Allen Chapel, a sizeable church which is still standing at the
corner of Gillamard and Jackson streets. The message was entitled "We've
Come This Far By Faith." It took the subject from the scriptures and
basically stressed that we walk by faith and not by sight. It remains my
favorite message to this day because I know that without faith, I would
not have been able to make it through the things that I have undergone.
The sermon must have gone well, because I was asked to preach at Allen
Chapel once a month. I continued to teach Sunday school each week
and spoke to the congregation every month until I got my own church
in 1962.

After I started preaching, I helped organize, with some of my old
friends from the bars, a group in Pensacola called the Toastmasters. I began
to notice my leadership abilities much more when I started preaching,
but knew that I needed to improve my speaking style. I did not have a
firm grip on my public speaking skills, but I knew I had a gift for com-
municating with people and possessed a pretty good delivery when I
spoke. Interestingly enough, Toastmasters focused on public speaking
skills. The organization taught its members the art of communication
and stressed the importance of proper speech mannerisms, eye contact,

hand gestures, and the like. I also wanted to stay in fellowship with my old friends and thought about starting a local service club to do so. I read about the Toastmasters in a magazine and brought it up to my friends at the bar. Everyone seemed real interested in forming a local chapter. We all agreed that black men needed a fraternal organization of some type in Pensacola, and none existed. This seemed an excellent opportunity to start one, so we did. I was elected the first president of the Gaveliers Chapter of Toastmasters Club 3397. Before I started preaching, I left Baldwin Dairy to work as a custodian at Baptist Hospital of Pensacola. Baptist allowed us to have Toastmaster meetings at their facilities. It was an organization like "rent-a-worker," but Toastmasters provided speakers. When groups needed somebody to speak at a public or private occasion, they contacted us and asked if we had anyone available who could appear. I began to cultivate my speaking skills with the Toastmasters. The group refined a gift that God gave me, and I applied what I learned to my ministry. I received my "Toastmasters International Certificate of Merit in Speech Training" on March 14, 1963. It was a great experience because it helped me personally and also gave black men a chance to join a civic organization. The charter members decided that Toastmasters would not have any racial restrictions. We knew how segregation felt, so we opened membership to whites and blacks. However, we never had a white person attend any of the meetings. I guess they did not feel the need to join.

As I continued to preach monthly at Allen Chapel, my reputation spread throughout the community and I began to fill in at other local churches. I even considered taking my own church after a couple of years, but knew that the AME Church moved their ministers around a lot and I did not want to leave Pensacola. At the urging of Rev. H. C. Calloway, I decided to join the African Methodist Episcopal Zion Church. The worship styles in the AME and AME Zion churches were basically the same, but the AME Zion preachers were not moved as frequently as AME pastors. There were also many more AME Zion churches in Pensacola, so my chances of staying in the area were higher than with the AME Church. Rev. Calloway also told me that there was a possibility that I could get my own pastorate in Pensacola, which is what I wanted. So I joined Rev. Calloway's congregation at Houser Memorial Chapel AME Zion Church. I continued to preach at local churches when called and filled in for a number of pastors, including Rev. Calloway.

One incident in particular stands out from Houser Chapel. On a Sunday morning that I had been asked to preach, I saw a man who lived around the corner from me coming home from a late night out. He used to "take communion" quite often. I knew he drank quite a bit because he was a friend from my bar days. As I left my house for church, I noticed the man stumbling down the road. He could barely stand and took one step forward for every five steps he made. I stopped, waited, and walked him down the street. It took us a while to get to our destination, but he turned to his home and I turned to the church. One older church woman saw me and said, "Come here, boy." I call her a church woman and not a Christian, because there is a difference. She told me, "You call yourself a preacher yet you walked down the street with a drunk man." I looked at that woman and said, "Let me tell you something. It was just a few days ago that me and that same man were getting drunk together. The Lord saved me and He is depending on me to help that man." Needless to say, I did not have any more problems out of her. But that is the kind of negative spirit that some people have.

In 1960, I preached on occasion at Houser Chapel, but was on call with local AME Zion churches and spoke when needed. I also had the opportunity at preach at several other churches in Escambia County. The one that I appeared at most was St. Paul United Methodist Church in Pensacola. They had a minister named Rev. W. C. Dobbins, who I got along with very well. I guess he liked my preaching style, because I filled in for him whenever he was away. I did not minister any particular church full-time, but I was not without work. I worked at Baptist Hospital as a janitor, filled in for a variety of churches when I was needed, most importantly at St. Paul's, and stayed active with my preaching. In 1961, I finally took my own church. It was Spring Hill AME Zion Church, which had about five members. Despite the fact that I had my own church, I continued to fill in for Rev. Dobbins at St. Paul's when he needed my help. He is the person, above all others, that awakened my social consciousness.

It was abundantly clear that blacks in Pensacola lived in rigid segregation. The realization became more obvious as I grew older. When I returned from Korea, the social injustices blacks endured became more obvious to me. I had fought in an integrated Army for my country. I was a patriotic American, but the privileges others in this country had were closed to blacks. I realized that the people I had fought against in Korea had more freedom in my hometown than I did. Black Americans had fought against people of other cultures who were given better treatment than those of us who were citizens. Public accommodations were the most prevailing form of segregation. They were also the most humiliating and most frustrating for the local black community.

Blacks had limited access, at best, to public accommodations in Pensacola. We could go into the Florida Theater or Sanger Theater on Palafox Street, the main strip of the downtown area, but we had to go to the balcony. We could ride on the city transit systems, but we could not ride in the front of the bus. If blacks needed a bus ride, they had to pay the same amount as whites but had to sit in the back. We could not go to Pensacola Beach and enjoy ourselves. We had to go to Wingate Beach, which was designated for black use only. There was nothing wrong with the beach itself, but it is where we had to go if we wanted to use area beaches. Blacks could shop in downtown Pensacola and spend their money at Woolworth's, Kress's, Newberry's or Walgreens's. But if a black wanted to eat a sandwich from their cafe, which was attached to the store, they had to go out of the building and get food from the take-out counter. We could spend our money in the stores and even their diners, but we could not sit down there to eat because we were the wrong color. If I was shopping and had to go to the restroom, I had to leave the stores and go blocks over to the Greyhound Bus Station on Balyn Street. The Greyhound Station had bathrooms for blacks, but the department stores did not. Those businesses reaped the benefit of black dollars, but treated us like inferior people. In places of employment around the city, there were no African-Americans in noticeable positions. The only black people that worked in stores downtown were the ones who went in there with a bottle of window cleaner, or a mop and bucket. And blacks were not to question the status quo. Race relations were great in Pensacola as long as black people deferred to whites and did not ask for anything. If any black deviated from the code and dared asked for something that our race had not had for years, they were characterized as "communist niggers"[7] or troublemakers. Blacks were expected to be happy with what we had, even though many of us were growing increasingly dissatisfied.

It was made completely clear that blacks lived in a segregated city, even though some had risked their lives for this nation. As I grew older, straightened my life out, and noticed these things, I kept remembering what my grandmother had to go through when I was a child. The conditions blacks lived with frustrated me to the point of anger, but I did not know what to do about it. I did not consider myself a leader; that was not my forte. I had not honed, and did not know how, the leadership skills that people claimed I had. I did not know how to vent my aggravation or change the situation until I met Rev. W. C. Dobbins.

I first encountered Rev. Dobbins through my ministry. He also noticed the rampant injustice that existed in Pensacola. He was not from the area and transferred to the city through the United Methodist church in 1959. Upon his arrival, Rev. Dobbins experienced the frustration of segregation in downtown Pensacola first hand. He soon preached on these issues in his church. He told his congregation and others who listened that, "We have got to do something about this. This cannot go on. We are human beings. We are Americans. We must do something to show whites that we are not going to continue living under these conditions." Before Dobbins arrived, Rev. K.C. Bass had spoken out against the treatment blacks received but there was no organized effort to fight segregation in public places. In 1961, though, William Curtis Dobbins changed things when he formed the Pensacola Council of Ministers (PCM).

The PCM was organized to tear down the walls that separated African-Americans and white society in the city. It was open to ministers of all denominations and was led by Rev. Dobbins. Only black pastors, however, joined. I signed up immediately after the organization formed, which was shortly after I became pastor of Spring Hill AME Zion. Rev. Dobbins woke the sleeping giant within me. I had no way of venting my frustration concerning black inequality and did not know what to do about it until I heard him speak. But he pointed things out that made me think, "I can do something to bring change." Dobbins preached on the righteousness of social justice. His belief, which became mine, stated that Christ was interested not just in the spiritual welfare of man. He was interested in the whole man. For instance, when Christ passed the blind man in front of the temple, He did not ask him what church he belonged to. He asked the man if he wanted to see. He took care of his physical needs first and then He took care of the rest of him. Peter and John once went to the temple to pray and saw a beggar sitting outside the building. He was lame, helpless, and begging for survival. The Disciples did not ask him to go to church. They instructed him to stand and walk. Then he went into the temple. My point, which was also the point Rev. Dobbins made, has always been that you take care of the total person. You must take care of the physical before tending to spiritual conditions. Nobody wants to sit in church and hear about how good it is to be "born again" or how great Heaven is if they are starving to death or have no roof over their head. Pastors must take care of all of their congregation's needs. Rev. Dobbins lived through the same indignities that I did, but he approached the situation with an insight and wisdom that was much more keen than mine. So my grandmother's experiences and my encounters in Pensacola led me to join the PCM with enthusiasm. I was an energetic thirty-three years old and had been inspired to fight for racial equality.

Between thirty-five and fifty pastors from a variety of denominations joined the PCM. It was Rev. Dobbins's goal to have every black minister in the city join the PCM, and almost all did. We were all dedicated to preaching on the same theme: social justice. All of the ministers began a united effort to alert our congregations of the conditions that existed for blacks downtown. From Sunday to Sunday, in pulpits at black churches throughout Pensacola, we preached the fact that whites did not treat us right in downtown businesses so we should not spend money where we are not wanted. We had two demands: the integration of the store lunch counters and increased black employment in the downtown stores that we gave our most business. The PCM had a strategy to achieve our demands. We would not act alone.

Florida's oldest branch of the National Association for the Advancement of Colored People existed in Pensacola. It had operated since 1917, but had done little to desegregate public facilities. I joined the NAACP in 1959. Rev. Dobbins, and nearly all black Pensacola ministers, were NAACP members as well. But Rev. Dobbins wanted to form another group to integrate public places, so he started the PCM. The PCM focused solely on the visible aspects of segregation. The Pensacola NAACP did fight several battles for local blacks. They later played a key role in the education arena and became the driving force behind the *Augustus* school integration case. The PCM led the way in desegregating public accommodations and was more assertive than the NAACP, but Rev. Dobbins realized that the two groups could accomplish more working together. Under the leadership of Rev. Dobbins, I joined the NAACP Youth Council after joining the adult branch in 1959. To me, the NAACP was the best way blacks had to make democracy a reality in our society. The Youth Council worked under the umbrella of the adult NAACP to bring young people into the civil rights struggle, and the PCM later supervised NAACP activity. The Youth Council first had about forty members from ages twelve to twenty-five, but it grew rapidly. I instructed the members on our responsibilities as citizens and we outlined how to best achieve our goal of ending social injustice in Pensacola. I later took over as advisor for the young people because I wanted the broader community to realize that young blacks were not concerned with brick throwing, looting, and burning buildings, as they were often portrayed by the white press. The Youth Council wanted to change policies peacefully by working within the framework of the laws of our land. We wanted to be the motor that powered the adult branch. There were, therefore, three groups working together under Dobbins's supervision by 1961: the PCM, the NAACP, and the NAACP Youth Council. Cooperation between the NAACP and the PCM was inseparable. All organization members worked together. For example, I belonged to the PCM, worked with the NAACP, and helped organize their Youth Council. It was a concentrated effort of all members of the groups. The NAACP really followed the lead of Rev. Dobbins and the PCM. They were almost as one group after Dobbins came to Pensacola, because so many belonged to both organizations. The assertiveness of all blacks increased under Dobbins's guidance, and the NAACP was no different. Most of our meetings were called jointly by the NAACP, PCM, and Youth Council. Even NAACP president Calvin Harris, Sr. deferred to Rev. Dobbins. We all worked together, but everyone considered Dobbins the unquestioned leader of the black community. There was total unity within the organizational structure. The two groups gelled and formed a stronger bond between local blacks.

In March 1960, I supervised a NAACP Youth Council project to write letters to many national variety store chains such as Woolworth's, W. T. Grant, and Kress, asking them to end their discriminatory tactics. We did it to stop the humiliation to black shoppers without resorting to the sit-in tactics that swept the entire nation at the time. Rev. Dobbins supported Youth Council efforts by writing a letter to the *Pensacola News Journal* that echoed our concerns. The paper printed the note on April 1, 1960. Dobbins revealed the ridiculousness of segregated lunch counters by stating, "It is interesting to try to imagine a person eating a bowl of soup standing." The Youth Council also wrote separate letters to downtown stores managers requesting them to voluntary desegregate their lunch counters. We received no reply, so on April 4, a group of about ten entered the Woolworth's in Pensacola and stood in their cafeteria. Our student spokesman, Raymon Harvey, gave a reporter a note which stated, "This is a phase of our protest demonstrations against unfair, unethical, and un-Christian practices of many nationwide variety stores." It promised more protests and said blacks would not shop in their stores during the Easter season. The *News Journal* refused to cover the incident, but word got out pretty quickly about what was going on. On April 6, five robed Klansmen marched into Woolworth's and offered their services to the store manager in case of future demonstrations. They claimed to represent Pensacolans who did not want violence.[8] Ministers who were NAACP members spread the message in pulpits that a selective

buying campaign had begun. It was very successful, as blacks throughout Pensacola refused to shop from stores we targeted. After the initial
campaign, Rev. Dobbins decided the city needed another organization
to compliment the NAACP and focused on the downtown situation.
Because ministers led the first boycott, he decided to unite them in one
group. The PCM was born.

In 1961, the PCM and NAACP first worked together to encourage white business owners in downtown Pensacola to hire more black
employees. We did not understand why they refused to hire blacks when
they were more than happy to sell their merchandise to black customers. At first, PCM and NAACP members approached business owners
individually. We went into the stores, told them who we were, and asked
them to consider hiring a black employee. Some said they would think
about it, others just ignored us. After a few weeks there were no changes
downtown, so the PCM and NAACP called for a joint meeting with
the Downtown Development, Incorporated, and they complied. The
Downtown Development group was like the Chamber of Commerce,
but it was a coalition of those who owned stores only where we made our
requests. Only merchants from the downtown area belonged, so it was
a key group in our struggle. Their president was a man named Murray
Wilcox. We met with him and a few other organization members in the
late winter of 1961 and repeated our concerns. We again asked businesses
to hire more blacks and integrate their lunch counters because of their
reliance upon black customers. A lot of them were not receptive at all.
One owner said, "We have our work force and it is what we intend to
keep," while another flat out said, "You cannot force us to hire anybody
that we do not want to hire." Most of those businesses were indepen-
dently owned, like Elebash's Jewelry, for example, and hired only family
members. They refused to make concessions because they said they
had to take care of their employees, who were often their relatives. We
repeatedly told them, "We do not want you to fire any of them to hire
us. Expand. Make room. You have the business, and much of it comes
from our community. What will it hurt for you to hire at least one Negro?" Most, though, did not budge, and our pleas fell on deaf ears. We

finally told them, "If you want to keep your business all white, then we will help you keep it all white." Rev. Dobbins took a page out of Martin Luther King Jr.'s book and suggested we start a selective buying campaign in downtown Pensacola. The PCM and NAACP agreed with the strategy and we made plans to mobilize the black community. The first public activity the PCM and NAACP organized was the purchase of a full-page advertisement in the *Pensacola News Journal*. We listed all of the downtown businesses that had segregated lunch counters and no black employees, stated our requests, and asked Negroes to not patronize the stores until they proved sympathetic to our plight.[9] We wanted to meet with the business owners first and give them an opportunity to respond to our requests. If we started a selective buying campaign without first discussing our problem with the proprietors, the protest would be unfair. They would have said to us, with just cause, "If you would have first come to us we could have worked something out, but you just went out and acted on your own." The PCM and NAACP asked on more than one occasion for the whites to hire a black, but they had a dogmatic refusal to integrate. We decided to meet them on the streets.

Rev. W. C. Dobbins brought direct action protest to Pensacola. He first spoke out against the social conditions that blacks endured in 1961, formed an aggressive organization of local ministers dedicated to civil rights, joined forces with the area NAACP, and organized a selective buying plan for downtown stores. To me, he was the master teacher. He taught me to agitate in the right way: peacefully without displaying hatred, hostility, or violence toward our tormentors. I have been called an agitator several times in my life, and I do not mind the label. In fact, I like being called an agitator because it reminds me of an important part of a washing machine. The agitator sits in the middle of the machine and goes back and forth to sling the dirt out. That has become my job; removing the dirt that exists in our society. And it was W. C. Dobbins who taught me to agitate. So we followed his lead once again when he suggested we use a new tactic in our fight for equality. The sit-ins would come to Escambia County.

3

BUILDING MOMENTUM: THE SIT-INS, SELMA, AND YOUTHFUL ENTHUSIASM

During the spring and summer of 1961, the Pensacola Council of Ministers, NAACP, and NAACP Youth Council organized a massive selective buying and sit-in movement in downtown Pensacola. Unlike the previous year's protest, the 1961 demonstrations lasted for an extended period and included hundreds of black participants. White businesses refused to integrate their lunch counters, so we prepared for the boycotts. The PCM decided that all of its ministers, our church members, and the NAACP Youth Council would be used. The response from the black community was overwhelming. Our congregations thought we supported a good cause. In fact, numerous parishioners told me, "It's about time we did something about the way we are treated downtown." Our community rose to the occasion and volunteered as picketers. The Youth Council was especially fired up about the demonstrations. They were young, energetic, and tired of being denied their rights. All they needed was a catalyst. I basically said "Let's" and they said "go!"

The PCM planned for two demonstrations to occur at the same time. We established picket lines to protest the lack of blacks working in the downtown stores, while sit-ins would occur in the dining areas to challenge segregated facilities. Rev. Dobbins organized the pickets while I helped supervise the sit-ins. Most Youth Council members wanted to participate in the sit-ins. The young people also made the signs for picketers. The signs had a variety of slogans on them such as, "Justice is Not Served," "Don't Shop Here," and "Your Dollar is as Good as the Next," among others. PCM representatives also passed out flyers and discouraged people from entering the stores. I participated in both the sit-ins and walked the picket lines. It took a few weeks to organize the campaign because we had to call for volunteers for both the sit-ins and pickets, and had to receive an assembly permit from the city. We told our congregations of the plan and posted ads in the newspaper that said when the boycotts would begin. The PCM and NAACP thought the best time to begin our activities was shortly before the Easter holiday. We wanted to strike when our actions would hurt businesses owners the most. By April 1961, the selective buying campaign had began. The NAACP national office, who was aware of what we planned to do, warned us to not use the term "boycott" to describe what we did, although that was our goal.

The picket lines were established first. Ministers announced their formation on Sunday mornings and declared that the PCM would meet there at a certain time in a certain downtown area the next day. The Youth Council designed posters and the ministers distributed them before the marching began. Other members and I met downtown, handed the signs out, walked to the targeted stores, and walked the picket lines. We walked all day sometimes, from morning in the hot sun until the shops closed. We also marched in shifts. Different ministers and concerned citizens relieved others at different times and continued the demonstrations. Citizens unaffiliated with any church also participated. Many protestors were from our congregations, but many were not. They were individuals who acted on their own accord. Sometimes so many people showed up that the ministers did not walk. We merely supervised and organized later gatherings. African-Americans in Pensacola were very determined to discourage others from shopping in those stores.

Those carrying signs walked up and down the sidewalk with two feet between us, like the local law required. We often walked in circles and formed a double barrier for those entering the businesses. Our presence was a discouraging factor to those who wanted to go into the stores, particularly blacks. Still, some slipped in through the back doors. There were several picket lines that were active at the same time in front of the stores we targeted. It was not hard to keep more than one going at once because all of the stores blacks used were located in downtown

Pensacola. The main goal of the pickets remained employment, and we pledged to keep walking until those stores agreed to hire some black people. During the spring and summer of 1961, the PCM, NAACP, and Youth Council demonstrated every day except Sunday. The Youth Council often came in when they got out of school in the spring and worked on the weekends. During the day when they were in school, the adults marched. The kids, like the adults, walked all day long when possible. The students brought freshness and a youthful enthusiasm to our work on the nights and on weekends. We decided to use their energy in a different way when school let out for the summer. Rev. Dobbins and I agreed that the Youth Council would initiate the sit-ins of segregated downtown lunch counters.

W. C. Dobbins suggested the sit-ins and gave me a key role in organizing and leading the demonstrations. The Youth Council initiated the sit-ins while the adults and other young people continued to picket outside of the stores. Some PCM members, such as myself, would monitor the sit-ins to protect the students and make sure that they remained non-violent affairs. The sit-ins and pickets were designed to work together and were conducted in conjunction with each other. The duties were split equally between the ministers, congregation, and young people. The youth acted as a liaison of sorts between the NAACP and the rest of the community. I divided the young folks into different groups and in early June 1961, we entered cafes at the same time in Woolworth's, Kress's, Newberry's, and Walgreens's and began the sit-ins.

We wanted to pack the eating areas for a couple of reasons. First, we wanted to protest segregation. That was the obvious goal. But we wanted to fill the restaurants so that nobody else could come in and eat. If the white managers refused to serve us, we wanted their business to collapse. For the first few days of the sit-ins, the young people and their adult supervisors simply sat at the counters and tables and attempted to place an order. Of course, we were always refused service so we sat there for hours at a time. After a period, other youths who had been walking the picket lines came in to relieve those who had been sitting. We often rotated in that manner. It did not take long for white crowds to begin gathering both inside and outside the packed dining areas.

Not only did the white workers refuse to serve us, but they and other white onlookers began to harass the young people. They underwent a lot of humiliation because white employees wanted to make sure that no one could sit down in the cafes. Whites called us names, while some students were burned with lit cigarettes. Battery acid was thrown on a few young people. Students saw a cook take an order from a black, prepare the dish, place broken glass in the food, and return it to the customer. One girl even had insecticide sprayed in her eyes by an enraged white man. The adult NAACP and PCM members who watched the violence appealed to the police for help, but they were no help at all. In fact, they laughed at what was going on and arrested young blacks for a variety of trumped-up charges. Students were arrested for trespassing, illegal boycotting, cursing in public, and disorderly conduct. The favorite tactic of the police, though, was taking items like flashlight batteries from the stores, placing them in the student's pockets, and arresting them for shoplifting. They never arrested the whites who burned us with cigarettes or threw battery acid, and they arrested few adult black leaders. They primarily picked out the young ones and hoped to cripple our efforts by discouraging them. The officers' behavior was just awful; it was probably the worst experience we had during the sit-ins. Their actions began a mistrust between blacks and law enforcement that exists to this day in Pensacola. We watched the police, people who were supposed to protect us, set up the young people and arrest them for something they did not do. Several students were given a criminal record for no reason at all. The mistrust and suspicion blacks had for Escambia County police began during the sit-ins but became a permanent aspect of our freedom struggle.

The harassment we faced during the sit-ins from whites backfired against them. Instead of discouraging the students or making us fearful, the tactics strengthened our resolve to fulfill the goals we set. The Youth Council made sure that we continued the protests regardless of what anyone did to us. The consequences simply did not matter. When we left or were dispersed to our duty stations in the morning, the students were determined to sit all day everyday if that was what it took. The arrests only encouraged us, because we knew we were doing the right thing. Despite all of the terrible things that were done to us, no black protestor ever responded with violence. It was difficult, at times, to maintain control because of the resistance we encountered. I did not notice white efforts or fully understand their desire to keep blacks in their so-called place until the sit-ins began. Whites then organized efforts to counter our organized efforts. The police and the people who owned and worked at the stores were the most resistant to change.

During the sit-ins, I never saw Ku Klux Klan members appear in full dress downtown. I imagine there were a lot of Klan members, but they were not identifiable. There were some who wore blue uniforms and some who stood behind the counters, but they were not obvious in appearance. Initially, only a few whites made comments concerning our activities. But the white crowds got larger the longer our boycotts continued, and they really grew after the sit-ins began. White workers, bystanders, and police officers did a lot of yelling, name calling, threw rocks, and did anything to discourage our efforts. Many whites did not like blacks being more assertive than they had previously been. It was during the boycotts that I was first called a "communist." I, and any other blacks who seriously fought for equal treatment, were declared communist sympathizers because we supposedly questioned the status quo in America and disrupted society. We followed the nonviolent, passive resistance, direct action methods that Dr. Martin Luther King, Jr., advocated and whites called him a communist, so that made us all communists by default. To whites, our actions were unpatriotic and we remained awful people to them. We were destroying race relations in their eyes, because we dared asked for something that belonged to us. It was a dignity as humans that was guaranteed to us by our God, not by the governor of the state of Florida or anybody else. In short, therefore, the downtown boycotts totally divided the community and demonstrated that blacks were unhappy with their social, political, and economic status in Pensacola.

When looking back at the demonstrations, it is important to emphasize that not all whites resisted our boycotts and not all blacks supported us. Few things are ever so cut and dried, and that is true even concerning our pickets and sit-ins. There were people in our congregations who disagreed with the PCM and NAACP tactics. They may not have vehemently disagreed, but many expressed reservations about the tactics we used to achieve our demands. They felt that if the ministers left well enough alone, things would work themselves out. I disagreed with that, as did many blacks in Escambia County. I felt the situation downtown had not worked itself out to that point, so why would it ever change? The business owners needed help to make progress, and we hoped to make their decision easier. I remember that my Uncle Sidney, a Church of Christ minister, told me, "You ought to be ashamed of yourself for doing all of that agitatin' and stuff. You ought to be working for God." I said, "That is what we're doing. We are working for God." There were some blacks who kept shopping in the stores we targeted, even if they had to enter through the back door. Others expressed a deafening silence because we dared rock the boat for them. Some told us that we were just making things worse, that things have always been segregated and there was no need to expect different. But the PCM members did not have to sell nonviolent resistance to most people in our congregation. During that time, people were real concerned with social affairs. It was only after the organizations achieved success that a lot of blacks started crawfishing, because they felt they had arrived. But in the early 1960s, local blacks basically felt that we were all in the same boat so we had to fight.

On the other hand, there have always been some whites, particularly preachers, who felt that we were not being treated fairly. The pastor of the Pensacola First Methodist Church supported all of our efforts, as did Pensacola First Baptist minister Rev. Jim Plights. Rev. Al Butler pastored Myrtle Grove Baptist Church near Escambia High School and publicly endorsed our boycott, and it is a wonder that his congregation did not run him off. There has always been a core of whites in Pensacola who supported us. Even some who were not preachers joined in our later marches and protests. I remember one public accommodation that allowed blacks in without any trouble was a Howard Johnson's restaurant owned by a white lady named Paula Johnson. We achieved what we did during the 1961 demonstrations because a lot of whites stayed away from downtown. I believe that a lot of them avoided the area because they supported what we were doing. They may not have supported us openly, but they agreed that it was only right for us to be able to spend our money in all areas of those stores. It was wrong for businesses to accept our money for goods in the store and for the sandwich and drink we bought, but only allow us to receive food from an outside window. Some whites noticed this and supported us with their absence. They may have supported us from the rear in silence, but that is where it was safest for them. Others spoke up on occasion. For example, during our boycotts a black lady whose name many Pensacolans are very familiar with but I will not call, went into the white-owned Miles Shoe Store in downtown Pensacola to buy a pair of shoes. She entered through the back door on Palafox Street so the picketers would not see her. The owner of the store told her, "You ought to be ashamed of yourself for coming in here to shop when your people are outside picketing for better conditions for you." The lady who tried to buy the shoes told me that story years later, and Miles became one of the first downtown stores to hire a black. So there were some white people who were very sensitive to our demands. I tell people all of the time that you have to be careful painting everybody with the same brush, because there were whites who sympathized with our efforts. All white people are not bad and all black people are not good. People are people. We all have the potential to act in both good and bad ways.

During the 1962 summer, the PCM and NAACP expanded the selective buying campaigns beyond national chain stores. We broadened the pickets against white-owned businesses that relied primarily upon black customers but refused to hire any African-Americans. On July 13, then, we targeted Nolan's, a grocery store where white owner Ernest Nolan refused to hire black cashiers. He also had a lunch counter and would not let blacks sit in the dining area. During our first month of protest, Nolan's revenue dropped ten thousand dollars. He lost 90 percent of his business before the year ended and tried to end our activities with legal action. He took the NAACP to court and tried to get an injunction against us picketing his business, but he did not prevail. Nolan's ended up hiring blacks in the meat department and as cashiers. When he died a few years later, he was about the only white man in that store. We converted him before his death! The NAACP Youth Council also took the sit-ins to the cafeteria at the Escambia General Hospital in the mid-1960s. The PCM estimated that at their peaks, the selective buying campaigns and sit-ins achieved 80 percent of its goals, even though the *Pensacola News Journal* refused to cover our activities.

The sit-ins, pickets, and selective buying campaigns continued throughout the summer of 1962. Some of the demonstrations carried over a little longer than that, but most of our demands were met by the time school started in the fall. When one store would meet our demands and integrate their counters or hire blacks, the PCM and NAACP stopped the protests against it. It did not take long after our tactics began to obtain results. Business owners saw an immediate loss of customers after the protests began, and some responded to our requests within the first thirty days of activity. When the boycotts began, particularly the sit-ins, downtown Pensacola became as deserted as a ghost town. White customers began calling the stores and canceling their layaway payments because they did not want to come downtown with us there. We damaged downtown businesses bad during the 1962 Easter season, but we were just getting their attention. For the remainder of the spring and into the summer, we almost crippled the downtown area. Businesses were hurting, and that was our goal. When an organization leads a selective buying campaign against a store, and 50 percent or more of their revenue comes from the group that initiated the boycott, the results will be drastic. If an owner loses half of his revenue, especially in a holiday period like Easter, the store will not survive. I do not care how stout-hearted anyone is; there comes a time when you are going to have to let that stout-heartedness go. Those white people we targeted were in business to make a living, not to entertain people's racism. If their livelihood was threatened by people they refused to serve, PCM and NAACP members believed that they would eventually find it in their best interest to open up to black customers. It was either remain segregated or survive. I think that when the pickets started some whites thought we were a joke. Then the sit-ins began, in earnest, and it showed them that we were are not playing. Slowly but surely, downtown merchants responded to our requests.

Elebash's Jewelry was the store that broke the ice and first hired blacks. A couple of other small, family owned businesses did the same shortly after the Easter season, and we no longer targeted them. One accommodation even integrated during our campaigns that we did not specifically target: the city transit system. Pensacola buses were still seg- regated when the sit-ins began. We were still sitting in the back of the buses and could not enter the vehicle through the front door. We had to enter through a side door. I really do not know how the bus system integrated. There was no big push to make them integrate, but they did. We believed the city desegregated the lines on their own. City managers saw the pressure the PCM and NAACP put on downtown businesses, and most blacks used the bus system to go downtown. They knew that sooner or later, we would target them, too. It is no coincidence that the mayor at that time, Eugene Elebash, owned the first downtown store that integrated. Maybe he realized that opening public accommodations was simply the right thing to do.

By the end of the 1962 Easter shopping season, Downtown De- velopment, Inc., approached me and Rev. Dobbins and asked for a meeting. We promised the group to first work through them, instead of through the police, the courts, or the government. After a few pretty tense meetings, Downtown Development informed us that some stores had decided to waive their racial restrictions and would hire blacks on a limited basis. About thirty stores promised to hire a qualified Negro. We understood that they had to make a living, but we wanted them to be fair. Our aim was not to send them into poverty. Well, maybe it was if they did not do what we asked them to do, which was both the morally and Constitutionally right thing. We merely wanted people hired based on their qualifications and not on their race. During the same time, for example, I had to pay a city bill and the white lady behind the counter could barely count. I told a city official, "We are not asking you to hire people that are not qualified, but if you are going to hire retarded white people, then hire retarded black people too." This is what the PCM wanted: fairness. Downtown Development had always been willing to meet with us, but it was never willing to do what we requested until our protests began. To them, any compromise would have been a surrender. Our requests never changed, but they had a dogmatic refusal to change until we met them on the streets.

The *Pensacola News Journal* announced Downtown Development's compromise in an article that announced "Merchants seek accord to halt Negro boycotts." The downtown merchant's association had met our demands, which had not changed since the campaigns began. They promised to hire black employees and most pledged to open their remaining dining facilities to everyone. Not all did, though, and that is why the boycotts continued throughout the summer as we had promised. The PCM told the owners that we had not used downtown as a whipping boy. We wanted justice throughout the county and would continue our activities at other shopping centers and drug stores, but their businesses were where the most blatant grievances existed. The owners admitted that they were hurting financially and would not succeed without black customers. But the businesses had reservations about hiring too many blacks at once. They did not want to lose all of their white customers because of our demands, because they needed customers of both races to recover. The PCM and NAACP knew that they had to go slow in their hiring practice. We did not want them to lose their white customers by being dogmatic about it, but we promised to resume the campaign if the integration process was too slow. We wanted to be reasonable with them and all we asked for in return was for them to be reasonable with us. It worked out. It was a win-win situation for white-owned businesses and their black customers. In February 1962, the *Montgomery Advertiser* labeled our movements "extremely successful" and noted that some Pensacola department, variety, and drug stores desegregated their lunch counters because of our efforts.[10]

African-American ministers announced the meeting's results to their congregations the Sunday after the downtown protests ended. We let them know that their efforts were successful. The stores had agreed to serve everyone based on their ability to buy and agreed to hire black people based on their qualifications. My congregation was joyous, almost ecstatic. The African-American community was not necessarily surprised, though, because the PCM had continuously preached that the right cause would prevail with continued pressure. One of the things that I used to say is, "If you want to see the results, apply pressure. If there is a rock that is sticking out of a waterfall and water constantly drips, drips, drips, on that rock, eventually it will loosen up. If water continues to drip after it loosens, the rock will finally fall." The black community responded by applying pressure to the merchants, city government, and resistant whites. Pressure in even small doses will eventually loosen and topple the biggest rocks, but it must be consistent. You cannot drip today and turn the faucet off tomorrow. You have to keep going. And the people, both young and old, male and female, black and white, did.

The constant determination of the local African-American community most impressed me during the 1961 sit-in and boycott campaign. At one point before the summer began, the PCM told our congregations that it looked as if the downtown merchants were not going to budge, so we might change protest tactics. The people said, "No. Keep doing what you are doing. We are behind you," which was extremely encouraging. There were still some, though, who said even after we succeeded, "You got the counters integrated, but the whites still do not want to serve you." My response was, "As long as I can go in a store and sit at the counter, and as long as the waitress says, 'What can I do for you sir,' and 'Thank you sir,' after I pay her, it does not matter how she feels." I did not care how whites felt after the counters integrated. Blacks could finally eat there. Racism was their problem, not ours. And it was interesting, because the same people in the diners who resisted black efforts during the sit-ins were the same ones there when the barriers were taken down. But they treated us with respect after our campaign, because they had no choice. It was a tremendous accomplishment, and the PCM and NAACP were extremely proud of the black community in Pensacola for their efforts.

Rev. Dobbins was around when the sit-ins came to a conclusion, but left about a year later. He did not stay in Escambia County very long because he was a minister in the United Methodist Church and, as all

Methodist ministers, he had to transfer often early in his career. But Rev. Dobbins was able to see the results of his leadership and tasted the fruits of what he had initiated. I think Pensacola, especially the African-American community, should never forget him. It was Rev. Dobbins who started the whole thing. He had nothing but respect from the black community before his departure. He opened our eyes to social injustices and we respected his leadership. He got the ball rolling, and I just happened to come in behind him and eventually built on his accomplishments. The biggest problem was that his departure left a huge leadership void within the black community. The civil rights movement in Pensacola all but died for a period after Dobbins left the area. There was no skipper for the ship. In fact, the Pensacola Council of Ministers dissolved as an organization after Rev. Dobbins's departure. The future of the movement was left in the hands of the NAACP and the NAACP Youth Council.

There were some fantastic followers among the city's black ministers. They were great preachers and even better people. H. C. Calloway, pastor of Houser Chapel AME Zion, was an integral part of the movement. He supported all PCM and NAACP activities and played a leadership role in both organizations. Years before the sit-ins began, for example, he protested the use of separate obituary columns for whites and blacks in the Pensacola newspapers. Rev. Calloway claimed, "At least we should be able to be together when we are dead," and the *News Journal* combined the two. He was a forceful, important part of the movement, but he claimed to be too old to assume a leadership role after Rev. Dobbins left town. He remained active in the local movement, but he was not its primary leader. Calvin Harris, Sr., was the NAACP President but was not a minister and, therefore, did not have access to the congregations that others did. Another key force in the local movement was Rev. K. C. Bass, who pastored Mt. Olive Baptist Church. Rev. J. S. Young, the Mt. Canaan Baptist Church pastor, and Rev. J. H. Kendrix also formed a solid core of dedicated activists, but they turned to me for leadership soon after Rev. Dobbins's transfer.

I gained a positive reputation among local blacks before the sit-ins began, but I became even more respected when Rev. Dobbins gave me such an important role in the demonstrations. I guess admiration of my style grew when we succeeded. I have always been good with people and consider myself a gifted communicator. I have always responded to people's calls, listened to their problems, and acknowledged their concerns. Several ministers suggested individually that I take the leadership role within the community after Rev. Dobbins left, but I resisted. I knew that despite our gains in employment and integrating diners, there were and are still things that African-Americans were not privileged to. Equality was an ongoing fight and there were things that needed to be done, but nobody wanted to lead the way. None of the ministers took the leadership position, and the movement nearly died as a consequence. There were people that had good leadership skills, but they did not want to exercise those skills. A group of preachers finally approached me and asked me to organize local activities. I remember that one person told me, "The people have confidence in you and they come to you when things happen in the community. We want you to take the leadership role." I accepted and promised, "I will do what I can." I have always claimed that my leadership role in Pensacola was thrust upon me. I never asked for it. The leadership role was nothing I sought and something I did not deserve, but the ministers that I highly respected saw fit to give it to me. I agreed to do what I could because of my commitment to God, my grandmother's influence, and the training I received under Rev. Dobbins. The Good Lord opened my eyes to racial prejudice, Rev. Dobbins instructed me on how to fight it, and my grandmother taught me the dignity all human beings possess. It had always been in the back of my mind, sub-consciously, that I was not comfortable in the role that I had been relegated to as an African-American. One reason I was never satisfied with my position in society is because my grandmother used to tell me, "Don't ever think that you are better than anybody else but for God's sake, do not think that you are less than anyone." She was an old country lady who probably would never dare do some of the things that we did, but that was her philosophy. She was the moving force behind me and everything I did. She constructed me, and I went back to her advice when I was approached to lead black Pensacolans. I agreed to do it based on the values that she taught me. I also agreed because W. C. Dobbins came to Pensacola as a stranger and took it upon himself to try and get some things done for those of us who had lived here for years and had very little to show for it. After I agreed to lead the community, several NAACP members and former PCM members went public with the decision. They told the press and their congregations that "H. K. is acknowledged as the leader in Pensacola." I felt both honored and important, but I knew what it entailed. I was up for the challenge.

The first issue I wanted to tackle as new leader of the local movement was black political involvement. Before he left, Rev. Dobbins ran for the state legislature. He was the first black to do so in Escambia County, and came pretty close to pulling off a win because due to the sit-ins, picketing, and selective buying campaigns, his name was very recognizable in Pensacola. The problem was that there were not enough black voters registered to ensure Dobbins's victory. We believed that blacks were involved in local politics on a limited basis only. African-Americans supported candidates when elections came up and let our presence be felt as voters, but we did not do enough to help other blacks register. Pensacola differed from other Southern cities during the early- to mid-1960s because we were able to register and vote without white intimidation. As a result, I decided to initiate a voter registration drive through the NAACP. Alice Kendricks, an NAACP member from Pensacola, volunteered to head the program. Most members participated, but Mrs. Kendricks became the most active person in that particular campaign. She assumed the personal responsibility of registering blacks to vote throughout Escambia County and really beat the bushes for our cause. We would find out who in our neighborhoods was not registered and put them on a list. On days that we specifically designated for registration, carloads of folks visited the people on our lists of unregistered voters. Mrs. Kendricks would go into those homes and literally drag them to the courthouse. She would tell them, "Turn off your pots, we're going to register." The NAACP Voting Program went beyond registration, though, and arranged rides for people who needed them on election days.

The churches were very important centers of political activity. They served as the headquarters of all registration and election campaigns in our community. In each black church there was a volunteer who made sure that every church member of voting age was registered. On election days, all of the church vans were used to take people to the polling places. That is how we made political assertiveness work for us during that time. Black ministers, including myself, preached that there was political power through the vote. We wanted to register 100 percent of black voters in Escambia County but, of course, did not meet our lofty goal. There have always been people who feel that their vote does not count. One vote does count, and I still stress that today. A lot of people were apathetic to our activities, but did not openly resist what we tried to accomplish. They possessed the mind-set, "My vote does not count because those white folks are going to do what they want to do anyway." My response was, and still is, "Yes, they will do what they want as long as you allow them to. If that is your attitude, if you really feel that your vote does not matter, it won't." Political activism seemed to work in Pensacola after Rev. Dobbins transferred from the area, thanks to his earlier steadfastness. The sit-ins and selective buying campaigns caused enough pressure to influence those in the political arena to acknowledge our requests and activities. But voting and political activity was only one of the early goals I pursued as the new leader of the local black community. The other objective was increased employment.

I maintained throughout my time in Pensacola that more blacks needed to be hired in local businesses. Blacks never held positions in proportion to our population in the area, particularly in meaningful, visible positions. We therefore pressed for more minorities to be hired in Pensacola stores after the successful 1961 selective buying campaign. At one time, I labeled Pensacola one of the most racist cities in America. I based that claim on the surrounding areas, both in northwest Florida and southern Alabama, where white resistance was not nearly as strong against African-Americans as Pensacola. This was a shock for many of us involved in the area movement, because Pensacola was a larger, more urban city that had people from all over the nation thanks to the local Naval Air Station. But there were some die-hard segregationists in

Pensacola that occupied high places and pledged to never integrate their work forces. One of the first campaigns I organized, therefore, targeted hiring practices at the Southern Bell Telephone Company.

Southern Bell did not have a single black employee, even though the majority of us owned telephones and used their services. Calvin Harris, Sr., president of the city NAACP, and I requested a meeting with Southern Bell representatives in 1964. We met them at the Roadway Inn on Cervantes and Palafox streets in downtown Pensacola to discuss our concerns. Calvin and I laid out our case and pleaded with them to hire one black, but they were persistent in their refusal. They told us, point blank, "No, we are never hiring any niggers." We got nowhere with those people but made sure that was their final answer before we left. They said it was, so we decided that all NAACP members who were ministers should pass the meeting results to their congregations. I also devised a tactic to resolve the problem. The phone company did not have coin counters or any technology they currently have to sort change, so I decided that all blacks should appear at the phone company personally and pay their bill in pennies to protest their hiring policy. Black ministers spread the word and the tactic began the next Monday. Southern Bell cashiers had to count out every single cent. You can imagine the long line of people that formed when each African-American paid their bills with about thirty dollars worth of pennies. The whites who came in had to stand in the long lines. They fumed and cursed and carried on with the manager. It was the first tactic that we used other than picketing and sitting-in, and it was very effective. The phone company reconsidered their policy hurriedly and hired a black worker within the month. It is so sad that it became necessary to take such actions in a free country where we talk about "the land of the free and the home of the brave." In order for blacks to be recognized as other than sub-human, to be recognized as full citizens, there were things we were forced to do. Other places hired blacks because they did not want to undergo what we had promised if they refused. Stores at the Town & Country shopping mall in Pensacola, for example, gave us no problem hiring minorities. After a period, we only had to make our presence known to business owners and tell them what we wanted. I never considered what we did as threatening because there was an option available for proprietors. They could choose to hire blacks or choose to survive solely upon white customers.

Pensacola movie theaters also remained closed to blacks after the downtown demonstrations ended. The Ritz Theater catered to blacks, but the movies were second rate and the facility was not clean. The public accommodations that existed for blacks were like the buses that hauled black children: inferior in every way. The main place that the NAACP and local ministers targeted was the Florida Theater, a racist stronghold. It was located in the middle of the downtown area on Palafox near Garden and Gregory streets, and was one of the few places that resisted integration during the 1961 campaign. The managers were determined that blacks would not enter their theaters. Calvin Harris, Sr., H. C. Calloway, and I requested a meeting with the theater's owners, who proved as stubborn as their managers. The owner and his family lived in Selma and possessed a chain of movie houses around the South. The oldest man in the group, who we assumed was the primary owner, had a hearing aid that he loved to use during our conversations. Every time we mentioned integrating his theater he would say, "I can't hear you! My hearing aid is not working!" We knew that was his way of playing with us. He would mention something about his bad battery and they would all laugh. He refused to take us seriously. If he refused to be civil, I decided it was time to shake things up. I told him, "Well, tomorrow we are going to put black people throughout your movie lines." We knew this would work because there was a real popular movie out at the time the theater was showing. I told him, "We'll put one black for every five white people you have wanting to come in. We are going to pepper that line with Negroes. Each one will try to buy a ticket, ask why they can not enter, and demand to speak with a manager. By the time they deal with a few black people and explain why they cannot come in, the white people in line are going to get disgusted and leave. If not, the white folks will be standing all day because we are not going to move. But I know that you cannot hear me, so our plans won't bother you." His hearing aid battery miraculously got fixed then and there because he told his group, "We need to go out and discuss this." When they returned to the table he had decided that their business did not need that kind of activity. They opened their doors to blacks the next day. After the Florida Theater opened, the ownership of the Sanger Theater integrated as well. The Sanger was where art programs, musicals, and plays were performed in Pensacola. Blacks could enter the Sanger, but we had to sit in the balcony. After the Florida Theater integrated, the Sanger management closed the balcony and allowed people to sit wherever they wished. The sit-ins had a direct bearing on many decisions whites made concerning blacks after 1961. Their success made every thing run a lot smoother for a time.

By 1965, I thought things were going pretty well in Pensacola. I led a group of enthusiastic and hard working blacks in the community who were serious about obtaining full equality. I also still worked with young adults in the NAACP Youth Chapter and preached full-time at Escambia Chapel AME Zion Church. Still, I wanted to do more. I was working as a janitor at a medical building on Jordan Street when the call went out for people to come to Selma and march with Dr. Martin Luther King, Jr., for black voting rights. In February, I heard the news that Jimmie Lee Jackson, a young black, was shot by an Alabama State Trooper during a voter demonstration in Marion, Alabama, which is close to Selma. Dr. King made his call on March 3. I remember hearing him say, "We must stand up for what is right," and I knew that the situation in Selma was anything but right. So I decided to leave Pensacola as a leader and go to Selma as a follower. I wanted to be part of what was going on there because I knew it was going to be historical. The overriding factor in my decision to go to Selma was my position as leader of the black community in Escambia County. I represented our entire community and knew I should represent Pensacola at such an important demonstration. I was young—thirty-seven years old—adventurous, and thought I was brave. I thought I was "Mr. Big Stuff" because of the role I had in Pensacola, so I wanted to lend my assistance to Dr. King and the national move-ment for civil rights. I was also familiar with the area Dr. King targeted, because I grew up in the county south of Dallas County. As a child, my grandmother and I often went to Selma to attend the picture shows on weekends. So I left Pensacola on Friday, March 5 after I got off of work. I drove my 1957 pink and white Ford Fairlane to Selma that night by myself to take part in the Sunday demonstration and had no idea what I was getting into. I arrived in Selma that evening and attended a mass meeting at Brown Chapel AME Church. The demonstrators also met there for most of the day on Saturday. My work schedule prevented me from being there until Friday night, although meetings were held in Selma for weeks before Dr. King called for the march to Montgomery.

I have a lot of memories about that weekend. I should have been aware what was coming for us on Sunday based on what happened Friday night. At the first prayer meeting I attended, law enforcement officers rode their horses into the crowded Brown Chapel. They literally rode horses into the church to persuade us to halt the demonstrations and disperse the group. Dallas County Sheriff Jim Clark was a rabid racist and used several tactics to discourage the people there from participating. We knew he would use violence against us if he could get away with it. But the marchers were determined to go through with the demonstration, despite the fact that Governor George Wallace promised to "use whatever measures are necessary to prevent a march."[11] The blacks in Selma had been through too much for us to desert them. The leadership present at Brown Chapel really had the full support of those in attendance. Hosea Williams, James Bevel, John Lewis, and Andy Young were all important parts of the march and spoke at the mass meetings I attended at Brown Chapel. In fact, I remember one of them assuring us during a meeting that Governor Wallace would not allow his troopers or guardsmen to hurt the demonstrators because there would be tremendous media coverage of the march. Some whites also participated in the mass meetings and the Sunday incident. A lot were ministers, some were students, and others seemed to be ordinary people dedicated to doing what was fair, just, and Christian. Whites helped us during the Pensacola boycotts, but never as many that showed up in Selma. I also had my first experience with Jesse Jackson during the weekend. When I look at him now and think back to 1965, I laugh. He was a young fellow at the time who was mentored by the leaders there.

The big moment in Selma came on Sunday morning. It was later referred to as "Bloody Sunday" because of what we encountered when we marched across the Edmund Pettus Bridge. We gathered at Brown Chapel and proceeded from the church steps. It took quite a while for the march to begin, but when it did we proceeded from the church in a double file line toward U.S. Highway 80. Hosea and John led the procession. Later reports estimated between three hundred to six hundred people marched, but it seemed like there were more of us than that. One thing that I learned throughout the movement is that the media could not count, particularly reporters in Pensacola. They always gave low numbers for civil rights gatherings to make it look like we were not as supported as we really were, and I suspect that also occurred in Selma.

It was several blocks from Brown Chapel to the Edmund Pettus Bridge. Every marcher was excited, yet solemn, about our mission. I was toward the front of the crowd because I thought I wanted to help lead the way. But I found out pretty quickly that I was not as brave as I thought. When the crowd came to the bridge, everyone saw the state troopers on horseback across the structure. We all knew that the troopers and national guard would be there, but the sight of them waiting for us in full riot gear was something I was not prepared for. I knew I was in over my head almost immediately because I did not expect this kind of resistance, and I do not think very many other marchers expected it either. I may have been naive, but I thought that George Wallace would not let anything bad happen to black citizens with all of the media that had gathered to cover the event. We heard their commander, Major John Cloud, tell Hosea through a bullhorn to stop because we were illegally assembled. I clearly recall him saying, "Take your people back to the church," "You will not be able to proceed," and things of that nature. But nobody was going to go back. I honestly did not want to face the consequences of not turning around, but we were too far along to retreat. All of us were dead silent, but we were in a position where running was not an option. The determination was there to continue from everyone, despite our reluctance and fear. I never considered quitting but did think when I saw all of those officers, "Man, I should not have come to Selma." I still say to myself today that if I had known what we were getting into, I would have stayed in Pensacola in the safe haven of the medical building where I worked. I was only a janitor, but I was not going to get beaten there. The officers refused to negotiate with Hosea and John, who asked to speak with Selma's mayor. The state troopers instead gave us two minutes to leave. Not sixty seconds later, the attack began. Some marchers avoided the brutality, but many did not. I was one of the ones that received the blows.

Despite the warnings officers gave, we held our ground. Then the attack came. The troopers saw that we were not turning around so they decided to beat us back. The first thing I noticed was the movement of the horses. Then I saw several of the mounted troopers wading through the crowd swinging their billy clubs at the protestors. Soon, I heard shots and noticed that tear gas was being used against us. Some of the demonstrators ran, some cowered down, and others grouped together. Many got beaten down, but no one fought back. People were screaming, crying, and falling like dominoes. I tried to cover up and avoid getting hit as the police neared me, but I was hit in several places. My knee took the worst blow. I was not in the position to count the blows or see how many times I was hit or who had hit me. All I know is that I hurt. The white onlookers, several of which had gathered, cheered and whooped as we fell. The scene was one of total chaos. I just lay on the ground in a heap dumbfounded. I began to cry because of my pain, but it was more psychological than physical. I could not believe that I witnessed people treating human beings the way we were treated that day. I went to a doctor in Selma the day after the violence and he discovered that I had a severely bruised kneecap. My knee was the only thing that bothered me after the attack. Degenerative arthritis later developed in my knee due to the hit I took in Selma. Others, though, had it much worse than me. I will never forget seeing the beating John Lewis took. He was the most severely beaten I saw. I believe the troopers tried to kill John.

As the troopers pushed us back to the bridge, many blacks retreated back to Brown Chapel and the police blocked off the area. I think they did it more to contain rather than protect us, as they later claimed. There

was chaos in the church as leaders tried to speak and restore order. A few
of the more injured protestors went for immediate medical attention.
Some of those gathered, including myself, later decided to cross the Edmund Pettus Bridge. It was what we came to do, and we were determined
to walk peacefully across it. A handful of us left the church a bit later
and began the walk to Montgomery. We decided, probably foolishly in
light of what happened earlier, that we were going with or without the
leaders. I am not sure how we made it past the police and the roaming
bands of white racists, but we crossed the bridge again that evening. As
a matter of fact, we walked to Hayneville. I determined after the morning encounter that even though I had to limp most of the way, I would
cross the bridge. The determination of some blacks increased after the
beating. We made it to Hayneville and camped out in a the middle of
a pasture that night. Blacks who lived in the town supported our stand
and brought us food and materials that we used to build a makeshift
tent. The next morning, we awoke to reality and headed back to Selma.
Without leadership and protection, we probably would not have made
it to Montgomery by ourselves. So I walked back to Selma, saw a doctor
about my knee, and drove back to Pensacola. I was unaware of the plan
Dr. King made for the following day.

After he heard of "Bloody Sunday" from Atlanta that evening, Martin
Luther King, Jr., announced that another march would occur on Tuesday,
March 9. I did not participate in the second or subsequent marches. I do
not know if I heard about them too late, if my job prevented me from
going, or if I was just scared, but I remained in Pensacola. On March 9,
Dr. King led the procession from Brown Chapel to the Edmund Pettus
Bridge but went no further. He led the crowd in a prayer, a verse of "We
Shall Overcome," and turned back. That night, white Massachusetts
minister Rev. James Reeb was killed by whites in downtown Selma
and black resolve, even as far south as Pensacola, hardened. Thousands
descended on Selma in the days after Reeb's murder, and on March 15
President Lyndon B. Johnson delivered his famous speech condemning
what happened during the previous days and promised a federal voting
rights bill. The Montgomery to Selma March began again on March 21,

and Dr. King led the way. I did not attend that event, but did meet some marchers in Hayneville after they left Montgomery on the twenty-fifth. I wanted to show my support of the march, and returned to help those with no ride from Montgomery to Selma. I will never forget that place for a number of reasons. I thought blacks might get attacked again in small towns like that one along the parade route. It was in places like Hayneville where whites showed blatant resistance toward civil rights workers. They hollered insults and such at any activist because we dared to try and gain voting rights. I saw a lot of hatred displayed all during that episode. Upon my return to Hayneville, I set up camp again in the pasture where I first stayed in the town on March 7. There were many more people in the area than there were a few weeks earlier, due to the national and historic magnitude of the Montgomery arrival. Soon after we pitched our tents, word spread that a white volunteer named Viola Liuzzo had been killed. She and a black SCLC member were giving rides from Montgomery to Selma for those who participated in the march. She drove through Lowndes County that night when a carload of Klansmen shot her. The reality of what we wanted to accomplish hit me then. People were willing to kill those who only wanted what everyone else had.

When I think back on it, my experiences related to Selma in 1965 are very painful. It was not a pleasant situation for those who marched for black voting rights. Those officers were there simply to stop us in our tracks. Our goal was just and noble, but it was not an easily obtained victory. I also learned that I was not as fearless as I believed. What I saw in Selma and later in Hayneville opened my eyes in a lot of ways. In spite of my fear and negative experiences, however, I do not regret going to Selma. It was an incident that made me a stronger person. It strengthened my faith in God and helped me realize that He is with His children, regardless of what happens to them. God protects and takes care of His people, and I witnessed this first hand in 1965. Only God kept more of us from being hurt worse, or even killed, on Bloody Sunday, and only God kept the march to Montgomery alive after the beatings we received at the Edmund Pettus Bridge. He can be called on and can be relied upon in times of social turmoil. Selma, therefore, only strengthened my faith

in Him. It gave me strength and made me more determined to do and
to pursue what I knew belonged to me. After that incident, I was not
about to let anything turn me away from fighting for the rights of my
people. Perhaps the biggest lesson I learned was how far some were willing
to go to keep blacks in their so-called place. The experience weakened
my faith in humanity. As foolish as it may seem, Bloody Sunday opened
my eyes to the reality that some people in this country were not human
as it relates to how they treat their fellow man. It has always bothered
me that human beings could beat nonviolent demonstrators as they did
us, merely because we demanded access to a right that the Constitution
provided all citizens. Furthermore, the march taught me that if you want
something, you have to go after it even if it costs you personally. Nothing
in this life is gained without sacrifice. I may have been afraid, and still am
on occasion, but I have always been willing to sacrifice. I have sacrificed
much during my life, and it all began in Selma. The march changed me
forever and directly impacted the Pensacola civil rights movement during
the next thirteen years.

When I returned to Escambia County, I began to get more personally
involved in the local movement. One way I went about doing this was
practicing what I preached. I had stressed that blacks needed to apply
for meaningful positions of employment, so I applied for a job with the
Florida State Employment Service. I began working with the organization
on April 12, 1965 and was the first black to work in the statewide office.
I worked in downtown Pensacola on Garden Street which, ironically,
was a short distance from the sidewalks we paced during the selective
buying campaigns. Due to my civil rights activism, many of the workers
there did not accept me with open arms. I had a boss at the Florida State
Employment Service, though, named Leighton Pierce, who supported
me 100 percent. I will never forget the first day I went to work there.
Pierce called a staff meeting and closed the office doors. He said that,
"We have a Negro that has been hired in this office, H. K. Matthews.
Some of you have said to me that if a Negro was hired in this office, you
were going to resign. At the close of this meeting, I am going to stay in
my office for thirty minutes for the purpose of receiving any letters of

resignation that you want to submit." He received none. I wanted to bridge the very wide gap that existed between the Employment Service and the black community in Pensacola, and thought my hiring was a positive step toward accomplishing that goal.

I was acknowledged as the spokesman for local blacks before Bloody Sunday, but really felt like the leadership role was totally mine when I returned from Selma. Black activity continued in the area after Rev. Dobbins left, but I wanted to do more after my experience with Dr. King. Calvin Harris, Sr., stepped down as president of the NAACP sometime after the 1965 march and I was elected to fill the void. Although I was the spokesman for the black community in Pensacola, I retained my position as director of the NAACP Youth Council. I wore two hats for the organization. The adult branch still mainly concentrated on employment, but the youth helped me realize that there were still many places of public accommodations in the city that had not yet opened up to blacks. We decided that the NAACP adult and youth members had to fight for integration in all public places. The YMCA, for instance, was one of our first targets after 1965. It was on Palafox Street in downtown Pensacola but remained closed to blacks. We found out a lot about the business because Hollice T. Williams, a key member of the NAACP adult branch, worked at the YMCA as a masseur and could not use the facilities they had. The NAACP wanted to change the situation through negotiations. Even though we had to confront many people and groups over time, I have always felt that negotiation was better than confrontation. When we had to use direct action protests, we wanted it to be a last resort. We were able to negotiate with the management of the YMCA and convinced them that we would not harm the building or their patrons. We just wanted to participate in their programs and use their facilities. I promised them personally that we were not going to rub off on anybody. Surprisingly, the YMCA administrators did not have a strong resistance to integration. This encouraged me to continue our fight for integration throughout the late 1960s.

I think a lot of areas that were segregated and finally integrated came about because black organizations sat down and explained our point of

Matthews, third from left on the top row, at the Florida State Employment Office in Pensacola. He was the first African-American hired at the state agency, 1965.

view with the business owners. There is, and always has been, a fear of the unknown. When people do not understand something they usually assume the worst. It is similar today when people see someone with a turban on their head. They automatically think that it is another Osama Bin Laden. Whites looked at black people during the 1960s and believed that we were going to rob, steal, and destroy their property. When we talked to those people, we first wanted them to know us as individuals. We then explained what we wanted. When it came to integrating public facilities, I stressed that black leaders were as interested in decent people patronizing their businesses as they were. We also stated repeatedly during our hiring pleas that we were not trying to force unqualified blacks onto their job rolls. The NAACP and I wanted skilled, qualified blacks representing their race in white-owned businesses. We wanted responsible blacks to use facilities previously closed to them. I always maintained, "We are not going to open the front gates and let any and everybody into your place of businesses." Hopefully, as good businessmen, they would not let anyone in, whether they were white or black, who would cause problems in their establishments. These were the points that I always made first, because I felt that whites simply did not know or have the opportunity to understand us as dignified human beings. Many simply acted as if we had tails and had been running around in the jungle. Our strategy of "talking before walking," then, brought down racial boundaries in many privately-owned facilities in Escambia County.

In the late-1960s, the local NAACP targeted skating rinks, bowling alleys, and theaters for integration. The Youth Council led the fight in these areas, and I organized the protests. Our young people wanted something to do on the weekends and these places refused to let them inside because of their race. There were some places of entertainment for blacks only, but they were often in dilapidated conditions and not appropriate hang-outs for our people of their age. One of the first places we targeted was Dreamland Skating Rink. Its owner, V. T. Wozniak, offered little resistance and issued a press release on May 20, 1968 that stated, "Because of numerous requests made upon the management by members of the colored race and the desire of the management to maintain harmonious relations with the public, and as a result of negotiations between the management and the local chapter of the National Association for Advancement of Colored People," their facility would operate on an integrated basis beginning June 4, 1968.[12] Other accommodations, though, proved more resistant. Fast Lanes and Liberty Lanes Bowling Alleys both initially refused to meet our demands. We picketed Fast Lanes first because it was located in downtown Pensacola on Palafox and Maxwell streets. After Fast Lanes integrated, we targeted Liberty Lanes. One night, the NAACP Youth Council, its adult sponsors, and I decided to go bowling but were not allowed inside the building. I asked why we could not enter but received no answer. We decided to mill around in the parking lot until someone called the police. I explained our situation to the cops and they left us alone. All we wanted was a response, and I guess at that time the police had not yet graduated from half-baked racism to full-fledged racism, so they did not bother us. Liberty Lanes found that with no police support, it was best for them to negotiate with us. They opened to blacks soon thereafter. Entertainment facilities were just one part of the NAACP Youth Council's campaign.

We targeted any public place that openly discriminated against blacks. One such place was a laundromat in Ensley, which is just outside of Pensacola. In the spring of 1969, Youth Council members told me that the business still had a large hand-painted sign that said "Whites only" outside of the building. That was the kind of practice we wanted to end, so I decided that we would do something about it. The biggest problem with the facility was that I discovered Meredith Lumber Company owned the business. They sold wood and supplies to blacks, but only allowed whites to use their laundry. Many blacks in the area did not have their own washing machines or clothes dryers and depended upon such establishments, so I determined that the youth would protest this activity in a unique way. If the business wanted whites only, that is what we would do. We would go to the laundry and wash only white clothes. We staged our demonstration on about June 15, 1969. Each person who went into the business took one piece of white clothing and put it in separate washing machines. White customers came into the laundromat, saw us, and turned around and left. We must have caused a big ruckus that day, because a large crowd of mostly confused whites stood outside of the building when the deputies arrived. The police were not mean and did not go out of their way to disrespect us. One officer approached me and said, "Y'all are going to have to go. This establishment is white only." I told him, "That is what we are doing. We are only washing white clothes. We are following the directions." He thought it was pretty funny but said, "You know what that means. As soon as your clothes finish washing, you are going to have to leave." I promised that we would leave when we finished our task. But we had to dry them first, and it took another hour or so to finish the chore. Nevertheless, we still felt that no laws were broken because we did not wash a single piece of colored clothing. I do not think they ever took down those signs, because Meredith Lumber closed the laundromat soon after our wash-in. I guess they did not want people to obey their signs after all.[13]

The NAACP Youth Chapter also continued fighting segregated dining areas. It is hard to believe, but even eight years after the downtown sit-ins some stores still refused to serve blacks at their lunch counters. We found that some places would rather close than integrate. Pleezing's Supermarket, for instance, had a lunch counter in it. The owner was a members of the original Florida Boys Quartet, Davis Whitfield. Rather than integrate the counters, he took them completely out and served no one after the Youth Council targeted his place. It was fine with us that he removed them, because it was equal treatment. Nobody ate at Pleezing's, regardless of color.

The Youth Council was really on fire to win full equality for blacks during the last years of the 1960s. I even got involved in two incidents at Pensacola High School because my reputation as a spokesman for the youth had spread throughout the county. In 1968, a group of black students in the Youth Council approached me and said they had asked for a Black History assembly at Pensacola High School, but the principal refused. I talked to him a few times about having a Black History Day at the school, but he still adamantly refused. All the students wanted was one hour, but I guess that was too much to ask. I suggested to the Youth Council that a demonstration needed to occur, and they agreed. On one school day soon thereafter, almost every black student at PHS refused to report to classes. Instead, they met me in front of the school and sat on the lawn. The principal wanted to know what was going on and I told him, "None of the students will enter that school again until they get a Black History forum." I left to return to my job at the employment office and had a phone call waiting for me when I arrived. A deputy asked me to return to PHS and get the students back in class. I told the deputy, "They are not going back inside until they get a Black History assembly." The news was relayed to the principal, who proved more accommodating and agreed to honor the request. I was honored as the first speaker for a Black History assembly at Pensacola High School. The following year, the Escambia County School Board instituted a Black History Day at all local public schools. The Youth Council's work at PHS, however, was not over.

In the fall of 1969, several NAACP Youth Council members who belonged to the PHS band told me that they had to play "Dixie" at halftime of an upcoming football game. The black students, who made up about a quarter of the band, protested the song because it offended them. I, too, find the song insulting because it talks about "the land of cotton where old times there are not forgotten." Old times and cotton fields only reminds us of slavery, and there was nothing good about those days. Blacks should not be forced to commemorate and reminisce about a period of bondage. The students voiced their concerns to me and did not want to play the song. Their next appearance was no regular school event, either. The PHS band was playing at the halftime break of a game the Naval Air Station football team hosted. They had a squad then and played teams from other Navy bases from across the nation. I talked to officials at the school once again and voiced our concerns. The PHS principal said that if the students refused to play "Dixie" at the Naval game, they would not get credit for band class. There was no compromise and no one was going to convince them to cancel the song. I said, "If that is your ruling, that is fine with us." We met the kids again and told them that the administration said they either had to play "Dixie" or fail the band course. The students still did not want to play the song, so I came up with a way for them to express their sentiments.

I told the students that when the band began playing "Dixie" at the halftime show, I wanted them to drop their instruments to their side and walk off the field. They agreed to follow the plan. Word must have gotten out that the Youth Council had planned something, because deputies monitored every move that I made at the stadium on game night. I finally asked one, "Can I help you?" He replied, "We know what you intend to do." I responded, "I'm sure that I am free to walk around during a football game. If you going to follow me, follow everybody. If not, you are harassing me, so leave me alone." They knew something was up, but they did not know exactly what it was and did not know how to stop it. As soon as the band began playing, the black students dropped their instruments to their side and walked off the field. They left the band shocked and in shambles. Some whites kept playing while others watched the students walk off the field. The blacks in the crowd started cheering. Most of them, anyway. I had two black parents who were angry enough to kill me. They did not know what the consequences would be for their kids or for them, and they thought that I was a bad influence on their children. On the other hand, whites in the stands were quiet. There was nearly dead silence from the white audience. It had to have been shocking for them to see black kids being so assertive. After the demonstration, PHS officials had a change of heart and did not fail any blacks for band class. That pretty much ended "Dixie" at Pensacola High School, but my fun with symbols that schools used for racist purposes was only beginning. While the Youth Council continued their fight for equality in the schools and public facilities, the NAACP adult branch focused on other areas of discrimination.

One of the most serious obstacles facing black adults in the late 1960s was the lack of meaningful employment opportunities. City positions with the Pensacola Fire Department and the Pensacola Police Department were limited for blacks. In fact, the few blacks who worked for the city police department patrolled only black neighborhoods and could not arrest whites. We arranged meetings with city government leaders, who proved very receptive to our requests. During the sit-ins and selective buying campaigns, city officials persuaded Downtown Development, Inc., to grant our requests. Rev. Dobbins and I believed that all of our protests against injustice were related. We may have targeted downtown businesses, but our success had an impact on minority employment with the city. Political leaders saw how we crippled businesses with our actions, and they knew that we would use the same tactics against them. We may not have been able to withhold finances from the city, but we could target city merchants once again until city leaders addressed our concerns. The NAACP was prepared to begin such a campaign and area businesses began pressuring city leaders to hire blacks like they did years earlier. I wanted white store owners to tell their political leaders, "If you do not hire any blacks, they will pressure our stores again until you meet their demands." City agencies also influenced other businesses to integrate because the city would suffer economic losses if several white-owned stores began closing at one time. All of our activity, therefore, was connected. The NAACP did not have to fight tooth and nail to have all of our demands met, and city employment was one example. We requested they hire more minorities, and it occurred.

Another significant issue to me was that no African-American belonged to the city council. In 1968, we had a chance to place a black on the body. A member of the city council died before his term expired, so NAACP members and my fellow ministers decided to act. A group of us approached the city council, which was responsible for the filling the vacancy, and asked them to consider appointing Hollice T. Williams as the first African-American to serve on the council. Hollice was the person who earlier brought up the situation at his place of employment, the YMCA, and he was a dedicated NAACP member. The city council responded to the request very favorably and placed him on the body. The NAACP saw no hostile reaction to the appointment from the white city council members.

There were some times that things between whites and blacks in Pensacola went fairly smoothly. Those instances were few and far between, but they happened. One such example occurred when some white leaders publicly credited the NAACP for keeping more "militant" groups like the Student Non-Violence Coordinating Committee (SNCC) and the Congress of Racial Equality (CORE) out of Pensacola. City leaders and businessmen appreciated the fact that we used negotiation as our main tactic, instead of public crisis. As long as white leaders cooperated with the NAACP's peaceful demands, I promised to personally keep outside groups from interfering in Pensacola's affairs. After the successful local sit-ins and the 1963 Freedom Summer campaign in Mississippi for example, CORE organizers approached me and wanted to organize more street demonstrations in Pensacola. I informed them that we had things under control and did not want to aggravate the situation needlessly. I did not have contact with them or SNCC until ten years later. However, *Pensacola News Journal* writer Mac Harris distorted my words and made me look more like an accommodationist that I was. He quoted me as saying that I told CORE representatives to "not go away mad" just "go away." He also reported that I said militant groups "prey on people who can't think for themselves—the hard core of unemployed who have nothing to do but sit around on the street all day. And the sad thing is, while people are out in the street getting dog-bit and tear gassed, those guys are up in a room somewhere reading about it." I never held such negative regard for any civil rights organization and did not express those words to Harris. It was an early example of the *News Journal's* fabrications they intended would weaken the black freedom struggle, but it was far from the last time the paper used such tactics. My thought process, which I shared with Harris, was quite simple. I did not want the civil disruptions associated with CORE and SNCC coming to Pensacola. I was also against, and still oppose, separatism of any kind. God created us all equally. The world is large enough for all of us to get along in but too small for any of us to destroy each other. As long as whites continued to cooperate with our demands and treat local black representatives with dignity, I saw no reason to bring other groups in. I often told local people that if a person is a clown, treat him like a clown. If he is a troublemaker, treat him like a troublemaker. But if he is a man, treat him like a man. The white establishment, up to the late 1960s, had treated us like men when we demanded they do so. That, however, began to change during a local hospital strike I organized in 1969. When local white treatment of black protesters changed and the NAACP refused to modify their demonstration tactics in response, I understood the benefits of bringing another group into the Escambia County civil rights movement.

4

THE SCLC COMES
TO NORTHWEST FLORIDA

As the 1970s began, I decided to end my term as NAACP president. When the first elections came after Calvin Harris stepped down, I did not run for office. I much preferred leading the NAACP Youth Council because there was more energy there, so I remained in that position. There was less conservatism on the part of the young people and I enjoyed working with them for this reason. They were interested in social justice and remained integral to the local civil rights movement until my stay in Pensacola ended. In fact, I was appointed State Director of the Florida NAACP Youth Council by the time I ended my term as leader of the Pensacola adult branch. The man who was elected president of the local NAACP was Rev. Billie Joe Brooks. I had a lot of respect for B. J. Brooks and we worked together on many projects during the next ten years. Brooks was a very tall man whose determination for the rights of his people equaled his imposing height. He did a lot for local blacks and remained strong in his beliefs until some incidents occurred during the late 1970s. He fought hard for what he believed in and was a good leader for the NAACP. Rev. Brooks pastored Greater Mount Lilly Baptist Church in Pensacola and also worked for the Florida State Department of Transportation. Local whites later used his job to drive a wedge between civil rights activists in northwest Florida. Still, he remained president of the local NAACP until his death in 1998.

One of the first times B. J. Brooks and I worked together as leaders of a protest was during an NAACP-sponsored strike at a local hospital. In 1969, there were no blacks in meaningful positions at Baptist Hospital of Pensacola. The only positions blacks held were as housekeepers. In fact, I worked as a custodian at Baptist years ago. In March 1969, twelve black female employees led by Mrs. Ruby Scott, an NAACP member, approached me and Rev. Brooks and voiced a grievance. The female housekeepers had to clean the halls with extremely heavy mops. The work caused feminine, back, and stomach troubles. The previous month, men used the heavy equipment but were removed for reasons that remained unknown. In short, the ladies wanted to be taken off of the heavy mops. They had already gone to the housekeeping supervisors and Executive Director of the hospital, Pat Groner, and asked him to provide lighter mops for the females, but their requests fell on deaf ears. Mrs. Scott suggested they come to me and Rev. Brooks, so it fell on us to resolve the situation. I scheduled a meeting with Pat Groner and we voiced our concerns. Brooks and I made no firm demands, although the hiring situation at Baptist was deplorable. We initially only asked them to take the females off of the heavy mops and to employ some black people in positions other than housekeeping. Groner, though, refused our appeals. We met with the housekeeping personnel, who were all black except for the supervisors, told them about our meeting, and suggested a strike. The employees wholeheartedly agreed and decided to walk off of their jobs. Twenty-two blacks began the strike and the NAACP established picket lines at Baptist Hospital.

The facility was integrated and relied on blacks and white patients for survival. After the strike began, the NAACP asked all blacks to patronize other hospitals. Whites also stayed away from Baptist because of the activities that went on outside the entrances. I worked at the Florida State employment service at that time but we still made sure volunteers picketed the hospital on a daily basis. When I was at work, other volunteers walked with the striking workers. Most of the picketers belonged to the local NAACP, but some did not. They had heard about the strike through their churches or the newspapers. I usually led the demonstrations at night. Pat Groner maintained the entire time that our activities did not affect the hospital. He even told *Jet* magazine, which covered the strike, that it was "business as usual" but he lied.[14] It was quite obvious that their business had slowed dramatically since the strike began. In fact, I counted the occupancy myself after the protests had been going on for a couple of weeks and the occupancy at Baptist Hospital had declined to between ten and fifteen patients. The strike reduced revenue considerably at Baptist, so I decided to extend NAACP efforts to another area hospital.

Black employees at Sacred Heart Hospital faced the same things those at Baptist faced: heavy mops for females and no blacks in meaningful positions of employment. In the midst of our campaign against Baptist during the summer of 1969, sixty-one black Sacred Heart employees approached me and asked for NAACP aid in their workplace. They complained, as well, about the general treatment white supervisors gave blacks.[15] This was especially upsetting because Sacred Heart was a hospital the Catholic Church operated. The NAACP's main goal, once again, was simply to have blacks hired in higher positions. Black leaders, including myself and B. J. Brooks, held a press conference before the strike began where we discussed our plans and demands. I made a statement that criticized the nuns who worked at the Catholic hospital. I said that, "The nuns are hiding their racism behind the cloth, but they are just as bad as other people." I wanted everyone to know how serious we took the hiring situations around Pensacola. The Sacred Heart strike was very successful; in fact, it did not last an entire week. NAACP members used the same tactics implemented at Baptist Hospital, including worker strikes and picket lines. We experienced success more rapidly at Sacred Heart because of the damage, both in finances and public relations, that occurred at Baptist.

The administrators at Sacred Heart refused to talk to me in formal sessions because of my approach. They publicly declared, "We won't meet with Matthews," and instead demanded to work through Rev. Brooks. He became our prime negotiator during the campaign, even though he demanded the same things I did. He just carried himself in a different way. We both knew that even though hospital administrators would not meet with me, the same thing would be accomplished if Rev Brooks met with them. They were bound and determined to show me my place, I guess.

That was fine, because our groups did not care who the person was that got things done. We just wanted them done. Brooks even said, "Matt, I will go if it is fine with you, but only if you do not mind." I was not present at the Sacred Heart meetings, but they agreed to the same terms that I would have proposed. That is the way Brooks and I often had to accomplish our goals. Local blacks worked together, even when another organization came to Pensacola, because we all wanted the same thing. Whites granted our requests because someone other than I negotiated on behalf of the black community. Many people thought that Rev. Brooks was a more civil voice than I was, and we played that image to our advantage when we could. So Sacred Heart also took women off the heavy mops, hired blacks in other positions, and put whites in housekeeping. The strike there ended on October 5, 1969.[16] The demonstrations against Baptist Hospital, though, continued.

Despite the settlement at Sacred Heart and the financial hit blacks dealt Baptist Hospital, Pat Groner and other administrators refused to satisfy NAACP requests. We must have been doing something right, because the administrator called the police on us more than once. I was even arrested there on December 10, 1969 with five other folks and carted off to jail. We were arrested for disturbing the peace, even though we were across the street from the hospital.[17] The arrests only strengthened black determination, and the number of protestors at Baptist tripled. After my arrest, I continued to lead the demonstrations at Baptist. Soon thereafter, Mr. Groner approached me and said that he would consider the employee's cases one by one. He finally agreed to hire all of the female workers and provided them with lighter mops. He also hired some people in other blue-collar positions and placed white people in housekeeping. I had some people to tell me after the strike ended, "What did you accomplish? You did not get those black housekeepers off of the mops." I said, "Maybe not, but we got some white folks on them." Because of our efforts, custodial work was no longer a job for blacks only. Administrators moved black employees into supervisory positions in the business offices, in the dietary department and, ironically enough, they even promoted a black to housekeeping supervisor. Now blacks in Pensacola view Baptist

Hospital as just another employer.

Protests against the employment situations at both Baptist and Sacred Heart hospitals were tremendous successes. For a long time when I went into Century Hospital, a hospital in another part of Escambia County, the guards called administration to tell them that I was in the facility. They watched me like a hawk because they thought I was up to no good. I went there innocently enough, usually to see somebody from my congregation, and the whole hospital was alerted that I was on the premises. One thing that really angered me during the demonstrations is that some blacks refused to support us. Two even crossed the picket lines at Baptist and went back to slinging those heavy mops. I thought it was a disgrace for all blacks to not support our efforts because it was a concern for all of them. I even stated that those who did not agree with us, particularly those who went back to work, deserved nothing more than to be humiliated and maltreated by the white power structure at the hospital. Although the NAACP organized each successful campaign, I thought that more could be done to further black equality in northwest Florida.

Even before I stepped down as president of the Pensacola NAACP, I felt that Escambia County needed another civil rights organization. The national NAACP had numerous rules that local chapters had to follow. The regulations were one reason I did not want to lead the adult branch. In my opinion, the restrictions made many of the organization's policies too conservative and slow moving. I did not want to check with the headquarters every time I wanted to arrange a demonstration or organize a campaign. People also realized that the NAACP was not as assertive as they had been in the past, and they voiced their concerns about the group's limitations to me. After Dr. King died on April 4, 1968, I made contact with Ralph Abernathy. He became president of King's organization, the Southern Christian Leadership Conference (SCLC), after the assassination. I was attracted to the group because Martin King was its founder and first president. I had nothing but admiration for Dr. King, his leadership style, and his organization. I admired Ralph too, but for different reason. He did not have what Dr. King had, as far as personal charisma. Nevertheless, I was always impressed with the SCLC and I felt it was time to bring another civil rights group to northwest Florida. In January, 1970, therefore, I organized the Escambia County SCLC.

Many people encouraged me to establish the SCLC in Pensacola. They, too, were attracted to the SCLC's philosophy and tactics. The SCLC was more dogmatic in pursuing its goals. The national office of the SCLC was very assertive in pursuing its objectives and that is the thing that most attracted me to the group. I was a go-getter and I did not mince words or play games. I wanted what I wanted, and I wanted for my people what I wanted for my people. When I say my people, I mean the underdog. I have been one of them all of my life. SCLC, then, championed some fights for white people and opened membership to all races. Black people in northwest Florida needed not just another voice, but a stronger voice that was not too restricted in its activities. We had to act gingerly with the NAACP because of certain regulations that they had. The NAACP, for example, could not use the term "boycott." There were other things that we did that the NAACP did not want us to do for fear of a lawsuit. Because of its caution, the NAACP had become a little weak in Pensacola. Some people had become reluctant to identify with the NAACP because of its feebleness. I told area residents that it was not the tactics, but rather the non-tactics of the NAACP that concerned me. I think that their push was watered down and I think that it came from the top.

Some people had also commented that "I'll never join the NAACP as long as H. K. Matthews is the president." I did have a brash air about me and thought that those who said that did not belong in the movement anyway. I just went after what I went after and did not care who agreed or who liked it. Throughout my life, I found that the only way you can please everybody is to say nothing. And when you do that, people say you are dumb. So I just said what I felt and let the chips fall where they did. Still, I used this as a way to open the door for B. J. Brooks in the NAACP. I told him, "It might be well if somebody else was elected to lead the NAACP. Why don't you consider taking it?" That is how the transition occurred. I told him after he became president that "some of the same people that said they were not going to join as long as I am president are going to say the same thing as long as you are president. It is just an excuse not to become part of the struggle for equality." Sure enough, that is what happened. I stepped down as leader of the NAACP because I was just elected to fill the void that Calvin Harris had left. When his term expired, that meant that my time was up. I remained director of both the local and state Youth Councils. I gave up some of my responsibilities with the NAACP because I was not entirely thrilled with their limitations. Not long after I became president of the Escambia County SCLC, Ralph Abernathy appointed me as the first president of the Florida SCLC. The statewide branch operated out of Quincy, Florida. After I became an SCLC official, I resigned as state director of the NAACP Youth Council. I could not serve as president of two groups, so I decided to focus on the newer organization. However, I remained director of the Pensacola Youth Council. That was one hat I never tired of wearing. My plate was still full, but the new positions brought me new energy and enthusiasm.

The black community in Pensacola responded favorably to the new organization, for the most part. Some individuals said I started the SCLC because I wanted my own group, but that was ridiculous. I did not want nor need my own "thing." I said that anyone who refused to join the civil rights struggle because they did not want to support me better examine themselves first. I made it very clear that the SCLC was not a group that was in competition with the NAACP, and encouraged many people to join both organizations. I led by example in that regard. I made it known that SCLC was an organization that had the same major goal as the NAACP, which was racial equality. We may have gone about achieving it differently, but SCLC was not in conflict with or in competition against the NAACP. I promised everyone that the two groups would work together and we did just that. The SCLC under my leadership, and the NAACP under Rev. Brooks's command, worked hand in hand. This strategy came in handy during big campaigns, like the 1973 push against Confederate symbols at Escambia High School. SCLC and the NAACP, therefore, often operated as one with the leadership composed of Rev. Brooks, me, and Rev. Raleigh N. Gooden, who was state president of the NAACP. Rev. Gooden appointed me state youth director of the Florida NAACP and was very committed to black equality. Although he was a Tallahassee, Florida, resident, he was always willing to come to Pensacola when we needed his help. He became an integral part of the 1970s struggle in Escambia County due to the combined efforts of the NAACP and SCLC. Within our first year of operation, the local SCLC attracted over three hundred members. About six hundred individuals belonged to the area NAACP. Most new SCLC associates held dual membership in the organizations, because Rev. Brooks and I emphasized the importance of joining each organization. We existed as one body, basically, because the leadership and membership of the two groups were so united. When all of the group's members gathered, Rev. Brooks and I acknowledged Rev. Gooden as the overall leader. Rev. Brooks and I were sub-leaders, but we all played major roles because Rev. Gooden only came to Pensacola periodically.

The Escambia County SCLC was split into three crucial committees. Rev. Nathaniel Woods organized membership drives and solicited support for our new organization. He coordinated the Field Staff Committee. I appointed Fred Henderson as chairman of the Labor and Industry Committee, whose purpose was to monitor all firms in Pensacola that did business directly or indirectly with the black community to ensure that fair hiring practices existed. If not, we found out why and took action against the offenders. Rev. Otha Leverette was appointed to head the Educational Committee. Rev. Leverette was a crucial part of our organization because he presided over a small group known as the Escambia County Community League. He brought those members into the group, along with fragments of the local Black Baptist Minister's Alliance. But his main duty with the SCLC was dealing with local schools to make sure black students, teachers, principals, and all employees were being treated fairly. I intended the SCLC to be a "catch all" group for all local blacks that transcended group divisions, and it did for a time. It was broken down into subdivisions because we had enough members of the SCLC to specialize in specific areas. Furthermore, I could not do it all. There were times when I needed somebody to depend on in particular departments. Even though I was president of SCLC, the group was divided into foremen and workers like any other job. Labor relations and education were the two most pressing issues for blacks in Pensacola. Public accommodations had almost become a reality but we were still on the short end of the stick as it related to equal treatment in the schools and equal employment opportunities. The last category was particularly important. I stated on numerous occasions that the lack of blacks in meaningful employment around Pensacola was so conspicuous that it was both sickening and frightening. I proclaimed that "America has defaulted on its promise to the black people of this country," and was dissatisfied with a system that kept blacks enslaved in some regards.[18] I felt that at the time, the SCLC possessed the best way to make the nation fulfill its promise to all citizens.

The biggest difference between the SCLC and NAACP in Escambia County was their leadership styles. There was no big difference in the age of their members or anything like that. I was just more vocal and adamant about what SCLC did. Our methods and reputations differed tremendously from the NAACP. I was perceived by people in the community who did not know me as a loud-mouthed rabble-rouser, a gadfly who was anti-white, which was totally untrue. Whites thought I was someone who supported anything if it involved a black person, which was also untrue. That was the perception, because that was what many wanted to believe. There were many instances where black people came to us and requested support and I said, "No organization will support you, because you are in the wrong." And I have never been one who wanted to pursue an avenue of wrongness. If people were mistreated, white or black, my organization tried to help. SCLC came to the rescue of some white people when they were mistreated. The only reason we did not defend more whites was because they did not seek our help. But SCLC never refused to help anybody if their cause was just. I feel that my role in life is to help all people, regardless of color. Still, I had a reputation in Pensacola as one who was hard to deal with. Rev. Brooks did not have that image.

It was often easier for B. J. Brooks to negotiate with local whites because his approach was such a contrast to mine. We used those differences to our advantage, like we did in 1969 during our demonstrations at Sacred Heart Hospital. Even though Brooks and I demanded the same things, he often got it because he was not me! I wore down the white leaders through my picketing and agitating, and they demanded to talk to Rev. Brooks. We set up each organization so that if the people in the SCLC pursued a goal, then the people in the NAACP pursued the same goal. Often this was easy because SCLC members were also NAACP members. As members of the NAACP they could not do certain things, but as card-holding members of SCLC they could do it under our banner. Our efforts were a true inter-mingling of two organizations. If one couldn't, the other one could. For instance, if the SCLC boycotted a store, the members of the NAACP that also belonged to the SCLC participated. They could not have participated under the umbrella of the NAACP because their national office did not approve of our strategies, but they could take part as SCLC members. The differences between the two groups were not hostile ones, but were just philosophical differences between the two concerning how we went about doing certain things. All of the activities that we embarked on, therefore, were basically joint ventures.

One activity that I initiated shortly before organizing the SCLC was the establishment of a public affairs television program on WEAR in Pensacola. I knew the station manager at the time, Milt Deraina, and he extended the opportunity for me to speak to the community on the weekly show. I used television time to express black concerns and explain the motivations behind the requests the local NAACP made. I was the group's president at the time and thought it was a wonderful way to reach out to blacks and whites in Pensacola. The show, which was called "Black Problems in Pensacola," came on television once a month for thirty minutes. It was a very effective tool in the black freedom struggle and I continued the appearances after becoming SCLC president. Most importantly, it publicized the fact that blacks were excluded from many privileges that other local citizens enjoyed. A lot of people did not know that the racial situation existed as it did at the time, and others did not understand why the NAACP, SCLC, and area blacks acted as we did. I used the television show as a means of publicly declaring what local blacks wanted. I wanted to bring activities, words, and beliefs blacks considered offensive to the forefront. Some whites acted in an obnoxious manner without realizing that it offended blacks. My analogy was that if a child thought four plus four equaled nine, they would believe it was true until someone corrected them. The show, therefore, was meant to correct the thinking in Escambia County, and I saw some improvements in race relations after the program began. I wanted to bring what blacks were thinking into living rooms across the viewing area, and it was successful in that regard.

"Black Problems in Pensacola" only solidified my role as the spokesman for Escambia County blacks. I always made a point to say that whites asked me every day, "What do blacks want?" I responded, "Make a list of what you want and ditto; that is exactly what we want. No more, no less. We wanted to be given the same privileges because we were created by one God." I repeatedly stated that we are endowed by our creator, not by the president, not by the governor, and not by the mayor. All citizens have all inalienable rights and should be allowed to pursue liberty and happiness because we are all equal in the eyes of God. I also stressed that exercising our rights did not mean that we were trying to take away rights from anyone else. The public needed to understand, and still needs to realize, that we were not trying to deprive white people of anything. We just wanted what was rightfully ours. I used a story on the show to illustrate my point: if two children are playing with twelve marbles and one had eight and the other four, the only fair thing is to take two from the child with eight. They are then equal and on a level playing field. That is exactly what blacks wanted, and it is the message I tried to spread on the show.

The public affairs program also helped change hiring policies at WEAR. After most public facilities in Pensacola integrated, hiring remained the SCLC and NAACP's top priority. One day on the show, I publicly criticized Escambia County's Monsanto Chemical Company for not hiring blacks in more advanced positions. The station's program moderator questioned me about SCLC complaints concerning Monsanto when I noticed something. I told him, "You know something, we are sitting here today on this program complaining about other places, and there is not a single black person working at WEAR. You do not have any black employees at this station." When I returned to tape the next week's program, they had hired their first black cameraman. So I know first-hand that the program had a direct effect on the life of at least one African-American in Pensacola.

In 1969, I also began writing a series of articles for the *Pensacola Call and Post*, a black newspaper in Escambia County. I continued writing for them after organizing the local SCLC. I entitled one of my first essays "The Black Man's Waiting Period is Over" and expressed what African-Americans wanted. I began the piece, "Black American have waited and waited, and prayed and begged to be granted their full rights under the Constitution. We have become tired of waiting. We intend to have what belongs to us right now." It may have had a militant ring, but it was how I felt at the time. I claimed that blacks helped build the United States but were denied full citizenship because "the white man has raped us of our labor and attempted to rape us of our manhood." Blacks washed white clothes and cared for white children, but whites did not have enough respect for us to teach their children to treat us as humans. Black housekeepers could not ride in the front seat of a white person's automobile, but those drivers would carry a dog in their laps. Racists and hate-mongers talked of how good they have been to blacks, and it was a lie. I wrote that "no sacrifice is too great for us" to force "the foot of the oppressor off our neck." I wanted our community to see the contradictions and know how we felt. The essay basically stressed that blacks were awake and would wait no longer for what was ours, particularly from some so-called white Christians who worked hardest to deprive us of our dignity. I also pointed out in capital letters at the end of my essay that I was not attacking all white people, but only those who fit into the categories I described. That did not matter much, because many whites labeled me anti-white or communist and no article could change their opinion.[19]

I also spoke to the black community through the newspaper column. I told blacks that many left the church because it failed to address issues such as poverty, illiteracy, and racism. In an essay entitled "The Failure of the Church in Dealing with Social Problems," I maintained that the church had to lead the civil rights struggle for blacks. I accused many pastors of restricting their messages to the narrow space behind the pulpit and not practicing their words in daily society. What people needed to hear from their ministers, I argued, is "how to make it in this affluent society of ours." "Our aim as ministers," I wrote, "should be to teach our people to rebel against slavery in any form and, if we must encourage our people to bow, let us encourage them to bow to none other than the most High God and not some Back Alley Racist." I thought that too many blacks, particularly ministers, had become wrapped up in watching out for their own interests. They did not want the boat rocked for themselves, so they kept quiet when it came to racial injustices. But this practice went against the teachings of Christ, and I said as much in the column. "We must restore the faith and confidence of people in the church and in our Religious leaders," I concluded, "by proving to them that we are interested in the total human being."[20] The community affairs program and newspaper column were excellent ways for me to get the message out not only to local whites, but also to local blacks. I promised that the SCLC would expose black "Uncle Toms" to the black community, and it was a controversial yet effective tactic.

As I fought for the employment rights for others in Pensacola, I began to experience problems at my own job. Many people who knew about my civil rights activities, either through the papers or first-hand experience, complained to the Florida State Employment Service in Tallahassee concerning my public work. L. F. Shebel, director of the state agency, investigated my activities on several occasions and put a lot of restrictions on me in 1969. For example, I alone was forbidden to discuss anything except Employment Service business on Employ- ment Service time. That was fine, but the harassment and intimidation tactics continued. The state monitored all of my out-of-work activities with the local movement, and I felt the attention was not warranted.[21] I foolishly resigned my job after organizing the SCLC because another opportunity became available. In 1970, I accepted a job as manager at a new apartment complex, the Escambia Arms. The owners painted this picture of how I would be able to pursue my activities without restraint, and the opportunity to work for the dignity of my people was the most important thing on my mind then. I was considerably younger then than I am now, and they convinced me to resign from the Florida State Employment Service. Still, all things work for the good for those working for His purpose. I resigned, but if I had not done that I would not have the family that I have now. All things worked out, but it took a long time for me to realize it.

Up until the last day at the employment office, my supervisor said, "If you want to reconsider, it is not too late." He told me, "If you keep this job, you would take the wind out of the sails of a lot of folks here." Even after working there for almost five years, some were still not used to the fact that I was in the office. They did not approve of my activities and I later discovered that they, too, wrote letters to Tallahassee complaining about my SCLC work. But I foolishly resigned, thinking the grass was greener on the other side. Escambia Arms changed owners a couple of years after I began working there and the new management replaced me with someone else. So I floated from job to job until I left Pensacola. I was also going in and out of jail on frivolous charges due to my civil rights activities, and potential employers did not want to be bothered with me. So I preached on weekends and picked up what work I could find during the week.

My employment status did allow me to continue my civil rights work, which spread into other parts of Florida during the early 1970s. When I was appointed Regional Director of the SCLC in northwest Florida in 1972, I began going to more remote places in the state's panhandle. This is when most of my arrests occurred. In all, I have been arrested thirty-five times because of my involvement and leadership roles within the civil rights movement in Florida and Alabama. My reputation spread fast among blacks and whites in northwest Florida and when something would come up, I was the first to hear about it. But before I was appointed Northwest Florida Coordinator, Ralph Abernathy wanted me to organize a state-wide branch of SCLC. We decided it would operate out of Quincy, Florida, and I organized our first membership rally in 1972. I consulted individuals from Tallahassee and Quincy to help plan the event, and we considered bringing in Shirley Chisholm to speak. She ran for the presidency that year, though, and she had already been in the area campaigning. We also debated on having a march through town or organizing a good old-fashioned mass meeting at a local church. We decided, though, to hold a mass meeting at an AME Zion church in Quincy and invited Ralph to give the address. He accepted our invitation.[22]

On the night of the mass meeting, people packed that little country church. It seemed like folks were hanging from the rafters. But time passed, and Ralph was not there. I thought he may have just been running late, but he never showed up. The crowd grew restless after a while, though, and I was put on the spot. I had no choice but to deliver a speech myself. I did not have any notes or any preparation, and people were there to see Ralph Abernathy, not H. K. Matthews. Needless to say, a Florida branch of the SCLC did not get off of the ground for a few more years. There was a lack of interest in the state for another civil rights organization and the drive to organize a Florida SCLC just died out after the failed rally. Ralph did get to Quincy, but he was a day late. He apologized and told me that he had to stay in Atlanta because he was having problems with his church. There was a movement to get rid of him as their minister because he spent so much time away from his home congregation. I told him that I had empathy for his situation, but "you really put me in a tight spot. Besides that, you put the SCLC in a bad situation. Those people came to see you, Ralph, and you never showed up." Despite the fact that a state branch failed to take flight in Florida at first, I became very active in northwest Florida due to my activities in Escambia County.

My reputation spread throughout the panhandle in the early 1970s. For instance, one of my first activities outside of Pensacola was in Crestview, Florida. Crestview is about fifty miles east of Pensacola and one hundred twenty miles west of Tallahassee. The NAACP president in Okaloosa

County, Rev. Clanston Seymore, contacted me and requested our assistance because a nine-year-old black boy was expelled from his school for supposedly asking a white girl of the same age "an unfair question." How could one nine-year-old ask another nine-year-old an unfair question? What exactly is an unfair question? I was still the NAACP State Youth Director at the time and it was my responsibility to go where I was called to handle issues involving young people. So I met in Crestview with Rev. Seymore and the superintendent concerning the child. I found out that when he was expelled the principal made him walk home, even though the boy rode the bus to school. They would not allow him to finish the day or wait on a ride. I asked the superintendent, "What did the boy ask the white girl that was so unfair?" He never told us. I said, "If you are not going to tell us what he said, we want him reinstated." He agreed to reinstate the boy but said he either had to walk back to school or his mother had to return him. I said, "The bus picks him up every morning and you made him walk back home, so the bus will bring him back to school." He claimed, "The buses are not running because it is the middle of the day," but I said, "Send one to go and get him." And that is what he did. The child was reinstated, but I never found out what the exact words of the "unfair question" was. That was one of my first experiences with the NAACP or SCLC outside of Pensacola.

I was familiar with many people throughout northwest Florida as State NAACP Youth Council, and got to know many others after I became SCLC Northwest Florida coordinator. My SCLC activities really took me outside the boundaries of Escambia County and put me in some interesting situations. I initially did a lot of work for the SCLC in Century, Florida. Century is forty miles north of Pensacola near the Alabama state line. A shopping store in Century, Hudson's Grocery, gave blacks a lot of trouble when they went inside. They were followed by managers, accused of shoplifting, and harassed in other ways. I went to Century and began a boycott against Hudson's that spread to other areas in the town. Consequently, black people stopped going into the store. My job as a SCLC representative was basically to let the white power structure know that I was around. This was 1972 and blacks were still being mistreated in places of public accommodations and public schools. I went wherever I was called to intervene on behalf of the SCLC in northwest Florida, because there were a lot of racist activities that occurred in the areas between Tallahassee and Pensacola. Many areas did not want the attention we brought, so they did the right thing when SCLC made our presence known. DeFuniak Springs was one place, however, that did not respond to SCLC demonstrations, so we resorted to other tactics.

DeFuniak Springs is the seat of Walton County and is about seventy miles east of Pensacola. The city's public school system suspended blacks in disproportionate numbers to whites. SCLC also found out that the schools removed black kids from class, while whites received no punishment for doing the same things. The school board would not acknowledge our grievances, so I came up with a new strategy. If they did not want blacks in the class, we would help them out. The SCLC established Freedom Schools at Greater Union Baptist Church in DeFuniak Springs. We pulled all black kids out of the public schools because of the high suspension rates. Our contention was that the infractions could have been settled in school, that white students were not being suspended, and that the blacks were often not involved in things that were serious enough to require expulsion. That was when integration first took place in DeFuniak Springs, and the SCLC believed that this was how white administrators vented their frustrations. The purpose of our Freedom Schools was to hit the school system in the pocket, because there was so much the state government allotted for each child that attended classes per day. If the attendance was down, that meant that the revenue was down for a particular period. The Freedom Schools were effective tactics because they hurt system revenues. School boards had little choice but to comply with our requests, and that is what happened in DeFuniak Springs. The Freedom Schools were so successful in DeFuniak Springs that the SCLC established them in Live Oak and Chipley. Yet our productive activities in those areas were not without peril. In fact, two events occurred in Chipley that nearly ended my life.

Chipley was an isolated rural town in Washington County about one hundred ten miles east of Pensacola and eighty miles west of Tallahassee.

Local schools integrated shortly before 1972 and black parents thought their children were not being treated fairly by teachers, parents, students, or administrators. Rev. R. N. Gooden, the NAACP state president, and I were in Chipley for an extended period during the winter 1972 school term. I later found out that I was the first black man to stay in a Chipley motel room.

Needless to say, the white desk clerk was not very thrilled about me being there. I think he is the person who gave the Ku Klux Klan my room number. Regardless, one afternoon I got a call from someone that I will never forget. It was a white man who said, "The Klan is coming to pay you a visit." I did not know who the caller was and have never discovered his identity. I called R. N. Gooden to tell him what had happened. He had stayed outside of Chipley and called me a fool for staying there. Rev. Gooden told me to "get out of the room now and meet me across the street from the hotel." I got out of that room in what is probably still a record time in Chipley! I met Gooden in a parking lot across the street from the hotel in my car. We knew my enemies would not recognize my automobile because the SCLC did not allow me to take my own automobile to out-of-town demonstrations. It was too dangerous for my car to be identified, so they rented a different car for me every time I traveled from Pensacola to Chipley. A few minutes after Gooden arrived, four Klan members in full regalia showed up knocking on my door.

I guess they thought I was still in my room because they stood around for a while. I do not know what they wanted to do and did not want to find out. I thought they would try to break in the door, but they did not. Finally, they left when I never came out of my room. That was one of the most interesting experiences I have had, and that is saying something. A few minutes after the Klan left, I went back to my room and called the local sheriff. I told him about my Klan visit and suggested that he already knew about it. He did not take me seriously and did not satisfy my concerns, so my response to him was, "I am in Chipley and I am going to stay in Chipley and nobody is going to run me out." It was another brash statement, but I made it. I also told the office that "I would appreciate the law not harassing me, but protecting me." For good measure, I called those Klan members "nothing but a bunch of yellow-back cowards" and promised that "if they break in on me, they might get me, but I'm going to make sure I get one of them before I go."[23] I did not care if they were officers or not, I was going to protect myself. I spent the rest of my visit in that same hotel room. The telephone and heat in each room was controlled from the hotel's front office, and the manager cut both off after the Klan visit did not scare me off. Someone also cut all four of my vehicle's tires. But it did not matter. I was not leaving that hotel, despite the fact that it was the middle of winter, my room was cold, and everybody in Chipley knew were I was staying. I was stupid to stay in that motel. I was stupid to allow those people in Chipley to talk me into staying in that motel. But I was no fool. I slept with a pistol under my pillow every night I stayed in Chipley, and took it with me everywhere I went after the Klan incident. My refusal to leave Chipley is probably when the assassination plot started. People just love me to death!

Rev. Gooden and I began organizing mass meetings in Chipley during the early 1970s to address our complaints concerning the schools. To protest the conditions, we decided to boycott all area businesses. I told them, "You do not need to shop in stores in Chipley until white treatment of blacks in this town changes." Rev. Gooden spoke to the crowds and supervised a lot of activity in Chipley, but the whites there viewed me as the main agitator. In fact, the protestors in Chipley and DeFuniak Springs came up with a chant they often repeated during our activities that infuriated some folks. It asked, "Hey, hey, have you had your H. K. today?" Many folks wanted me and SCLC out of that city and would go to any length to get us out. There were even two prominent blacks, including a black deputy, who steadfastly opposed what the SCLC tried to accomplish. The local deputies pulled me over in my automobile repeatedly for no reason after our nightly meetings ended. It was harassment, plain and simple. But I always thought that police harassment was a sign of progress, because it indicated that they wanted you out of their hair and resorted to such tactics to accomplish it. Those two Chipley blacks had spoken to the white community and criticized me and Rev. Gooden for coming to their city. One night at a community meeting in early 1973, one of the men came to the church where local activists met. I noticed him in the crowd and thought it was strange for him to show up. Several adult SCLC members in the congregation also thought it was suspicious. They watched him closely because they had a feeling he would do something rash. He had made it very known that he was against everything that we were doing. I kept speaking to the crowd and noticed a ruckus at the back of the building. A crowd surrounded the man, whose last name was McDougal, and were hitting and kicking him. I had to leave the pulpit and keep our members from beating him to death. I later found out that he had a pistol in his jacket and made a move to grab it when the crowd pounced. We pulled him to his feet and questioned him. Some of our supporters said that if he did not talk, they would beat answers out of him. I did not condone the activity, but I did want to know who was behind the plot. He admitted that a group of local whites had sent him to the church to kill me. He rattled off several names, and most were known Klansmen. I wondered how this person got into the church because law enforcement officials were supposed to guard the building every night. Sure enough, Deputy Potter, the black who was speaking out against our activities, was sent by the sheriff to guard the church that evening. He denied knowing anything, but we believed that he was not there to protect us. It was the old idea of "the fox watching the hen house" in practice. The really sad part of the assassination attempt is that McDougal's daughter was one of my biggest supporters, and she was in the congregation that night. The SCLC eventually achieved all of our goals in Chipley, but it was a constant struggle that took many visits, meetings, rallies, and demonstrations to see the fruits of our labor.

During the early 1970s, the Escambia County SCLC also became more involved in local affairs. In particular, we addressed hiring practices in Pensacola stores and industries. The first company we negotiated with in the area was Monsanto Chemical Corporation. We were aware of their mistreatment of black employees because our SCLC Labor and Industry Committee Chairman, F. L. Henderson, worked there. Monsanto demoted him from a lucrative position and tried to fire him because of malfeasance on the job. That was another obstacle local blacks faced, and still encounter, in the struggle for equality: they are the last hired and the first fired. Monsanto definitely had ways of getting rid of people they did not want working there because the plant was not unionized. We thought the company had at least two other reasons to fire Henderson. Not only was he a key member of the SCLC, but he was also one of the few blacks that happened to have a supervisory position at that time. The SCLC problem with Monsanto was not their refusal to hire blacks, but the treatment of those they had employed. We decided to make our presence known and established pickets at the plant's main gates that charged that racism existed within the company. I am very careful about making that charge, but it was evident in this case that Henderson was demoted to remove a black from the position he held. He eventually got his higher level job back, and other blacks received promotions. Henderson stayed at Monsanto until his retirement.

SCLC also became involved with the Montgomery Ward department store when it came to Pensacola in the early 1970s. When it first opened, the store hired a lot of people for part-time work. Several SCLC members worked at Montgomery Ward, including the wife of Pensacola police officer Jesse Dean. But Montgomery Ward provided an example of how businesses often hired blacks, used them while they could, and got rid of them when the first opportunity presented itself. All of the part-time people were laborers who stocked the store and prepared it for the grand opening. After the store opened to customers, they fired all of the black people and retained the white folks. We did not appreciate the decision, so SCLC initiated a campaign against Montgomery Ward. After all of the blacks were fired, I authorized county SCLC Labor Representative F. L. Henderson to speak to the Montgomery Ward manager on behalf of our organization. He said that he made no headway and could not get the manager to hire back any African-Americans he fired. I decided to accompany Mr. Henderson to Montgomery Ward the next morning, and we again reiterated our requests to store management. Yet he still refused to hire blacks. I said to him, "Since you refuse to hire

these people, when you come to work tomorrow we are going to have a
picket line outside your store. Since you just want white people to work
in here, we want to make sure that your clientele is white." They would
not hire people who supported their store, so we decided to not support
their store. Evidently, he called the Montgomery Ward home office in
Chicago and said, "These niggers are threatening to boycott this store."
After I got home, not three minutes passed before I got a phone call from
Chicago. The man on the phone said that "I understand that you are
talking about picketing Montgomery Ward." I said, "Yes, I surely am.
We plan on beginning it tomorrow and have planned a meeting tonight
to tell our people about it." He said, "Let me tell you something. I told
that manager that he better not have a picket line in front of that store.
What I want you to do, Reverend, is to find Ms. Dean and take her to
the store in the morning. She is going to work as a full-time employee."
What the manager of the Montgomery Ward at the mall did not know
was that the man he called and reported the SCLC picket lines to was
black. The husband of that man's aunt, Dempset Smith, belonged to the
church that I pastored on Eighth Avenue and Brainerd Street. It's interesting how things often work out. When I took Ms. Dean to Montgomery
Ward the next morning, that manager wanted to know if I knew anyone
else who needed a job. He was there about three or four days before he
lost his job at that store.

A similar situation happened in Fort Walton Beach, which is in
Okaloosa County. I got a call requesting SCLC help concerning the local TG&Y. It was a local variety store that many blacks frequented. We
jokingly called it "Turnip Greens and Yams." The TG&Y had wrongly
accused some black children of stealing and literally ran them out of
the store. I organized a mass meeting and listened to other testimonies
of further mistreatment at TG&Y. I told those in attendance that I did
not know what I planned to do about the situation before I arrived,
but had decided to adjourn the meeting early and march immediately
to the store. It was about 7:30 P.M. and the store did not close until
nine. We marched there to demand fair treatment, and the next day
the manager was gone. The company had him shipped out. There are

several other instances where we used the same tactics to influence hiring policies and influence fair treatment of all customers in stores around the Florida panhandle. For instance, the SCLC got black cashiers hired at local Pak-A-Sak stores. The major chain stores offered the strongest resistance to equal employment opportunities. It seems that the SCLC had to threaten every large chain that came to Pensacola with some kind of action before they did what they were supposed to. We had to petition J. C. Penney's in University Mall and Gayfer's at Town & Country Plaza. It is shameful that we had to do these things in order to get what should have been ours already.

Throughout my work with the SCLC during the early 1970s, I stressed that our fights were for basic dignity. We did not want anybody to give us anything. We wanted the doors opened, though, so we could get it ourselves. I have always asked why a lot of African-Americans talked about wanting a piece of the pie. I maintained that I did not want a piece of the pie, I wanted the recipe. Give me the recipe and I will make my own pie. The SCLC did not want handouts or special treatment. As African-Americans, we have had special treatment all of our lives. We had to watch white folks get jobs we could not have. We had to sit behind them on the bus. We wanted equal opportunity, and the SCLC was dedicated to ensuring it existed for blacks in northwest Florida.

The organization also conducted investigations into situations concerning blacks and law enforcement officials that seemed suspicious. In July 1970, for example, two black teenagers drowned at Pensacola Beach. It was rumored that they had been murdered and the sheriff's department wanted to cover-up the crime. After the incident, I headed a committee of six people under the SCLC banner to investigate the rumors. I chaired the committee and Beno English, Admiral Leroy, Christopher Crenshaw, LeRoy Boyd, and Louie Holland conducted the investigations. Our goal was to check the facts surrounding the deaths of Beulah Mae Glover and Willie J. Huff III to substantiate concerns of foul play. We also made suggestions to ease the tense racial situation in Pensacola. We interviewed the parents and other relatives of both victims, recorded facts about each person at the time before their disappearance, and talked to law enforcement officials about the procedures they took to help find the bodies. We were also briefed by the mortician, pathologist, and his assistant about the condition of each body. In August, the committee concluded that the two teens died because of an accidental drowning. However, we did cite a complete breakdown in law enforcement procedures. We discovered that the sheriff's department initially refused to search for the blacks because the sun had set. The person who reported the two missing were told to walk up and down the beach and they would probably find the kids. We cited the careless attitude and claimed it was an example of why the black community did not trust law enforcement officials in Escambia County. We also discovered that white police had a reputation for harassing blacks at the beach, and stated our concern.[24] To my knowledge, the sheriff's department never addressed the grievances. The SCLC, though, soon had another chance to address police attitudes towards Pensacola blacks.

One issue the organization never tackled was higher wages for minorities. For the most part, blacks were hired on the same wage scale as whites. I have no doubt that some places existed where blacks who had worked for ten years made the same wage as they did after working there for ten days, but the SCLC's main focus was making sure that businesses hired blacks. Employment was the key to improved conditions. Slowly but surely, when merchants realized that hiring black people at their public or private business did not damage their sales or business activity, their resistance subsided. Business owners see no color but green, and when they hired a black worker who did a competent job, wage increases or other rewards often followed. Our challenge, from the SCLC point of view, was to get blacks in the workplace and they would take care of the rest themselves.

The SCLC and NAACP, therefore, participated in several joint ventures to promote racial equality in Pensacola during the early 1970s. We were not in competition with each other, and I made sure that people understood that the two groups cooperated at every chance. The SCLC and NAACP were very involved with media relations, educational activities, public housing policies, government participation, and hiring practices, and used traditional forms of protest to achieve our goals. The SCLC petitioned to make Martin Luther King Jr.'s birthday a state holiday in Florida and called the state's reimposed death penalty "a legal lynching" for blacks and poor whites. But one issue in particular brought me into a bitter, direct confrontation with the local white establishment: the symbols used at Escambia High School. Escambia High was known as "the Rebels," and "Johnny Rebel" was their mascot. Johnny Rebel was a white boy dressed in full Confederate gear who ran along the sidelines at sporting events waving a large Confederate battle flag. The flag was the school's official banner, and "Dixie" was the fight song at EHS. I have never been against the use of such symbols per se, and I do not think blacks object to their fundamental existence. A piece of cloth or word in and of itself is not offensive. What offends me is white *misuse* of the symbols. The intent behind the use of a word or flaunting of a piece of cloth is offensive. When the flag and "Dixie" are used to intimidate, scare, or just remind blacks that they are not welcome in a public place, they need to go. This is what was going on at Escambia High School soon after the school integrated. The local SCLC and NAACP Youth Chapter decided to confront the issue in 1972. In short, I was not ready for the resistance and hatred whites displayed. The conflict over the misuse of symbols at EHS permanently influenced race relations in northwest Florida and made me a marked man.

5

'Rebels,' Riots, and Freedom Schools: A Community Divided

Before the Escambia High School symbols controversy, there had been a lull in civil rights activities in Pensacola. In fact, I spent most of my time outside of the county representing the NAACP or SCLC. Locally, things had gotten pretty quiet. The SCLC and NAACP were still working together, just rocking along with our usual activities. We were still involved with media relations, education activities, and hiring practices in Pensacola. With the Escambia County schools situation, the bond between the SCLC and NAACP became even tighter. In my opinion, the SCLC was still a lot more focused on obtaining equality than the NAACP, but Rev. Brooks was deeply involved in the symbols issue and eventually brought outside assistance to our cause. For the first time since the sit-ins, we began holding mass meetings for the black community during the crisis. The episode also brought Rev. Raleigh N. Gooden to our area, who became a close friend of mine and remained a vital part of the local movement for the next three years.

A lot of racial tension and mistrust between whites and blacks came from the school situation in Escambia County. The schools had integrated under a court order, but there were still several problems that I got involved in during the late 1960s and early 1970s. For example, we had the episodes concerning "Dixie" and the Black History program at Pensacola High School. I later led the campaign to have a white principal fired for telling one of his black students that the youth was "acting like a nigger." However, the school board called it a "misunderstanding" and refused to take action against the principal. The episode demonstrated that local blacks did not want a person in office who would say something that they knew would deliberately antagonize blacks. I also appeared before the school board on a few occasions to protest the lack of funds going to schools with a black student majority. Some black institutions, such as Booker T. Washington Middle School, actually shut down against the wishes of many area residents, while several schools remained open that were nearly all-white. Washington Middle School later opened again, but it was renamed to honor a local white. Many in the black community felt completely nauseated by the decision. It was my assertion that only token integration had occurred at many schools, and funds were going unequally to schools with white majorities. Furthermore, there were many white teachers, principals, administrators, and school board members that blacks considered to be racist and bigoted. The school board had enlarged the gap between the races by rewarding white officials who resisted integration. Blacks simply wanted equality in education and knew our children would not get it unless they went to school with whites. I addressed the school board many times on behalf of the black community, but board members resisted any changes. They tried to inform me of my standing by repeatedly referring to blacks as "nigras," a demeaning term, against my wishes.[25] In other words, blacks were still a long way away from a fair and just unitary system of education in Escambia County. The most problems, though, came from the largest high school in the area, Escambia High School.

Escambia High School had approximately 3,500 students, only about 10 percent of which were black. I knew a lot of the African-American students at EHS and still had my finger on the pulse of the young black community as local NAACP Youth Director, so I was very familiar with the atmosphere that existed at the school. Racial problems first surfaced during the 1972–73 school term near the end of football season. The team went 0–10 and many black parents wanted the county school board to fire the incompetent white head coach and promote his black assistant, but they refused. The squad's lackluster showing led white players to accuse the few black team members of not playing hard and deliberately missing plays, which was ridiculous. As a result, some fights broke out between whites and blacks on campus. Escambia High principal Sidney Nelson even suspended classes before lunch on November 17 because of the fighting and high racial tension. After the school closed, a sick individual called Principal Nelson and told him that "somebody needs to hang" for causing the disturbances. Rumors were spreading like wildfire throughout the community, and it seemed like the *Pensacola News Journal* reported all of them. The paper said that the principal was stabbed, that blood was splattered in the halls, that black students overturned buses, and that police had to shoot tear gas into the school. It was obvious from reading the papers and listening to white school officials that they placed most of the blame on black students, despite the fact that whites outnumbered them nearly ten to one. EHS didn't open until noon the next day after a faculty meeting with school superintendent J. E. "Bud" Hall. He stationed county and city police on campus, set up a student human relations committee at the school, and discussed having a night session to relieve overcrowding.[26] Hall and other school administrators did everything except address the reason black students were upset.

The main problem that existed at Escambia High School was the white misuse of certain symbols. The school was supposed to be integrated, but Confederate symbols still represented the student body. That was insensitive, but not inexcusable. The frustrating aspect of the "Rebel" name and mascot, the playing of "Dixie," and the waving of a Confederate battle flag was that white students used them to blatantly insult blacks. Again, it was the misuse of such symbols that angered the black community, and that misuse intensified toward the end of 1972 as almost daily attacks on students occurred at EHS. The situation got no better when the school reopened. Fights continued to break out and tensions were still high. Whites sprayed "KKK" on school walls and the initials remained there for weeks. A few white students even showed up wearing white Klan hoods. Despite the nature of the harassment, many more blacks were suspended from school than whites. Deputies even sent a caged car to school to pick up those arrested on campus, like they were common criminals. To make matters worse, two state officials unnecessarily involved themselves in the matter. Florida House of Representatives member R. W. "Smokey" Peaden came to his home district and promised a grand jury investigation of the situation at EHS. Before he got into politics, Peaden was a Pensacola police officer, so we did not trust him one bit. Close on his heels was the self-proclaimed "banty rooster" himself, State Senate member W. D. Childers.[27] Their actions during the conflict proved that neither man was fit to be a state official. While whites addressed the situation in their own way, blacks also prepared for a confrontation over the racist use of those Escambia High symbols.

In November of 1972, students came to me in larger numbers and explained what they encountered on a daily basis at Escambia High. White students taunted and harassed them. They waved the Rebel flag in their faces as a symbol of defiance. Common sense allows someone to know that blacks are not particularly fond of what the flag represents, but waving it in a black person's face while saying, "Nigger go home" is a pure insult. It was also a sensitive time in the area's history. School integration was just getting off the ground, and the harassment meant more in 1972 than it does even today. What I mean is that people with a different culture entered a school that the majority did not want there. And then people waved objects in their face and told them to "Go back to where you came from," "We don't want you here, nigger," and "This is our school." The people at EHS, including instructors and administrators, did not want blacks there and they made their feelings known by displaying that flag and singing "Dixie." It was harassment, plain and simple. It was bad enough that the school was nicknamed "the Rebels." But whites took the Rebel flags which, by the way, mean much more than an innocent school symbol to blacks, and used them to make black students feel uncomfortable. Student clubs like the "Rebelaires" chorus group were not open to blacks. Those kids were being threatened and intimidated every day with those images, and they were getting fed up. I think every black parent that had a child in Escambia High School, even though there were not very many, brought this situation to my attention. All of them did not come at one time, but they wholeheartedly supported the actions of those who did approach us. Parent after parent told me and

Rev. Brooks, "We are fearful of sending our children to Escambia High because the intimidation is getting worse." The local black leadership decided to schedule a meeting with the county school board to discuss those issues. Dealing with the school board concerning the symbols was like pounding our heads against a brick wall.

The Escambia County School Board was very reluctant to do anything about our concerns. NAACP and SCLC representatives, including Rev. Brooks, Rev. Leverette, and I, met with the board a few times about the issues at EHS, but they never took our complaints seriously. The most vocal members were Peter Gindl, Richard Leeper, and Carl West. Leeper chaired the board. They told us one time, "This is our school and these are our symbols. We have had them there for years and we are not going to change them. These kids are just coming to this school starting trouble." We felt that they viewed black students as outsiders, so to speak, and they were not changing any symbols to accommodate them. Or us, for that matter. The entire board had a bad attitude when we first met with them. Their mood was worse than what we had encountered with other institutions. They were much more hostile, bitter, and closed to compromise than many other whites we had dealt with up to that point. I knew from the beginning that the struggle at EHS would be a little different than our previous battles.

In response to what was going on at Escambia High, the SCLC and the NAACP called a mass meeting to discuss the situation with area blacks. The initial assembly was so successful that those in attendance wanted to keep meeting until we resolved the situation. The mass meetings continued for the next several weeks, on almost a nightly basis. Rev. Brooks and I even invited Rev. R. N. Gooden to join our campaign. Rev. Gooden was the state NAACP field director and operated out of Tallahassee. For all intents and purposes, he moved to Pensacola during the next three months. He also added a spark to our mass meetings and joined our discussions with local white leaders. Rev. Gooden, Rev. Brooks, I, and sometimes Rev. Leverette continued meeting with the school board. We repeatedly voiced our opposition to the EHS mascot and nickname, but got nowhere. As a result, our mass meetings kept growing. We held the assemblies at Greater Mount Lilly Baptist Church, which was the church that Brooks pastored, and Leverette's church, St. John Devine Baptist. We met there because the churches were able to hold the crowds. We had overflowing audiences as the month progressed. People literally stood outside listening to the messages being delivered. The meetings were so successful that police officers patrolled the churches during the assemblies and harassed those who stood outside, or questioned people as they left the assembly. It got to the point that we had a local group of men who called themselves "Deacons for Defense" who stood outside of the building during mass meetings to protect those of us on the inside. The Deacons were armed and were stationed in the most visible places to prevent trouble. We were not a violent group of people, but as Rev. Gooden said in one sermon, "You bother us, and we will bother you back."

As the month wore on, the situation at Escambia High only got worse. It seemed that the number of deputies stationed at the school grew each day. During one incident, a white boy sprayed mace into a black deputy's face, while other white students pelted blacks with rocks. Police arrested almost fifty people for trespassing during that event. Things grew so bad that whites who did not attend EHS came to the school to start trouble. The school closed again in the middle of December due to racial fighting. To make matters worse, the black community had no trust in the Escambia County sheriff's department, which was supposedly the agency to protect innocent students. In particular, we did not trust or like Sheriff Royal Untreiner or the head of his riot control squad, Jim Edson. They were both bona fide racists and had bad reputations for the way they treated blacks. In fact, deputies arrested a black math teacher for disorderly conduct because he did not get out of their way fast enough to satisfy them. The intervention of Peaden and Childers did not help matters at all for black students. Although school officials told each that blacks had problems with the Rebel flag and "Dixie," Childers dismissed our complaints and promised he would get down to the "real problem." He promised his white constituents that "we will have peace" and "no concessions will be made" concerning the symbols, which he said "are a part of the heritage of Escambia High." He even called our actions "ridiculous" and told a reporter, "You haven't seen any white groups trying to get the name of Booker T. Washington High School changed after integration, have you?" The *Pensacola News Journal* did not help the black cause, either. They repeatedly tried to make black leaders look like troublemakers, labeled Rev. Gooden an "outside agitator," and published letter after letter from white readers who condemned or ridiculed our movement. For example, one letter that referred to blacks at Escambia High said, "Let them get out and stay out; they shouldn't be there in the first place."[28] There was no settlement concerning the situation when schools closed for Christmas break, but the NAACP and SCLC decided to act before classes resumed.

Both groups continued to hold mass meetings through the holiday season. Rev. Brooks, Rev. Gooden, and I listened to what black students and parents told us. We also met separately to plan a course of action. What we decided to do was present the school board with a list of concerns. If they were not addressed, we would pull all black students out of the county's public schools. We even decided that Brooks would present the school board with our requests. Rev. Gooden was not originally from the area, and everyone just loved me too much. So we thought Brooks was the obvious choice to talk to board members. We came up with a list of things the NAACP, SCLC, and local blacks wanted at Escambia High: the elimination of all Confederate images, more black teachers hired, the removal of sheriff's deputies from the campus, a black assistant principal, the removal of all KKK signs and other racist references from school grounds, an immediate suspension of anyone who wore a Klan hood to school or was caught writing the letters on school property, all charges dropped against each student arrested during the disturbances, and the maximum period of suspension for anyone caught with a weapon in the building. In addition to the stipulations, we also objected heavily to Peaden and Childers's involvement with the situation. Gooden's involvement ensured that the state NAACP would support our goals. We set the end of the holiday break, January 2, as the school board's deadline to act. We knew that all of our demands would not be met overnight, so all we wanted was evidence that the board would negotiate with us in good faith. We wanted some sort of compromise to come from the dialogue, but we knew we had to get the school board's attention. Rev. Gooden read the demands at a mass meeting and they were very popular. No one present voiced opposition to the list, so Rev. Brooks scheduled a meeting with three school board members for December 21. The rest were out of town for the holidays. Needless to say, the board members who were there were not very happy with our demands or our promise to boycott county schools. They were especially unhappy with our request regarding the inflammatory symbols. One board member, Richard Leeper, told us that "if the students want to play 'Dixie,' no one could stop them." Other than a few defensive comments like that one, the board pretty much dismissed our petition. But our boycott promise did get their attention. In fact, Leeper told the *Pensacola Journal* that the walkout threat "was a cruel exploitation of school children."[29] They could not afford to ignore us for long.

I have learned throughout my years of fighting for black folks that there is one thing that whites will always pay attention to: their pocketbooks. The NAACP and SCLC did not want to pull kids out of the schools. We wanted them to get the best education available and improve their lives. But we believed that they could not focus on their studies with all of the junk at Escambia High. We did not look forward to a walkout, but we were ready to follow through with it. We knew the boycott threat would get the attention of white leaders because of all of the money at stake. In December of 1972, there were 14,400 black students in Escambia County public schools. If every black walked out, the school board reported that they would lose forty thousand dollars a day in state funds. The amount of funding was determined by the average daily attendance per school. I figured the amount was probably even higher, because that is the figure the school board told the media and those folks did not want us to know that we could hurt them. Several local white officials responded to the NAACP list. Smokey Peaden and W. D. Childers promised to be at EHS when classes began. Board member Peter Gindl said that any student who boycotted county schools would not be allowed to make up missed work and would be given unexcused absences. I would like to know how they planned on distinguishing the boycotting students from others who missed school. EHS principal Sidney Nelson made a sorry attempt to compromise with our demands. He promised to hire a black assistant principal and said he would form a biracial committee of students and parents for future problems between whites and blacks at the school, but said nothing else about our main requests.[30] Regardless of white actions, we continued to hold mass meetings on the topic nearly every night through the holiday season. The closer we got to January 2, the more determined blacks were to hold out until the board addressed our concerns. The students, in particular, were fired up. We were ready to call for the boycott when we got unexpected news from the county school board.

Shortly before our mass meeting on New Year's Day, 1973, school board chairman Richard Leeper contacted Rev. Brooks, Rev. Gooden, and me. He told us that the school board had reached a decision and they would voluntarily stop using the inflammatory symbols at EHS. The board issued a moratorium on "Dixie," the flag, and the Rebel mascot and nickname. We were absolutely thrilled and could not wait to announce it at the meeting. The crowd was simply jubilant when they heard the news. The NAACP and SCLC decided to give the board thirty days to make a permanent decision regarding each item or the boycott would go on as planned. But halfway through the meeting, we got another call. I thought the matter was straightened out, but we discovered that Childers, Gindl, and school superintendent J. D. "Bud" Hall publicly repudiated the decision. Childers said the board had no authority to decide a school's nickname, and Hall agreed. We thought the matter was settled, but Hall told us that the battle was far from over. He ended all arrangements regarding the mascot, song, and flag, so we told the congregation that the boycotts were on once again. It was a real roller coaster ride. The mass meeting went from celebration, to disbelief, to anger. That call was really a blessing in disguise, because it intensified the effort of everyone in attendance to win the battle. The school board had lied, and hundreds of us found out about it at the same time. When schools opened the next day, we wanted to make sure that no black child was in class, so Gooden, Brooks, Leverette, and I went over the plans with everyone there. The boycott began the next day, and the effects were felt immediately.

On January 2, 1973, most black parents pulled their kids out of all public schools in Escambia County. The *Pensacola News* reported that attendance was down in some schools by 50 percent, and they could not count. If the local paper reported that a black campaign was half successful, it was probably about 90 percent effective. They always inflated numbers to make movement leaders and supporters look bad, but not even they could explain away all of those empty school buses that motored around the county. W. D. Childers took the lead in resisting our struggle. He said our tactics were nothing but "blackmail" because we used economic issues against the board. He was on campus when EHS opened and he had some bitter words regarding our tactic. Childers said that the boycotts were "a success" because there were no blacks in schools disrupting classes. He stated that there was a better learning atmosphere throughout the schools because blacks were not there. That embodied the arrogant racism we dealt with. But Childers did not stop at insulting every black in the county. He even issued a warning to our local NAACP president and movement activist, B. J. Brooks. Childers threatened Brooks's livelihood by saying, "Since he is on the state payroll, and his salary is paid by state dollars, I can't understand why he would call for this insurrection against the school board." Rev. Brooks worked for the Florida Department of Transportation but had taken some personal time off to help organize the campaign. I called the thinly veiled threat "economic genocide." It was not the last time such tactics would be used to fragment movement leaders.[31]

The response from the black community was tremendous during the EHS symbols crisis and school boycott. I hate to say this, but the black community often does a lot reacting instead of acting. Pensacola was no exception. We reacted to a crisis. I used to tell black folks all of the time, "If you are black, you have had a crisis all of your life. You are in a crisis until you die out of it. One after the other, we're involved in

constant crisis." We continued to meet each night during the boycott
and strengthen our resolve. Rev. Gooden even announced that we would
initiate a downtown selective boycott for the following weekend. I had
personally seen the effect blacks could have on those businesses, and
felt we could bring the same pressure on downtown institutions that we
brought during the 1962 sit-ins. It was the most effective tactic blacks had
in demonstrating their power and solidarity, so the boycott was planned.
We promised area merchants it would continue until our problems were
addressed. Black leaders also organized downtown demonstrations during
the school campaign.

On January 4, Rev. Gooden, B. J. Brooks, NAACP state president
Otis Williams, and I led a massive demonstration from a downtown
park to the county school board headquarters. Each of us spoke to the
crowd from bullhorns, as nearly one hundred police officers in riot gear
surrounded the school board building. I told them that if "Senator
Childers would have left it alone, the problem would have already been
worked out." It was then that I called Pensacola "a racist, red-necked
community." I also said that one of our main problems was that some
black parents ignored our pleas and sent their children to schools during
the week. I called those people "a bunch of dumb niggers" and said "we
got to deal with those folks." Gooden promised Peaden, Childers, and
school board members that white and black voters who wanted peace
in the area would remove them from office at their first chance. Some
black EHS students even spoke and promised not to return until the
flag was gone. There was absolutely no doubt how those kids felt about
the symbols, and it galled me that the white establishment ignored the
pain the flag, song, and name caused. Interestingly enough, before our
demonstration began, Childers and Peaden promised to withdraw from
the school situation if the NAACP and SCLC would do the same. But
it was too late. They injected racist fervor into the situation and we had
responded. Regional NAACP officials were even on their way to Pensacola
from Atlanta, so there was no turning back for us.[32]

The *Pensacola News Journal*, as usual, did their best to undermine
our efforts during the school boycott. On January 5, the *News* published

an editorial that criticized local black leaders. The article declared that
students should determine the symbols and nicknames of their schools,
not adults or activists. It read, "Frankly, we are most disturbed that black
leaders seem to have chose Escambia High's team name, Rebels, and its
fight song, 'Dixie,' as the primary cause for complaint in this situation"
because we were "entirely wrong." Blacks should leave the issue alone,
the paper argued, because the nickname and theme "are the long-stand-
ing tradition" in county schools. The article also gave a warped history
lesson and defended the Confederate flag as "part of the proud traditions
of many whites whose ancestors fought a war not for the continuance
of slavery but in defense of what they believed was their constitutional
right to govern themselves." Despite the best efforts of both print and
politicians, our boycott came to a temporary halt less than three days
after it started.

On January 5, the NAACP officially ended our boycott of public
schools in the county because the school board reached a formal compromise regarding the EHS controversy. The board announced that
students at Escambia High should "immediately address themselves to
the moderation or elimination of every racial irritant that can be identified." A biracial student group promised to write new words to "Dixie,"
while the principal decided that a student vote would decide the fate of
the flag and nickname. The student vote did not exactly thrill me, Rev.
Gooden, or Rev. Brooks because there was no way that the huge white
student majority would elect new symbols, and every side involved knew
it. It was no surprise that Peaden and Childers gave the student vote
their blessing. As a show of good faith, though, we called off downtown
boycotts scheduled to begin the following weekend. What really broke
the ice and made SCLC decide that we were going to let the students
go back into the public schools is that we pledged a judge would settle
the matter. We allowed the kids to go back to school while the NAACP
and SCLC organized a court case against the symbols. Still, the schools
opened with no problems. Superintendent Hall said that all work could
be made up from the previous week, and there were no police officers
present on the EHS campus when blacks returned to classes. We urged

all blacks to maintain their good behavior and avoid any confrontation with white students.[33] We even held a press conference to express our satisfaction with the temporary resolution and invited Representative Peaden and Senator Childers to our mass meeting that night. For some reason, though, they did not take us up on the offer.

The SCLC and NAACP boycott of Escambia County schools made state and regional news. The *Atlanta Daily World* called it "the first recorded case of a successful, or at least partly successful, action against the racist practices which are defended by some on the grounds that they represent a link with tradition." A state representative from Miami introduced a measure in the Florida legislature to outlaw the playing of "Dixie" and other racially inflammatory songs at school functions. Naturally, Childers and Peaden vowed to fight the legislation. Yet despite moderate success, the fight was far from over for black students. Not even a week after blacks returned to EHS, whites students threatened their own walkout. I thought it was ironic that whites were prepared to use the same tactics to get their way that they had condemned us for using. It seemed that white students and parents were already growing impatient with the uncertain status of their beloved symbols and wanted immediate steps taken to retain "Dixie," "Rebels," and the Confederate flag. They were like a spoiled child who was not getting his way, which is really what many whites were. They were used to getting their way with black folks, but this time we were more determined that right would prevail. On January 11, over three hundred whites left the school when a trophy draped in a Confederate flag disappeared from the trophy case. It turned out that a staff member had removed it for safe keeping but when administrators realized what was happening, the whites had already left. Several of the students marched immediately to the downtown school board building to speak with board members. They demanded an immediate majority vote to decide what to do with Escambia High's images. The parents were so fired up that a society formed called the Concerned Parents and Students of Escambia County (CPSEC). The group's founder, Otis Davis, was a lieutenant in the sheriff's department, which gave us further reason to distrust the local police.

The CPSEC was so upset concerning the EHS symbols issue that they arranged a meeting at the Pensacola Municipal Auditorium on the evening of January 12. Over four thousand people attended and discussed a white student boycott of the school. Childers and Peaden appeared and addressed the audience. They announced that earlier in the day, EHS Principal Sidney Nelson had promised them a majority vote on January 16 regarding "Dixie," the flag, and Johnny Rebel. If they did not get the vote as promised, they urged all whites to boycott Escambia High. They blamed all of the current problems on blacks from outside of the area who "came to disrupt, to tear down the area." Furthermore, Peaden claimed that blacks "did not want an education for their children." I taped a WCOA radio news report of the meeting, which turned into a shouting match where several whites grabbed the microphone and talked about the boycott. Students even spoke at the event. One, in particular, stood out to me. He told the audience that if whites did not boycott the school, "Then you ain't a Rebel." The *Pensacola News* reported that later that night, whites in automobiles with Confederate flags flying from them assaulted innocent blacks throughout the city.[34]

At our next mass meeting, Rev. Gooden and I encouraged black students to stay out of classes at EHS. We could no longer guarantee their safety on the campus. Black students had been attacked, pushed against walls, threatened, had flags flaunted in their faces since their return, and the harassment was getting worse. The NAACP and SCLC decided to hold blacks out of county public schools on Monday, January 15 in recognition of Dr. Martin Luther King, Jr.'s birthday. The demonstration would continue on January 16 to protest the EHS vote. But at the MLK celebration service, we urged them to stay out of all schools as long as "Dixie" and the Confederate flag remained at Escambia High. "If the school needs the symbols to remain open," I told the audience, "then we want to close the school." Common sense would have told anybody that there was no chance for the African-American students to win the vote because they were outnumbered one hundred and fifty to one and a half, or close to it. But by that time, it did not matter what any black person said or thought. The vote was going to happen regardless of what we wanted.

On January 16, students at Escambia High School voted whether or not to keep the "Rebel" name, to retain "Dixie" as the school's fight song, and to determine if Confederate flags would be allowed at official school functions. Whichever side got the majority of votes would win the election. The whole process was a joke and the black community protested its inherent unfairness. The problem was that the symbols offended a minority of students who felt unwanted at the school, and administrators let a student vote decide what to do. The black community felt that adult school officials needed to step in and do the right thing, but they took a cowardly way out. We felt that the vote represented a total betrayal of our previous agreement with the school board, who had caved in under white pressure. The NAACP and SCLC asked that no blacks attend EHS on the day of the vote, and that is what happened. The student vote went as expected; it was not even close. Students kept "Dixie" by a 2239 to 290 vote. 2354 voted to retain the Rebel mascot, while 179 objected. The flag remained at EHS functions by a 2257 to 179 vote.[35] What amazed me is that at least 179 students voted against each of the items. Principal Sidney Nelson and the Escambia County school board announced that it would honor the student's wishes at EHS, so the black community decided that we would resume our boycott of local public schools in protest. We added a new demand to our list: the removal of Sidney Nelson as principal of Escambia High School. He was obviously incompetent and could not fairly resolve the symbols controversy. During the second boycott, though, we prepared for the long haul and brought a new weapon to our movement.

We had been preparing for the likelihood of another school boycott since the term began, so the SCLC began organizing "Freedom Schools." NAACP members participated and Rev. Brooks fully supported the idea, but the schools were an SCLC initiative under my leadership. I was prepared to urge black students to never set foot in county public schools again, and many in the community agreed with me after the so-called vote at Escambia High School. I did not want the children to suffer from missing the classes, so I decided to pull a page from the mid-1960s civil rights movement and establish black-operated Freedom Schools in Pensacola for the students who boycotted the public schools. The first thing SCLC had to do was find a place to hold the schools. We needed big gathering places with several rooms that the white power structure did not control, so we turned to the local churches. The main school was located at Allen Chapel, one of the largest black churches in the city. It was also located in the downtown area and was easily accessible for many black families. We also established the schools at Rev. Brooks's church, Greater Mount Lilly Baptist Church, and Rev. Leverette's church, St. John Devine Baptist. This time when we pulled black students out of the county schools, they had a place to go for an education. We did not get them all, though. There were some blacks that attended the public schools, but a vast majority of them attended the Freedom Schools.

The response from the black community was tremendous. It had to be, if the school were going to work, because parents had to support them and workers had to come from the neighborhoods. I felt then, and still feel now, that the EHS symbols issue was the most important issue black people in northwest Florida encountered since the segregated lunch counters and lack of job opportunities in downtown Pensacola. The establishment of Freedom Schools, therefore, was the biggest project to come from the local black community since the 1962 sit-ins. We did not have any problems from a lack of support. We were supported by the parents, who brought kids to school and taught some classes. Most of the teachers were people from our community that had either retired or worked night jobs. We taught regular classes, but stressed the African-American contribution to the subject. This was especially true in the History and Literature classes. I wanted the Freedom Schools to function like regular schools. The classes were divided by age, and we even had group assemblies. There were some classes that we did not teach, but the main point was to make sure black students did not attend public schools. A purpose of the Freedom Schools was to reduce the revenue that the school system received, and we accomplished that goal.

I was not at all surprised with the response that the black community gave the Freedom Schools. People were fired up about their rights then.

During that time, a lot of things had not infiltrated into the community as they have today, like drugs and crime. People were focused on issues, and the Escambia High School situation was an issue in our community that had to be resolved one way or the other. The Freedom Schools also had a great impact on our area. Representatives from the Community Relations Office of the Justice Department from Atlanta came in to examine the situation. Whites were also up in arms about what we were doing. W. D. Childers wanted every student who attended the Freedom Schools permanently taken off of public school rolls and he wanted those who organized and drove students to the school arrested for a variety of trumped-up charges, including contributing to the delinquency of a minor. He also wanted the National Guard stationed at public schools in the county. School officials also tried to make Freedom Schools look like a failure by padding their roll books, and the local papers made derogatory comments about our schools. They said that outside of Allen Chapel, reporters could hear black students inside chanting "black power," and "soul power." That was a blatant lie. The fact that so many whites went to such efforts to discredit our schools indicated that we were achieving our purpose.

I took a lot of criticism from the white community for organizing the schools. They said I hurt the children and deliberately tried to start trouble between whites and blacks in Pensacola. Those were absolute falsehoods. Trouble existed between the races in Pensacola long before I got involved in the movement. Still, I was always the source of a lot of white rage in Escambia County. What my white critics, and many blacks, did not know, though, was that I helped keep potential trouble out of the area many times. One such instance occurred during the operation of the Freedom Schools. Representatives from SNCC, CORE, and a Black Panther group approached me soon after the schools began. They offered their assistance in any form we needed but I rejected their help. I told them, "We do not want to have here what we have had across the country, in regards to the racial violence that often comes with your help. We will handle the situation on a local level." I personally told representatives from each of those organizations, "Let us deal with the current situation in our way first, and if it comes to the point where we need your help, we will let you know." But we never needed their kind of assistance. Through my individual efforts, then, I kept those radical elements out of Escambia County during the time that we held the Freedom Schools. Even in retrospect, I am glad that I never requested their assistance because we did not need a city torn apart by violence. Pensacola was already divided enough, and the SCLC never considered resorting to physical force. Our goal was never to see how destructive we could be. We were trying to be constructive through legal means, which seemed to be destructive to the other side.

The Freedom Schools were open for several weeks. During the evenings, SCLC and the NAACP also continued to meet on a regular basis. White organizations continued to meet as well during the period. The state NAACP president discussed pulling all blacks out of public schools throughout Florida as a show of support for us, but nothing ever came of it. After the EHS student vote, Rev. Gooden introduced a Tallahassee attorney, Ed Duffee, to Pensacola's black leaders. He agreed to take our case against the school board and EHS symbols all the way to the United States Supreme Court, if necessary. On January 19, Duffee filed a suit with the federal district court to outlaw "Dixie" and the racist symbols at Escambia High. The suit named the county school board as the defendant and was filed on behalf of black EHS student Belinda Jackson and her mother, Merenda Kyle. Duffee claimed that the mascot, name, and flag were "racial irritants" that violated Jackson's Fourteenth Amendment rights and her right to participate in an integrated school system. The Freedom Schools continued to operate as we waited on Judge Winston Arnow to hear the case.[36]

On January 24, we finally got our day in federal court. Black students and civil rights leaders, including myself, testified against the symbol usage. Duffee dropped his claim against "Dixie" because a little-known state law prohibited school boards from regulating school songs. We still got our point across about how white students used Confederate symbols to antagonize and intimidate blacks. Students told the court how whites shouted racial slurs at them while displaying the Rebel flag or singing

"Dixie," and I talked about what the symbols meant to black people. Belinda Jackson summed it up when she said the symbols "reminded her of slavery." The day after the hearing, Judge Arnow ruled against the use of the Confederate flag, Johnny Rebel mascot, and "Rebel" nickname at Escambia High School. He issued a temporary injunction against each of the items. The right cause had prevailed; the bigots and racists had lost. Judge Arnow cited a 1970 Louisiana case and Fifth Circuit Court of Appeals ruling that declared the Confederate symbols "racial irritants" and "impediments to the operation of unitary school system." Ed Duffee knew that this precedent existed and used it in our case.[37] The black community was absolutely delighted with the ruling, but I knew the fight was far from over.

Judge Arnow gained a lot of respect from the black community because of his courageous ruling. He was a fair jurist. He did not cater to wrong, and that was how we prevailed. We stressed the righteousness of our struggle against the symbols, and Arnow saw them and their display as devices of white hatred. He said, "Black students are now a part of the school and their race should be taken into consideration when dealing with the symbols." Again, I stressed the misuse of the symbols, not their use. I told the court that our kids were in a school that was already predominantly white and had only recently integrated. The white students did not want them there and used the flag as a show of disregard for the blacks. The school was already being called "the Rebels." The name was established and perhaps we could have lived with that, if not for the fact that when the first blacks entered that school whites started flaunting those symbols in the face of African-American students who were there because of a court order. Even though they were the minority, blacks still had a right to be there. The Confederate symbols were misused by whites to demonstrate a hatred for integration. You can misuse anything, regardless of what it is. It can be good, but it still can be misused. And Judge Arnow saw this. In my opinion, he was a very fair judge, not just because of what he did for us but because of his demeanor on the bench. He let us state our side and he eventually deemed the symbols "racial irritants." He stated that he would determine the permanent status of

Escambia High's nickname and mascot at a hearing later that year.

I was not surprised that the verdict was in our favor. In spite of the defiance that a lot of white parents and some white politicians demonstrated, including Smokey Peaden and that puffed-up W. D. Childers, a lot of people in the community were on our side. And not just African-Americans. Many white people saw our point of view and offered their encouragement to me in private. It has been my experience that there are a lot of white people who are concerned about the fair treatment of everybody. They may have kept quiet, which really did not help us at that time, but that is how they felt. That is why it perturbs me when I hear an African-American try to categorize any person who has white skin. The reason it bothers me is because they are wrong in stereotyping all whites as "like this" or "like that." I also dislike it because I am used to being the recipient of that type of categorizing and I know it is wrong. This is what disturbs me so much about the war on terrorism; we label everyone who wears a turban as a potential terrorist. When they bombed the trade center, the terrorists did not go in there beforehand and tell all of the blacks to get out. They did not care who died. I have experienced some white support during all of my campaigns, but there are always some who have no regard for anybody's rights except theirs. Peaden and Childers, in particular, did not have a kind response to our concerns. And it was not only whites who resisted our efforts. Some blacks could not see the big picture and spoke out against our campaign and tactics. To me, as well as to Rev. Gooden, Rev. Brooks, Rev. Leverette, and most of the black folks involved, this was not a battle between white and black. This was a battle of right versus wrong. Whites, though, perceived it as a racial battle because they were the ones who often said, "Those niggers need to go back where they came" and used the Confederate icons in a racist manner. Those people had tunnel vision, and in their tunnel the only thing they could see was white. Judge Arnow's ruling, therefore, was not popular with most white people. In fact, Peaden and Childers began raising money for the coming court battle and hired a lawyer from Tampa to defend their interests. On January 26, as we expected, the school board appealed Arnow's decision.

Black students returned to public schools on January 29 because of the temporary injunction. They felt everything would be better for them, but I knew better. The NAACP and SCLC stressed at our mass meeting that the boycott was not officially over, but many still attended class at Escambia High School. On the first day of school, there were no incidents. Over twenty county deputies patrolled the campus and everything remained pretty quiet. It was like the calm before a storm. School officials abided by the temporary injunction, and I believe that this was when the reality of the verdict really hit the white students. The "Rebel" name on the football stadium's press box was covered with a huge sheet. All Confederate flags were removed from the building. The Johnny Rebel costume was retired. Tape was even placed over the offending logos on the basketball court. Two days after blacks returned, fights broke out between over two hundred students while blacks waited to board school buses after the day had ended. Some of the blacks who saw the fight begin said that the riot control officer at the scene, Sgt. Jim Edson, watched as a group of white girls assaulted some black females. Police arrested three whites and two blacks for fighting, including Belinda Jackson. Principal Nelson later suspended seventeen black students for participating in the incident.

News of the fight traveled fast to Tallahassee. Governor Reuben Askew ordered state troopers to stand by near Escambia High in case another broke out. Smokey Peaden was told about the incident at the state legislature. He told several people in the capital hallway that "those niggers make me so mad . . . If I had anything to do with it, I would get a shotgun—no, a submachine gun—and mow them down." A Tampa newsman heard the inflammatory statement and reported them on television that night. The black community in Pensacola was outraged. Rev. Gooden even suggested that the state house impeach Peaden for his racist comments. What made the situation even worse was that Peaden admitted that he made the statement, but said that he did so "in a joking manner." Why would anyone, much less a public official, joke about killing children during a sensitive time? Instead of impeaching Peaden, the house speaker praised him for being "man enough" to apologize.

Royal Untreiner said that Peaden, as an elected official, had "a right to say" what he wanted.[38] Peaden made a statement about killing black folks and got rewarded for admitting it. That was the situation we dealt with not only in Pensacola, but throughout the state of Florida.

As February began, the school board made some changes in an attempt to end the renewed NAACP and SCLC boycott. We had operated the Freedom Schools for nearly a month, and the absences were putting some heavy financial strains on the county school system. The board ordered more police to Escambia High. Over fifty officers patrolled the campus and promised to protect blacks from white attacks. A grand jury also promised to examine the disturbances and investigate our complaints of white harassment and wrongdoing at EHS. Because of the efforts, the NAACP wished to end the boycott. I wanted to keep the Freedom Schools going, but the walkout officially ended on February 9, 1973. Black students returned to all local schools that day, including Escambia High. Once again, there was an extended period of calm. But white administrators were not allowing blacks to make up any work they had missed during the boycott, contrary to the promises that they made to us. On March 22, more trouble engulfed Escambia High. This time, though, I was caught in the middle of it all.

As the school term ended for EHS students, teachers still refused to allow black students to make up any missed work. Many of them, as a result, would have an "F" in their classes and their permanent records would be affected. Rev. Gooden, Rev. Brooks, and I met with Sidney Nelson a couple of times to express our concerns. We told him that the school board said the students would be allowed to make up work they missed while they were in the Freedom Schools, but Nelson said the board did not have the authority to make that decision. We insisted that they were allowed to make up the work. Give them unexcused absences, we said, but do not allow them to suffer academically. We were also concerned about the disproportionate number of blacks who were suspended, and brought this to the principal's attention. But Nelson refused to let the students make up any work. On the morning of March 22, nearly all of the blacks attending EHS walked out of classes, went to the gym, and demanded to speak to Principal Nelson about their missed assignments. He first called the sheriff's department and asked them to disperse the blacks sitting in the gym. When the twelve deputies arrived, Nelson finally spoke to the blacks and promised to "work something out" if they returned to class. As the students left the gym, whites gathered outside and harassed them as they exited the building. One thing led to another, and more fighting broke out between the students. This time, though, the fracas was much larger. It was a full-scale riot.

After the fighting began, someone called me at work and told me what had happened. They said I was needed on campus because they could not do anything with the black kids. I cannot remember who made that call; it was either the assistant principal, Chris Banakas, or Superintendent Bud Hall. They also called more officers to the scene. Before the fighting stopped, police had arrested thirty-five blacks and fifteen whites, despite the fact that whites had started the fighting once again. When I arrived at the school, the officers had the riot somewhat under control. There was still a lot of hollering and bickering being exchanged between the two groups, which the police had separated. Several parents, mostly white, had also arrived on campus by the time I appeared. I went into Sidney Nelson's office to find out what was going on. He updated me on the situation and said that school had been canceled for the remainder of the day. He said they called me because they felt that I was the only force in the community that the black kids would listen to. I was in the office getting ready to go out onto the courtyard where the black kids were loading up on the buses, when several white parents began trying to break the door down to get me. They were shouting and cursing and could not wait to get their hands on me. I guess they were going to give me a party or something.

When the police finally cleared the mob out of my way, I walked to the buses to see what was happening. One of the kids saw me and ran toward me saying, "Rev. Matthews, they are going to take us to jail." I assumed that this is what the police or school staff members had told them they were going to do as they loaded them on the bus. The assistant principal stood beside the bus and told me, "They are not going to jail, they are going home." On the strength of that statement, I got a bullhorn from one of the deputies, stood up on the steps of the bus, and announced, "Nobody is going to jail." When I said that, the deputies moved in and arrested me and several of the students. They took us to the county jail and kept us in an outdoor pen for about two hours before they charged us with a crime. When they announced the charges, it was inciting and encouraging a riot because I had promised the crowd that nobody was going to jail. I only made the comment because that was what the school official told me and the students were scared to death.[39] To show the inconsistency between the charge and my release, the officers allowed me to sign my own bond and the bonds of all of the other children who were arrested. Encouraging and inciting a riot was a felony. Why would they allow an accused felon to sign the bonds of several kids and his own before they released him?

When I went to trial for the felony charge, the courtroom was packed. Not only were people there from Pensacola, but folks I had been working with in DeFuniak Springs and Chipley came as well. The trial was pretty comical. I remember that during a recess, the deputies who had arrested me were outside the courtroom arguing among themselves because they could not get their lies straight during their testimonies. One officer stated, "He said this," while another claimed, "No, he said that." An all-white jury found me innocent because all I said was, "Nobody is going to jail." I did not say it in a threatening manner, and I had not committed a crime. I just said it based on what the man there had told me. That was not, by far, the first time I had been arrested in Escambia County. It was, though, the first time that I had been charged with a felony and put on trial. My next felony trial would not go as smoothly.

After the March 22 incident and my trial, many more deputies and auxiliary officers were stationed at EHS. They stayed there for the rest of the school year. There were some minor incidents, such as fights between a few black and white kids, but nothing like what had happened in the previous months. Our mass meetings tapered off and each organization, the SCLC and the NAACP, decided to let the symbols situation work its way through the court system. Judge Arnow waited until public schools were on summer break before he made his next decision concerning our case. On July 11, 1973, the judge determined the permanent status of Escambia High School's controversial mascot, nickname, and flag. "If the use of these symbols was one of the causes" of racial violence at the school, he argued, "it's time to get rid of them." So once again, whites and blacks argued their cases in front of Arnow. The courtroom was more packed this time than it was during the first hearing. I imagine his first ruling and the fact that students were not in school contributed to the larger audience. School board attorney Ed Barfield said the symbols did not cause any violence. Principal Sidney Nelson blamed black students for all of the trouble and claimed, "White students resented their rights being taken away." Our arguments remained the same: the symbols were racial irritants and were misused by white students to antagonize blacks. Emotions were so high that Judge Arnow canceled the public hearing after one day of testimony because he feared it would increase racial unrest in the community. Instead, he told attorneys from both sides to prepare a written argument that summarized each.[40] Once again, Judge Arnow proved to be the fair jurist that I knew he was.

On July 24, Judge Winston Arnow permanently banned Confederate images from Escambia High School. He released his fourteen-page opinion to the public, and it was a powerful argument for justice. The judge called the symbols "racially irritating" and said they "generated a feeling of inequality and inferiority among black students." He also declared that they were "a source of racial violence" at the school. Furthermore, Arnow called the Confederate battle flag "a symbol of white racism" that was used "deliberately for the purpose of offending black students." He also noted that as our protests against the images intensified, "the symbols became a greater source of racial tension and violence." He supported his ruling by saying, "The use of such symbols at the school is likely to continue to be a source of racial tension and a cause of disruption." He concluded, "Hopefully, this court's order will not only protect black students from intimidation but will also help to achieve a more stable education environment for all students."[41] The black community was once again pleased, but not surprised with the ruling. I knew that right would prevail, and I had been preaching it to our community for the last eight months. Area whites responded to the order with increased outrage and bitterness.

The Escambia County school board voted to appeal the ruling less than twenty days after Arnow reached his decision. They also allocated fifteen thousand dollars of county school funds to the maneuver. We did not believe that was fair at all. That money belonged to the taxpayers, both black and white. Now our money was being used to support what we had been fighting against. Naturally, the *Pensacola News Journal* editors tried to inflame the situation. They could have at least kept quiet, but that was not their style. They questioned the ruling, said it "disappointed" their staff, and declared, "We reject Judge Arnow's decision." The article mocked our demands by calling them "willy-nilly" and asked, "What's going to be a 'racial irritant' tomorrow?" The editors also called "Afro hair-dos" and "the clinched fist of black power" offensive to them, and pointed out that "courts never banned the Swastika." The suit did achieve one goal. Escambia High principal Sidney Nelson quit his job because of the "mental and physical exhaustion" the symbols issue had caused him. Still, his successor was no friend to the black community. Assistant principal Chris Banakas was promoted and was probably more dedicated to fighting local blacks on this symbols issue than Nelson was.[42]

Local blacks waited while the school board appealed Arnow's ruling. Things kind of died down while the NAACP and SCLC waited on the next move. Rev. Gooden went back to Tallahassee, as did W. D. Childers and Smokey Peaden. Some incidents happened at Escambia High School, like fistfights and such, but they never amounted to much more than isolated scuffles. We continued urging black students to remain calm and act mature during times of harassment, and they did. I was very proud of the way our kids handled themselves during the episode. For the most part, they reflected great restraint. As bad as it is to ponder, the incidents could have been much worse than they were. Thank God that no one was killed during those riots.

I still belonged to the NAACP but my major role was with SCLC. By this time, the NAACP Youth Council had almost dissolved. I was still their leader, but many of the kids that were involved and real active in the late 1960s and early 1970s had graduated and gone on to college or done other things. As a result, I do not think there was much of a youth group affiliating with the NAACP because all of the previous forces had left and my main focus had become the SCLC. I was still working in conjunction with Rev. Brooks, and we both kept Rev. Gooden updated on what was going on in Escambia County.

Tensions between whites and blacks remained high during the 1973–74 school year, and continued to build under the surface. For example, Escambia High School had no mascot during their athletic season. The football team called themselves the "110 percenters," because they considered themselves 110 percent Rebels and were 110 percent against changing mascots. I do know that the name change did not help, because that team did not win a single game in 1973. On our side, the public activity declined. During this period, I traveled back and forth to Chipley, DeFuniak Springs, and other places in the state. My experience with the EHS situation made me an expert of sorts with racial disruption in schools, so I went all over Florida as both an SCLC and NAACP representative advising school boards and civil rights groups on specific issues they faced. In 1973 and 1974, then, the local NAACP and SCLC continued to meet but were not as vocal or assertive as they had been in the recent past. That changed with two incidents that occurred in December, 1974. In one month, racial hatred reached heights that I had never seen in Pensacola.

6

THE SHOWDOWN BEGINS:
DECEMBER 1974

At 10:15 A.M. on December 1, 1974, a nineteen-foot fishing boat was found drifting in Pensacola's Santa Rosa Sound. Little did anyone know that the discovery would begin a month that changed history in Escambia County. The boat belonged to five men from Atlanta, Georgia named Robert and Marvin Walker, who were not related, Leroy Holloway, Jr., Lonnie Merits, and John Sterling. They had come to Pensacola on a fishing trip, as they had dozens of time before. The circumstances surrounding the men's disappearance raised suspicions almost immediately among many in the local black community. The *Pensacola Journal* reported that the boat sank, but it had not. The Coast Guard could not conclude there had been an accident after searching the waters for almost an hour, but still assumed that the men "had drifted away or had been hit by a big wave." They called conditions surrounding the discovery "weird" and said all five were probably "safe on land or in the water."[43]

When the Coast Guard discovered the empty boat, the keys were in the ignition, the throttle was idling, and the gearshift was in neutral. Even though the motor was engaged, the anchor had been dropped. Its line, though, was broken. It was not frayed, but there was a clean cut like someone had sliced it with a knife. Inside the boat sat a tackle box, an ice chest, and their life preservers. A Coast Guard representative told the media that if the men had been tossed out, all of their gear would have been too. Two gas tanks also sat in the floorboard of the boat. One was full but the other was nearly empty, which made no sense if the weather or waves were strong enough to knock five grown men out of the boat. The Escambia County sheriff's department found a camper and trailer belonging to Robert Walker at a nearby boat launching ramp. All of their lunches and more fishing equipment were found inside. Coast Guard boats from Pensacola, Mobile, and New Orleans searched the sound for two days after discovering the empty boat. Airplanes eventually joined the search, but no one was found. Director of the Escambia Emergency Services M. K. "Buck" Renfroe had years of experience working in and around the Gulf waters and said the bodies would begin to surface by the middle of the week if the men had drowned.[44]

As the days passed and no bodies surfaced, some folks in the black community began to question whether the disappearance of who we called "the Atlanta Five" was a boating accident.

White officials, though, were quick to proclaim that there was no evidence of foul play. Rescue workers had not found anyone a week after the men vanished, yet continued to insist that they either had an accident or were picked up by another boat. The sheriff's department, which headed up the search, began to quote a mysterious "eyewitness" who said he saw the five black men anchor from the stern and recalled terrible weather that morning. One of the most interesting witnesses the *Pensacola Journal* dug up was a black man named Joe Sullivan. Sullivan claimed that he saw the Atlanta Five the day before their boat was found. He had this so-called encounter on a Friday evening, which we later proved was impossible. Regardless, Sullivan told the newspaper that he talked to the men and begged them not to go out in the choppy waters. He said, "The bay was just plain bad that evening and I knew I wasn't going out in it very far" because of the high winds, rain, and fog. Also, he remembered that night was beginning to fall. Sullivan said the "five big men" went into the water anyway with two sitting on each side of the boat and one steering. Sullivan also said they were all drinking beer and that their boat was packed with ice coolers, which were both lies. He claimed that two of the men stepped onto a sandbar and flagged a water patrol boat, which we never verified. Sullivan stated that the last time he saw the Atlanta Five, water was sloshing up over the sides of their vessel. He told the *Journal*, "They would go down in a waves and you couldn't hardly see them when they did. They didn't even have on any life preservers in that kind of water . . . It's a shame about them men, but they didn't have any business going out on a night like that. I told them not to go."[45] It was no coincidence that the *Pensacola Journal* reported Sullivan's story one day after I announced that Rev. Ralph Abernathy and the national Southern Christian Leadership Conference were coming to Pensacola to conduct their own investigation into the disappearances.

A few hours after rescue workers found the Atlanta Five's empty boat, they contacted each man's family and told them the men had probably drowned earlier in the morning. Each family disputed the conclusion and doubted very seriously that any of the men had drowned in the Santa Rosa Sound. All of the men were experienced fishermen and had come to Pensacola fishing together on several earlier occasions. Robert Walker's wife told the SCLC that her husband had taken their family to the area every year since 1952 and insisted they wear a flotation device each time they went into the water. In other words, he knew what he was doing in a boat and was familiar with Pensacola's waters. Marvin Walker's wife reported that before he left for Pensacola, he promised her, "I don't swim, and you can be sure I'll wear a life jacket." She also checked on the search party's findings each day after they informed her of the supposed accident, but said that local officials would not answer her questions or provide her with any additional details. A couple of days after the disappearance, Leroy Holloway's sister-in-law, Georgia Holloway, received an anonymous call from a man who said he talked to Robert Walker earlier in the day. The caller said none of the men had drowned and that all of them were still alive. He hung up soon after giving his information, but the strange conversation inspired Holloway to contact the other men's relatives and tell them what happened. Doris Mason, John Sterling's cousin, and Marvin Walker's wife decided to visit Pensacola on December 8 to find their missing relatives.[46]

The two women first tried to talk to local law enforcement and rescue officials concerning the case, but they were rebuffed in the efforts to obtain cooperation and information. When Mrs. Walker and Mrs.

Mason both heard rumors that all five of the Atlanta blacks had been kidnapped, they decided to visit places they had been on prior fishing trips. According to Mrs. Mason, she went into a bait shop and met "a big, fat, old man with stringy hair and about fifty years old" who said all five of the missing men came into his store to buy fishing supplies the morning they disappeared. The owner said the black men started a heated argument with him over bait prices and he told them to leave his property. He claimed the men returned to the shop shortly later and apologized for insulting him, but the owner told the two women, "If that nigger Sterling ever comes back, I'm going to get him." Mrs. Mason and Mrs. Walker also visited the missing men's favorite local bar, Abe's 506 Nightclub. A waitress there told them that a black policeman informed her that a group of whites kidnaped the five men and held them "in something that looked like a castle" thirty-eight miles north of Pensacola. Mason and Walker tried to find the building, but never discovered it. They returned to Atlanta without finding their loved ones. Each family heard about the Pensacola trip and decided to take their story to SCLC president Ralph Abernathy.[47]

Rev. Abernathy made contact with me soon after he talked to the Walker family. He contacted me because I was the highest ranking SCLC official in the area. Abernathy told me that he had enough evidence from the victims' families to think that someone had kidnaped or even murdered the five fishermen. After he told me the entire story, my suspicions also rose. These missing five men were not people who would go out into choppy waters and leave their life jackets under their seats. There are so many things that occurred on that fishing trip that it was not beyond a reasonable doubt to believe wrongdoing occurred. First of all, their time cards had them leaving their jobs in Atlanta at 5:00 P.M. on November 30. SCLC investigated those cards because a few people, including Joe Sullivan, claimed to see them launch their boat into the sound before nightfall that Friday. There was no way that they could have been in Pensacola at the time when Sullivan supposedly had his encounter with them, because work records proved that they were still in Atlanta. It was a blatant lie and Sullivan later admitted as such, as did a reporter for the *Pensacola News Journal* who researched the story. SCLC also discovered that a man contacted Escambia County authorities and said that he had helped the five men off of a rock pile after their engine broke down Friday evening and pulled them into service station, but he never saw him again. We concluded that the sheriff's department never investigated this claim thoroughly. The way their boat was found also confused me. Gas cans and tackle were still in the boat, despite a disaster that was big enough to knock all five men overboard. We also discovered that all of their lunches and bait were left in the camper. If they were going on an all-day fishing expedition, why would they leave bait and their meals on shore? Furthermore, Abernathy found that the Coast Guard turned the boat over to the men's families before the sheriff's department investigated it for possible evidence. The big picture just did not add up for SCLC, so Ralph Abernathy came to Pensacola. Soon before workers found the first body, SCLC leader Ralph Abernathy released a statement that read, "I call upon black and white people of good will to go with me to Pensacola and search for the bodies."[48]

On December 12, 1974, the national SCLC got involved in Pensacola's racial affairs. Soon after Abernathy announced his intentions on December 10, investigators finally found one of the Atlanta Five's bodies. County investigators declared that Marvin Walker died from drowning and proclaimed "no foul play" was involved with his death. Search coordinator Buck Renfroe said Walker wore two pairs of pants, heavy work boots, two shirts, a sweatshirt, and a heavy jacket. All of the additional clothes supposedly weighed over fifty pounds. SCLC thought it was very ironic that after our president said he was coming to town, the bodies started appearing. That added to our suspicions that something was not right with the whole incident. The bodies of Robert Walker and John Sterling appeared only hours before Abernathy's plane landed. On the day he arrived in Pensacola, Rev. Leverette and I met Abernathy and two SCLC officials at the airport. Rev. Abernathy was accompanied by his assistants, SCLC Communications Director Tyrone Brooks and SCLC Vice President Bernard Lee. We immediately held a press conference where Rev. Abernathy proclaimed everything the organization believed to the public. He claimed the Atlanta Five "were victims of foul play and possibly murder," but went even farther. He stated, "The black people are afraid" of speaking against racism in Pensacola and promised, "We're going to expose how backward this section of Florida is." He further charged, "It is commonly accepted in this community that these men were taken and beaten and killed by racists, segregationist forces in Pensacola Beach. We don't intend for this to be another case where black men are destroyed and nothing is done about it." His comments started a fire storm in Escambia County, but I stood behind him completely. I felt, and I still feel, that those men were killed. As a reward, I guess, for my commitment, Ralph formed the northwest Florida branch of SCLC and named me its coordinator.[49]

After the press conference ended, all five of us began to investigate the drownings. We went to the morgue, visited University Hospital where two of the bodies were being examined, and met with Sheriff Royal Untreiner. I did not view the bodies and did not want to. All of the officials from Atlanta did, though, and one thing in particular stood out. One of the men, I forget exactly which one it was, wore glasses. They were not the kind that hooked behind the ear, either. They had straight arms. But officers told the coroner at the hospital that when he washed up on the shore, he still had his glasses on. He had supposedly been in the water several days and washed up on the ground, but still had those glasses on. That was one of the suspicious stories that we were fed during the investigation. Rev. Abernathy also asked to view the bodies of Robert Walker and John Sterling. Hospital officials had told their families that each body was so unrecognizable and decomposed that no one should see them, but Ralph demanded to view them. After he saw the bodies, Abernathy questioned the identities of each man. He said that each body was in almost normal condition. We all wondered how those two bodies remained submerged for twelve days in salty water that was full of fish yet appeared in such normal conditions. Ralph went so far as to tell the press, "We were shown two fake bodies" at the hospital. Rescue leaders also told us that they had not found all of the bodies because the water was much cooler than they thought and each man had on layers of heavy clothes. The cold water was supposed to keep the bodies from surfacing as quickly as they first estimated and the weight kept them submerged longer.[50] Those facts may have been true, but at the time we had heard so many false stories that we did not know what was legitimate and what was being used to complicate our investigation.

After our group left the hospital, we searched in vain for the suspected bait shop but did not have a lot of time to discover it. Ralph left Pensacola on the same day that he arrived. He had to travel to Boston that evening but continued to support our efforts through daily phone calls and updates. He asked the United States Attorney General, William Saxbe, to organize a Justice Department investigation into the incident, and told our story to the *Atlanta Journal Constitution*. Ralph also called the governors of Florida and Georgia, Reuben Askew and Jimmy Carter, and requested their assistance with the matter. Governor Carter, in particular, became involved with the case. He actually told us that he would support the SCLC program.[51] I do not know how much real support he gave, as I saw very little action from his office. He was the governor of the men's home state and may have given lip service to satisfy potential voters there. Ralph and I had a very good relationship, and I was disappointed that he did not do more to support local SCLC involvement with the Atlanta Five case. After he left Pensacola, he only returned once more to support our efforts. I think he dropped out of the case because of the politics he was involved with in Georgia. Ralph simply became too interested in his own political career to help SCLC struggles. His political ambitions interfered with his focus on SCLC duties. Around the time of the Atlanta Five incident, he decided to make a run for the congressional legislative seat that Andrew Young vacated because he took another appointed position. Many SCLC members begged Young to not surrender that seat because we knew if he did, another African-American would not fill the position. But Ralph was going to run for it and, consequently, he began to crawfish on the Atlanta Five situation. I do not think he used the Atlanta Five to bring attention to himself and the national SCLC, but I do think that after he got involved somebody got to him and said, "You better back off this issue if you want to win the Congressional seat." And that is exactly what he did.

Rev. Abernathy returned to Pensacola a few days after workers discovered the bodies of Lonnie Merits and Leroy Holloway. They had searched for the men for fourteen days and found two within seven hours of each other. On December 15, the head sheriff's department investigator, Gary Cooper, released autopsies concerning the dead men. He concluded that each man drowned and said, "There are absolutely no signs of foul play involved." Soon after the autopsies came out, Ralph began to soften his stance concerning the Atlanta Five case. He said that the men probably drowned accidentally, but he refused to apologize for calling Pensacola a racist city. The sheriff's department closed its probe on December 17 and concluded that each man drowned, and the Justice Department refused to launch an investigation into the event because they concluded that not enough evidence existed to suggest foul play. That did not surprise me. I felt that the Justice Department, especially in 1974, protected blacks only when pushed to the wall.[52] In addition to the outside support of the investigation falling through, the little support the Atlanta Five had in Pensacola also disappeared.

When the men first disappeared, Otha Leverette and I agreed about their possible murders. But after Abernathy said the five men were probably not killed, Leverette also began to express doubts. He told local reporters, "It's a mystery how they died, but I don't believe now there was foul play." Rev. B. J. Brooks and the local NAACP never grabbed onto the Atlanta Five case. I think Rev. Brooks felt that we were barking in the dark. He always contended that there was no solid evidence that the men were actually killed and that we were going on suppositions and suspicions instead of solid facts. He told the *Pensacola Journal* that the charges Abernathy made concerning white murderers "are untimely. They were made before the facts were gathered. I don't think sufficient evidence has been brought about to justify valid charges of foul play." So Brooks did not jump into that fracas with us concerning the case. Ralph did not help matters by coming in, making all of these loud proclamations, and leaving me to clean up the mess. I continued to maintain that there was room for local authorities to do more regarding the case, but no one acted. This only added to SCLC mistrust of the sheriff's department. If they would have only taken a few more steps as a show of good faith to the black community, I would have felt better concerning their role in the investigation. But they refused to listen to us, which was common. I was pretty much on my own at the end of December concerning the Atlanta Five. Tyrone Brooks was the only national SCLC member who supported me. He called the situation "one of the biggest mass murders this state has ever seen" and said the sheriff's department was guilty of withholding evidence from our investigation. But he supported from a distance. I was alone on the matter.

The local SCLC called community meetings concerning the Atlanta Five situation from almost its beginning, but it was one cause that never really caught on in our community. I think it was due to a lack of vision on the part of the national chapter. The attitude that permeated our community did not help the matter any. It is kind of like death. People really cry when there is a funeral, but they do not really get upset until the hearse backs up to their door. The hearse was not at the back door then, so to speak. These were not people that anyone in Pensacola knew. These were not people that they had heard of until they disappeared. The demand for justice in their deaths never caught on and eventually, the whole thing just died. I still say that many locals believed, "These were people from somewhere else anyway. So why bother?" But I continued to make pronouncements to the media like, "There are still too many unanswered questions" surrounding the case. I even stated, "As far as Dr. Abernathy's remark about Pensacola being a racist community, I agree 165 percent. Pensacola is one of the most racist towns I've ever been in."[53] The *Pensacola News Journal* and Sheriff Untreiner did nothing to prove my beliefs wrong during the event, either.

Local whites acted as they normally did during times of racial uncertainty in the area; they treated blacks like we were just trying to start trouble. This was especially true for the *Pensacola News Journal* and the Escambia County sheriff's department. The newspaper called Ralph Abernathy a "demagogue" that they compared to the infamous Mississippi governor Theodore Bilbo. Its editors also said that Abernathy's words

increased white racism in Pensacola. Sheriff Royal Untreiner proved
even more hostile to our activities than the local press. Untreiner was the
elected sheriff during most of my civil rights activity in the area. He was
a former FBI agent and a bona fide racist; a complete bigot. Untreiner
stood in the way of everything local blacks tried to accomplish, and it
began prior to the Atlanta Five. He was sheriff when we were arrested
for the Escambia High School incident, so his resistance did not start in
December 1974. We were already well acquainted with each other. The
only thing Untreiner told me and Rev. Abernathy that he would do to
assist our investigation of the Atlanta Five situation was ask State Attorney Curtis Golden to call a coroner's jury to research the deaths. I told
him, "My confidence in the State Attorney's office is about as much as
in this ashtray getting up and walking out of the room," because Curtis
Golden was cut from the same cloth as Untreiner. The sheriff told us
point-blank that he would not assign any investigators to the case. "You
have to have a reason to investigate five murders when it appears to have
been an accident," he said.[54] I publicly accused Sheriff Untreiner of lying
and trying to cover up what happened to the Atlanta Five. I do not think
he had anything to do with the disappearances, but I think he knew what
happened to them. Untreiner also had his henchman, Sgt. Jim Edson,
on hand during our demonstrations. Jim Edson was a riot control officer
whose lies eventually did me in. But there was a mistrust that developed
between local blacks and the sheriff's department after Untreiner was
elected. His predecessor, Bill Davis, was a sheriff for all citizens. Davis
would not allow his deputies to mistreat African-Americans. But when
he left office, the department reverted back to the "good ole boy" situation. There was quite a bit of mistrust already between the community
and the sheriff's department before December 1974. And then Wendel
Blackwell was shot.

On December 20, 1974, a tragedy transpired that shook Pensacola
to its very foundations. At about 10:45 that night, a twenty-six-year-old
Escambia County Deputy named Douglas Raines killed a black man. It all
began when Raines was dispatched to answer an armed disturbance call.
On his way to the scene of the crime, he saw Wendel Blackwell leaving

the Club 400 in a green Plymouth Fury. He said that Blackwell left the club at a high rate of speed and went down the wrong side of the road, so he decided to follow him. It is my contention, which was later verified and became accepted as fact in the African-American community, that Raines followed Blackwell because a young lady named Deborah Jones was in the car with him. We later learned that Jones was having an affair with Doug Raines, and he was upset because she got into the car with Blackwell.

Raines turned on his lights so Blackwell would pull over. The young man was scared, though, and ran from the deputy's car. It was unwise of him to not stop, but he did not. Raines radioed for help and Deputy Roger Tyner joined the chase. We later found out that both Tyner and Raines had civilians riding in their cars with them, which violated sheriff's department rules. Raines had not even been with the department one year, but his brother-in-law, retired United States Marine Sergeant Darrel Lynn Mumford, was in the car with him. The two deputy's cars chased Blackwell for fifteen minutes through the area and onto Highway 29, where the young man finally came to a stop in the grass median when Raines bumped his car from behind. Raines drew his pistol, ran up to Blackwell's car, and ordered him to get out. What happened next remains a matter of contention in Pensacola.

Raines claimed that Blackwell "made no indication of moving at all" and "reluctantly" got out of his car while keeping the right side of his body shielded from view. Another deputy later said Blackwell exited the car quickly. Raines also claimed that he told Blackwell to put his hands on the car's roof, but he cupped them instead behind his head. From a distance of three feet, Raines shot Blackwell in the back of his head with a .357 magnum revolver. Raines claimed that he saw something shiny in Blackwell's right hand when he uncupped his hands to put them on the roof of his car. He said that Blackwell was pointing a .22 caliber pistol at him so he shot in self-defense. Two other whites at the scene said they never saw Blackwell point a pistol at anyone. To make matters worse, the guy who rode with Raines admittedly handled Blackwell's gun before investigators arrived. He said that he did not want Blackwell to use it against anyone, so he moved it from the scene. But how can a man use a pistol after being shot in the head with a .357? The funny thing is that none of the later investigators ever suggested that Mumford may have taken that gun out of Blackwell's car and put it under his head. Deborah Jones fled the area, but no newspaper or official report noted her presence anywhere that night. When the official investigation of the event began, detectives found a pistol that they claimed belonged to Blackwell lying under his head and immediately cleared Raines of any wrongdoing before the investigation even began. He was never even suspended for the crime. The department, though, did give him two paid days off after the event because of his "emotionally upset" state.[55]

The news of Blackwell's death shook the black community in Pensacola. I did not know him very well, although he was my cousin. But his death only began our ordeal. The hours progressed into a day, and then two days passed. The reports that surfaced concerning the killing became increasingly disturbing. When blacks in and around Pensacola heard what had happened, they were outraged. The NAACP and SCLC decided to do something to protest this action or we knew that it was open season on black folks in Escambia County. The sheriff's department finally agreed to investigate the shooting but State Attorney Curtis Golden headed the probe, and no black leader trusted him to do anything positive for our community. For several reasons, then, the name "Wendel Blackwell" became a rallying cry for black folks in Pensacola after December 20, 1974.

I met Rev. Brooks the morning after the shooting took place and discovered we were on the same page; there were just too many suspicions and strange stories circulating about the incident for us to remain on the sidelines. The real disturbing factor to me was that when the sheriff's department released its official report of the event, they did not dispute that Raines shot Blackwell with a .357 from a distance of about three feet. I thought police were trained to disable potential threats, not blow their brains out from point-blank range. Why not aim for the arm or leg? Rev. Brooks and I felt that good policing would not dictate that you kill a man from a close distance when you could disarm him. The other

thing that bothered us was that no one seemed to mind that Darryl
Mumford, Raines's brother-in-law, admitted he tampered with evidence.
It disturbed me for two reasons. First, what was a civilian doing messing
around with potential evidence? Most importantly, though, we believed
that it was a dropped gun. Common sense explains our reasoning on
this point. If someone is hit with a .357 magnum, they are not going to
just lay down and drop a gun exactly where they fall. But this is what
the sheriff's department claimed happened, and it represented an insult
to the intelligence of the entire black community. We simply did not
believe that Blackwell had a gun in his hand or that it was lying under
his head when he fell. Someone, either Raines or his civilian rider, put
it there. The suspicions Rev. Brooks and I had only increased after we
talked to Deborah Jones.

On the morning after the shooting took place, Ms. Deborah Jones
called the SCLC and NAACP wanting to speak with me and Rev. Brooks.
Neither of us knew her, but people relied on our organizations when they
had problems. She happened to be one of the few blacks working at the
Pensacola News Journal, and knew about our group's activities. We paid
a visit to Jones to find out exactly what happened to Wendel Blackwell.
She told us that she was with him at Club 400 that night and they both
left in the same vehicle. Soon after, Raines followed them with his lights
on. When they pulled over, Raines first tried to pull her out of the car
because they were lovers. According to Jones, Raines was an extremely
jealous person. She ran from the scene though, during his altercation
with Blackwell, and shots were fired. She ran down the highway and
another motorist gave her a ride home. That was all Jones had time to
tell us at that moment because she was running late for a prior commitment. She was in a rush, so we said that we would talk to her later. But
neither Rev. Brooks nor I got the chance to go back and talk to her. She
died four days later.[56]

I felt that Brooks and I made a big mistake after we talked to Deborah
Jones. We told too many people, including the sheriff's department, that
we had spoken to Ms. Jones, knew what really happened that night, and
planned to talk to her again and pursue charges against Doug Raines

and everyone who helped cover up the incident. Brooks and I were on one accord concerning this issue. We gave our information to Rev. Otha Leverette and Rev. R. N. Gooden and they agreed that Raines murdered Blackwell. We initially had an eyewitness to prove it, but we talked too much. You do not alert people to what you know or what you plan to do in such a volatile situation. When you do, it is no longer a surprise and folks will take measures to block your efforts to expose the truth. On December 26, Deborah Jones's body was found under an overpass near Washington High School. She had been strangled and her body was thrown off the bridge. We investigated the situation and discovered that some nearby residents saw a camper in the area that matched the description of one Doug Raines owned. We also discovered that Jones lived in a trailer that was registered to Raines. We furnished all of this information to the sheriff's department, but they chose to do nothing with it. In fact, the Deborah Jones murder case remains unsolved. In 1999, I met with a deputy in Pensacola about reopening the case and gave him all of the newspaper clippings and information that I had concerning the murder. He returned the clippings about a year later and I have not heard from him since. I thought the police were supposed to look into unsolved murders, but that must not be the case in Escambia County.

The NAACP and SCLC wanted something besides a departmental investigation into the Wendel Blackwell shooting, but we were not satisfied with what we received. State Attorney Curtis Golden headed the second investigation and proved as incompetent as the sheriff's department. Golden has never been fair when it came to civil rights, so the black community knew we would not receive justice through his efforts. Golden asked the Escambia-Pensacola Human Relations Commission to investigate, but they were more dedicated to pleasing the white power structure in Pensacola than they were in finding truth. Golden made other announcements in an attempt to exonerate Raines that only angered black people. For example, Blackwell's mother claimed that Wendel did not own a gun. She went to the sheriff's department to view the weapon deputies had confiscated, but Golden denied her request because he said it was evidence. The state attorney's verdict, then, was no surprise.

On December 27, Curtis Golden officially concluded that Doug Raines shot Blackwell in self-defense. Golden also went to great lengths to prove that Blackwell had a gun in his hand when Raines shot him. At the press conference where he announced his investigation conclusion, Golden stated, "With intense inquiries we have definitely established that Blackwell did have the gun on him before the shooting" occurred and pointed it at Raines. The attorney's office traced the gun to Eddie Lanier, who had sold it to Leroy Beasley on the night of shooting. Beasley supposedly gave the gun to Blackwell hours before he was killed.[57] According to Golden, that proved Blackwell had a gun when Raines shot him. Yet it did nothing of the sort. Even if Blackwell had the gun in his car that night, it did not mean that he had it in his hand when he was shot. And it surely did not explain how it ended up under his head after he was shot at close range. But Golden maintained that the gun's history cleared Raines. The conclusion insulted our community and demonstrated how Curtis Golden deliberately ignored black concerns in Pensacola. The state attorney publicly promised he would share his findings with Brooks and me on December 31, but the meeting never took place.[58] If justice would prevail in the Blackwell incident, I knew that it would have to come through the united efforts of the entire black community. The SCLC and NAACP, therefore, planned mass meetings to organize such activities.

The community started meeting the night after Blackwell was killed. They were sponsored by both the NAACP and SCLC, and Rev. Gooden once again came to Pensacola to participate in and help organize the movement. The sessions that we held after Blackwell's death were hot meetings. They were heated because the black community was fed up with the inequality that existed in Pensacola. First the Escambia High School battles, then the Atlanta Five, and now a murder. It was the final straw, so to speak, for many of us and the atmosphere that existed at our meetings after December 22, 1974 was electric. The core group of black leaders, which consisted of B. J. Brooks, R. N. Gooden, Otha Leverette, and I called for the firing of Doug Raines, who shot Blackwell and was the person we believed to be behind the death of Deborah Jones. So we held mass meetings on a nightly basis where we voiced our displeasure with the current racial atmosphere in Escambia County and stated our newest demands. Those meetings were the largest Pensacola had ever had. We met at Greater Mount Lilly Baptist Church, the church that Rev. Brooks pastored, and it was packed every night. Folks literally sat in the aisles and stood against the walls. Attendance did not wane for months and we met every night except Saturday and Sunday. We usually had a break and did not meet then. The community's tremendous response to the latest round of mass meetings did not surprise me. The shooting was a crisis that hit close to home. A lot of people knew Blackwell and a lot of people knew Deborah Jones, so their murders galvanized the black community. I really believe that blacks in Pensacola had not seen the numerous lies the sheriff's department spouted until the Blackwell killing. Each of us spoke at the assemblies each night, with Rev. Gooden usually giving the nightly message. I even recorded one of our meetings in January, 1975, on audio tape.

The recording is a good example of how the meetings usually went. The atmosphere resembled a church revival and that was how we wanted it. The people there were willing to fight, but we wanted to keep them focused that our struggle was a Christian fight for human dignity. The meeting opened with several songs, including "The Battle Hymn of the Republic," "Nobody Knows the Troubles I've Seen," and "Precious Lord." We also had several prayers before the message was delivered. On the tape, a man who led a prayer declared, "Thank God for Martin Luther King, John F. Kennedy, Robert Kennedy, and R. N. Gooden." Then Rev. Gooden, who was president of the state NAACP at that time, delivered the message. He began by saying, "We are in the throes of a confrontation with the white power structure. We want freedom and justice. We're tired of waiting on it; we want it now." On this evening, he titled the sermon "How Much Do You Owe?" It focused on what blacks owed those who had struggled and even died for the rights they often took for granted, and used Romans 1:14 as its Biblical reference. The gist was that someone had fought for their jobs, for the rights of their children to attend schools equally, and for their salaries. Now it was time for blacks to return the favor by participating in the struggle for justice in the Blackwell situation. Self-sacrifice was always our theme. Gooden cited Paul as our ultimate example and deemed him "another great fighter for freedom and justice," which were long overdue in Pensacola. He promised that by the time our campaign ended the "whole nation might know that black people in Pensacola are going to fight for freedom and justice." He stressed the idea of self-sacrifice by telling the audience that all of us, as leaders, may lose everything we had. But he echoed my feelings by saying that it did not matter because "if I lose it all, I lose it for my folks." One of the last things he said in his message that night was posed as a question. He reminded the crowd of our duties and asked, "Will you be an Uncle Tom or will you be a man?"[59]

Rev. Brooks spoke in the pulpit that evening after Rev. Gooden finished his message. He said that Gooden's sermon "should have converted some Uncle Toms" and warned "high stepping, half-breed niggers" in the crowd who may have been against us. He also told of several threats individuals had made against his life, and announced that he carried a gun in the front seat of his vehicle. He offered several other encouraging words and stated, "If we drop the ball and forget about this, white folks are going to have a field day beating niggers' heads" throughout the county. After B. J. concluded, I gave an update on local happenings and announced our plans for later in the evening. I first told those in attendance that "we have been leaving God out of the movement and this is probably the reason why it hasn't been more successful than it is." I then told them about an incident that had recently happened at a downtown grocery store named Coates' Market. The store's owner already had a well-deserved reputation as a racist. He had shot and killed one black in front of his store and got away with his crime. He always said in a loud voice when blacks were present, "If I kill me three or four more niggers, I guess the rest of them will go away." Well, his wife had choked a little black boy because he dropped a glass bottle of Coke in her store and broke it. I told them about the event and announced plans to boycott Coates' Market the next morning. I gave a meeting time and place and said we would picket both of his area shops. I reminded those in the congregation that "we're going to have to teach every cracker in this city a lesson. Every last one of them. There ain't no sense in playing tiddlywinks with crackers and playing hanky-panky with niggers." I also announced plans to take our grievances to Governor Reuben Askew in Tallahassee to make him respond to the Blackwell situation "one way or another." We were doing this for every city and every black resident in Florida. But we could not forsake local circumstances either. Before I closed the assembly, I asked everyone in the crowd to go with me to the county jail to picket for a while that night. We could not forget to let Royal Untreiner know that we still loved him.[60]

The taped meeting reflects how our nightly assemblies went. Folks sang and prayed, someone gave a sermon, another offered their encouragement, and someone else gave an update of our plans and activities. The person who performed the tasks changed each evening, but Rev. Gooden, Rev. Brooks, and I spoke to the crowd every night. Most of the time Rev. Leverette did as well, but for some reason he did not speak during the taped rally. I have been asked before, "H. K., why did you tape so many of your meetings and press conferences?" The answer is quite simple: I did it to protect myself. I had been misquoted so many times by the *Pensacola News Journal* that I knew I had to have a record of what I said in public to defend myself against some ridiculous accusations. I did not make the recordings for historical purposes or anything like that. I never really considered what we were doing as historical, to that degree. We were just fighting for what was rightfully ours. And I did catch the *News Journal* in a few lies. For instance, they reported once in the late 1960s when I was president of the local NAACP that I promised to "turn Pensacola upside down and burn it." I never said that, and for some reason I had taped that address. What I said to the audience was that "with or without your help we are going to turn Pensacola upside down." I never said anything violent, or anything that could have been interpreted as such. And I had the tape to prove it. I went to the paper offices that morning, stated my claim, and played my tape of the previous evening's meeting. The paper retracted their comment in their next edition.[61] If I would have had any sense about the matter, I would have sued them. But the tapes that I had protected me from further allegations that white leaders made. Interestingly enough, I received an amusing note after the retraction was published. Someone mailed me a postcard of a famous picture of Dr. King at the Highlander Folk School in 1957, which supposedly proved that he was a communist. On the back of the picture someone wrote, "Beware. We know about the tampered tape." Regardless of the threat, I continued my practice of taping public gatherings at which I appeared. I have about thirteen tapes from the period that still exist, but threw away dozens more because the tapes eventually became fragile and broke.

Another thing the SCLC and NAACP tried to practice during the mass meetings was consistency. We tried to repeat the same demands every night. One practice that we criticized after the killing of Blackwell surrounded civilians riding in a deputy's squad car. We did not want any civilians, blacks or whites, in the cars with officers. Rev. Gooden even told all of our congregations that if they saw any police cars coming through their neighborhoods with a civilian in them, they needed to stop them and force the civilians out because they were breaking the law. One of our main points was that suspicion surrounded Blackwell's shooting because an ordinary citizen with no police training, who was not even supposed to be in a patrol car, supposedly found the gun that Wendel was alleged to have in his right hand. We maintained that this proved nothing. It was not against the law for Blackwell to have a gun in his vehicle. The main demand that the entire community made, though, was that the sheriff's department remove Doug Raines from his position.

The termination of Douglas Raines was our primary request because we felt that he was a murderer. Like Rev. Brooks told the audience one night, Doug Raines had to leave the sheriff's department or "we are going to close this county down." We also wanted him to take a lie detector test concerning that night's events but it, too, was ignored. To have any of our demands regarding Raines met, we had to go through Sheriff Royal Untreiner. Rev. Brooks, Rev. Gooden, and I met with him on several occasions to voice our concerns, but Untreiner virtually ignored us. He eventually took Raines off of the street and put him on a desk job, but the county still employed him and it was unacceptable to SCLC and the NAACP. On top of the transfer, Untreiner upheld Raines's action and defended him repeatedly. Our nightly mass meetings were what united blacks during the Blackwell crisis. We met on such a regular basis that our activities extended beyond the sanctuary. After we had our rally at the church, we would leave the meetings and take our demonstration to the sheriff's department. That is when the chant started.

When the evening services ended, carloads of us would go to the county jail, stand on the grounds, and recite a number of spirituals and civil rights chants. We had several chants, but one of our most popular was one I called the "Two, four, six, eight" song. It went, "Two, four, six, eight, who will we incarcerate? Untreiner, Raines, the whole damn bunch." The chant started almost immediately the first few times we went to picket the department, and it summarized what the black community wanted; we wanted that murderer Doug Raines and the person who protected him, Sheriff Royal Untreiner, put in jail. It was that simple. We did not mean for it to be a threat; it merely vocalized our greatest demand. Criminals belonged in prison and in our minds, those men were two of the biggest criminals in the county. We did not like crooks, even if they were crooks in uniform. We did not like murderers, whether they were civilian murderers or murderers in uniforms. And we especially did not like people who upheld murderers in uniform. Rev. Brooks, Rev. Gooden, and I felt that Untreiner was as guilty as Doug Raines because he supported and harbored him. Raines should have been fired and tried for murder, but Untreiner instead put him in a place where he would not have to come in contact with folks. At one point, we also added Governor Reuben Askew's name to the "Two, four, six, eight" chant. He was a Pensacola native, but we felt that he did not do enough to bring about justice in Escambia County. At the prison, we chanted civil rights slogans, we sang songs, and we prayed. My favorites were what we called "the freedom songs" like ""We're Not Going to Let Nobody Turn Us Around," "We Shall Overcome," and hymns of that nature. We also assembled signs for our gatherings. It was a full-fledged civil rights demonstration with a jubilant atmosphere. Each night, anywhere from two to five hundred people of all ages, and sometimes all colors, would demonstrate for an hour or more in front of the county jail.

On January 8, Curtis Golden finally agreed to launch a grand jury probe of the Blackwell shooting. But things got off to a bad start, as far as the NAACP and SCLC were concerned, because Golden appointed black Pensacola attorney Nathaniel Delmond to lead the investigation. He was hand-picked by the establishment and was used to give their conclusion from a black mouth. Gooden stated early in the investigation that local blacks would not support Golden's grand jury because "hand-picked establishment blacks" were deciding what to do with Doug Raines. Gooden also promised to involve the national NAACP in the matter and declared, "This is not a small matter to be handled locally. It goes all the way to the national level of this organization, and they feel there has been a lynching down here."[62] The eighteen grand jury members, including three blacks, listened to almost five days of testimonies concerning the shooting. They interviewed over forty witnesses, including Escambia County sheriff's deputies, the Escambia-Pensacola Human Relations Commission members, Deputy Douglas Raines, Wendel Blackwell's family members, ambulance drivers, and everyone who was on the scene after Raines killed Blackwell. I led protests outside of the courthouse where the grand jury met because I knew what they would conclude. We picketed on the sidewalks and carried signs that proclaimed "Justice is Color Blind" and "Justice Now." Gooden called the period "showdown week" between Pensacola blacks and whites and repeated that "nothing short of the removal of Deputy Doug Raines will satisfy us." He also promised, "If this local grand jury does nothing, we will camp on the capital grounds" in protest. "We will fill up the roads between here and Tallahassee with blacks going to the governor to protest the lack of justice" for blacks in Escambia County.[63] The grand jury's decision tested our commitment.

On January 23, the grand jury released a report that declared Raines's shooting of Blackwell "justifiable homicide." The document said Raines "acted in a reasonable and prudent manner," "believed himself to be in imminent danger of death or great bodily harm by Wendel S. Blackwell who was armed," did nothing to intensify the situation "leading up to and including" the shooting, and could not legally face suspension from the department. Furthermore, the grand jury praised Royal Untreiner by saying he "acted lawfully in his handling of the investigation and could not be removed from his office" for any reason. The jury only made seven recommendations to pacify SCLC and NAACP leaders, the most forceful of which encouraged the sheriff's department to recruit, train, and hire more minorities as officers. The grand jury even had the audacity to ask dissatisfied minorities to "make a concerted effort to ride with regular deputies under the sheriff's office present policy" so that we "will more fully understand law enforcement duties and dangers."[64] The decision was a gross miscarriage of justice that made me increasingly bitter, angry, and disturbed. B. J. Brooks called the "discriminatory" report a "mockery of justice" and promised "a long struggle" for racial equality in the area would follow. I told the local media that the conclusion legitimized the murders of black motorists by white deputies and demonstrated that "I must be prepared to be killed if I exceed the speed limit" in Pensacola. I also promised that we would "get Doug Raines off the sheriff's department if we have to go to the Supreme Court," and warned, "This is the last time a black man will be killed in Pensacola and nothing is done about it."[65]

The "justifiable homicide" finding disturbed me tremendously, to put it lightly. This was one of the things that most angered me during the entire ordeal; the county law enforcement structure could not adequately police itself. But that is what they attempted to do. It did not surprise anyone that the grand jury returned a justifiable homicide ruling, because they had done so in many instances where the members of the sheriff's department had shot and killed young Afro-Americans. One white man on the police force named Lucien Mitchell, for example, had killed at least three young blacks. And each time a grand jury investigated we heard "justifiable homicide." Even before the Wendel Blackwell situation, then, blacks in Pensacola believed that local police could kill us at will. We protested each one of the killings, but it did not help our cause. It did not help matters in the Blackwell situation either, but we fought back as a more united community for a period after his death. Soon after the grand jury released their report, Brooks, Gooden, and I organized a trip to Tallahassee.

On January 31, we took our demonstration to the state capital. The NAACP and SCLC formed a motorcade to visit Governor Askew himself. I had considered Reuben Askew a personal friend of mine for years before the Blackwell incident. As a matter of fact, he always told me that I was the first person to suggest he run for the governor's chair when he was in the state house of representatives. He never let me forget my encouraging words, and he was a good governor. He was always friendly towards the right cause. For a time we did use his name in the "Two, four, six, eight" chant, but I felt that he was unaware of our plight. If we had the chance to give our side, I felt he would listen. So we planned a demonstration on the capital steps. We believed that going to Tallahassee was a crucial step in the local movement. About one hundred of us gathered for nearly an hour on capital grounds when Governor Askew said he would see me, Rev. Gooden, Rev. Brooks, Wendel Blackwell's widow Elaine, and Rev. Leverette.

I do not remember exactly what Askew said in our meeting, but he sympathized with our cause. Otha Leverette told the governor, "Unless something is done, any day Florida can go up." He also said that "if another black is shot" by a white deputy in Escambia County, "we are going to be walking in blood. There will be bloodshed."[66] Askew promised that he would persuade Sheriff Royal Untreiner to hear our concerns and make some changes in the area. He even said that he would do what he could to have Raines dismissed. The bottom line is that the governor listened to our side of the story, acknowledged our grievances, and expressed his frustrations about what was going on in Pensacola. The meeting satisfied us to the point that we removed his name from the "Two, four, six, eight" chant for the rest of our struggle.

The only negative point of our successful meeting with Askew was the way the white power structure treated us when we returned to Pensacola. Brooks, Gooden, and I knew that the pressure would increase when we got back home. We had taken our case to the governor and he criticized the actions taken by the sheriff's department pertaining to the Blackwell situation. After we came back from Tallahassee, we knew that the department would do everything they could to stop us and the movement. We were getting out of hand to them, and had no business involving the governor in local affairs. They thought black leaders, me in particular, were getting real sassy. The intimidation and Hitler-like tactics increased after our session with Askew. One of the biggest problems in the whole affair is that the Escambia County sheriff's department simply ignored black concerns. I believed that the situation would have been less tense if Untreiner would have listened to NAACP and SCLC representatives from the beginning and at least tried to implement some changes. But he steadfastly refused. The Blackwell situation angered us, but it angered us more that we were being ignored. We had absolutely no trust in the local law enforcement officers, regardless of their color. I often said that during that time, "It is open season on blacks in Pensacola." There was even a black policeman who acted as an informant for the local media and the county sheriff's department.

Rev. Gooden, Rev. Brooks, and I knew that somebody was going downtown after our mass meetings and telling everyone who was interested what we had said during the assemblies. A city policeman, whose name I will not recall, took information from the mass meetings. At the time, though, we did not know who was doing it. We had armed Deacons for Defense members standing outside the church to make sure that if anybody made a move, that they would hardly be able to tell about it later. We let everyone, including the police, know that we had armed security watching out for us. We did not hide that from the deputies and actually wanted them to know that we were protected. This is probably one reason that the city's white leaders wanted to know what was going on in our meetings. I knew that the sheriff's department placed an informant inside the assemblies because the *Pensacola News Journal* printed speeches that we made at the meetings the day after we delivered them. And the *News Journal* enthusiastically supported any activity that worked itself against Afro-Americans. That is about as simple as I can put it. It was just like the integration of the schools. Judge Harold

Carswell was an obstructionist as it related to school desegregation and the Pensacola area supported him. But we knew that somebody from within our community gave the paper their information, but there was no way for us to tell who it was. I even began joking that the police know we were coming to protest in front of the jail after our meetings before we even decided we were going down there. The NAACP and SCLC knew, therefore, that there were traitors in our camp. In 2000, I finally found out who gave away all of this free information. A good friend of mine saw me in Pensacola and made an interesting comment. He told me that during the mass meetings a policeman confessed to him that he recorded many of our meetings and took the tapes downtown to the sheriff and state attorney. The interesting part is that he was a black police officer who was supposed to have been in the church to protect the movement leaders. But he told my friend that he did it and apologized for this actions. He said that his supervisors at the station ordered him to make the recordings and he complied because he had to keep his job. I understand, and I hold nothing against that man today. He did what he did out of fear of losing his job, out of economic necessity, and out of the need to feed his family. He told my friend that he did not want to make the recordings because he sympathized with our claims, and I believe him. But if he had not recorded our meetings, he would have been fired and Untreiner and Curtis Golden still would have found someone else to do their dirty work.

As January ended and February passed, our demonstrations downtown and at the sheriff's department only grew larger and the people became more insistent upon justice. We continued our selective buying campaigns against local stores, asked blacks to not buy bread or milk at any county grocery store, and even asked parents to not allow their school children to use their school's lunchroom facilities. This went back to my theory that if you want to hear a white man holler, squeeze his dollar. We wanted to do any and everything possible to show the Pensacola power structure that we meant business. Most of our downtown demonstrations attracted more than five hundred people. We even staged a mock funeral for Wendel Blackwell during one of the protests, and marched from Lee

Square to the courthouse with a hearse and coffin. Rev. Gooden gave the eulogy for Blackwell. He said that we "reached out" to local whites for help during the murder investigation and "drew back our hands" to find them "covered with the blood of Wendel Blackwell and written in the blood were the words 'justifiable homicide.'" At one point, he said that at least death freed Wendel "from all the oppression and injustice going on in this country." He told everyone there, including newspaper reporters and deputies who watched the proceeding that "the black people standing on these steps are willing to die for justice."[67]

By February 1975, therefore, Pensacola was thoroughly divided because of the murder of Wendel Blackwell. The NAACP, SCLC, and many local blacks were determined that right would prevail in the county during this crisis. The mass meeting were growing in numbers and showed no signs of slowing, as did nightly demonstrations at the county courthouse and sheriff's department. We knew that many whites in the area, particularly Royal Untreiner and Curtis Golden, grew tired of our activities and had no plans to address our demands. In particular, they wanted to shut me up. What I did not know was that they planned to silence the movement by eliminating me from the area.

7

THE ARRESTS AND THEIR EFFECTS

T he NAACP and SCLC continued to organize mass meetings after we met with Governor Reuben Askew in Tallahassee on January 31, 1975. The forums actually energized movement leaders, particularly myself, because I thought the governor would intervene on our behalf and work to ensure racial justice in Pensacola. In fact, a few days after our meeting at the state capital Governor Askew called Escambia County Sheriff Royal Untreiner and urged him to meet with NAACP and SCLC representatives to hear our grievances. Untreiner agreed to meet with us on February 21, which was the first time during the Blackwell crisis that he acknowledged any black leader. We welcomed the opportunity to present our perspective to Untreiner, but we did not expect much to come of the meeting. He harbored who we believed was a murderer and showed no signs of addressing our main request, which was the termination of Douglas Raines. While Rev. Gooden, Rev. Brooks, and I awaited the meeting with county officials, we continued our mass meetings and demonstrations at the sheriff's department. Each occurred on almost a nightly basis. The church continued to overflow with folks who were fed up with the way blacks in Pensacola were being treated. After we returned from Tallahassee, the congregation actually spilled outside of the assembly hall and into the street. When the meetings ended, usually between three and five hundred people carried our protest to the jail. We followed the same routine every night at the Escambia County jail; we marched, sang, carried protest signs, and prayed. What we did not realize, however, was that we were being monitored by one of Royal Untreiner's most trusted assistants.

From February 6 to February 18, Sergeant Jim Edson filed nightly reports that documented our activities at the downtown jail. Jim Edson commanded the riot and crowd control division of the Escambia County sheriff's department. I knew Jim Edson before the Blackwell situation because he was often one of the main deputies in charge of calming the chaos that consumed Escambia High School two years earlier. We even joked at times about meeting so often on the campus. Yet Edson was a hard-core racist who did everything he could to harass blacks and impede racial justice in northwest Florida. Because of his stance on blacks in general and me, Rev. Gooden, and Rev. Brooks in particular, Edson became the person who carried out most of Royal Untreiner's dirty work against movement leaders in Pensacola. Edson's lies eventually caused me to spend time in state custody. Before he had the chance to send me down, though, he was hard at work documenting our activities at the jail.

Edson's reports recorded several details about each of our gatherings. He wrote down their precise locations, the number of people who participated in them each night, and how long the demonstrations lasted. He also noted if Rev. Gooden, Rev. Brooks, Rev. Leverette, or I attended. Although I did not find out about the reports until years after the protests took place, they contribute further to my belief that law enforcement made a concerted effort to quiet specific black leaders. Edson's notes also reveal that our demonstrations grew larger as February progressed. On February 11, for instance, he wrote that thirty to forty vehicles blew their horns as they circled roads that surrounded the jail. On February 18, he noted that "approximately seventy" vehicles brought demonstrators to the facility. In addition, Edson called the gatherings "orderly" in his earliest reports. He noted that many of us only carried signs and dispersed quietly after a short period. He wrote that our main goal seemed to be the termination of Doug Raines, which was correct. As the month passed, though, we staged longer protests. Edson seemed concerned that the demonstrations were expanding and noted that Rev. Gooden, Rev. Brooks, and I were "the ringleaders." He wrote that only we delivered speeches to the group, led them in songs, and conducted chants, which was incorrect.[68] As the nightly visits to the county jail grew, so did the officer's obvious contempt for our presence there. Edson's field notes demonstrate that as the month passed, the sheriff's department's desire to end our gatherings increased.

The prison demonstrations were peaceful and often festive affairs. We really had a good time down there, despite the reason for our protests, and blacks showed no violent intentions whatsoever. But Edson saw things much differently. He wrote that we hurled profanities and insults at officers, which was a lie. He also said that numerous deputies filled the sheriff's department building beyond our view "in the event there would be any trouble." I do not know if there were any officers there who were waiting to break up our meetings, but I do know that there was never any reason for them to use force against us because we never posed a threat to anyone. One of Edson's most important reports was dated February 19. The sergeant wrote that B. J. Brooks and I led a chant which stated, "Two, four, six, eight, who will we assassinate? All of these deputies." He reported that, "They were referring to us and pointed to the five members of the crowd control squad that were standing in front of the door." We never, ever, used the word "assassinate" in that chant. The word we used was "incarcerate" and we had used it numerous times in our protests since Blackwell was killed in December. But Edson did not stop there. In a report dated February 20 he noted, "Now they have gone to the practice of referring to us as pigs" in "the most vocal demonstration that we have had at this time." He even admitted that several officers followed us home in unmarked vehicles! This began a concerted set-up for the leaders of the Pensacola civil rights movement. It was obvious that we were not going anywhere and that the establishment would have to deal with us in one way or another.[69] But none of us, including me, had any idea that the department would use terroristic tactics to silence black dissent in Escambia County. Still, we hoped that some issues would be resolved at the February 21 meeting between Untreiner, Rev. Gooden, Rev. Brooks, and I that Governor Askew requested. The forum never took place.

The main problem we had about any meeting with Sheriff Untreiner was the location. He wanted to have it in a public setting with members

of the community and local media present, and planned to have it in the
auditorium of the Escambia County Health Department. I, in particular,
was against this idea. I knew that it would be hard enough dealing with
Untreiner in private, much less when he had his white disciples and
members of the press watching his every move and recording his every
word. It was the perfect setup for a white-wash by the sheriff's department;
Untreiner would simply justify his actions and defend Doug Raines's
actions and we did not want to hear it. Furthermore, I knew Untreiner
would avoid the major issues if a crowd was present. He even intended
for white audience members to ask black leaders questions. We knew they
would only vent their frustrations to movement leaders. We definitely
did not want to answer questions from angry white folks. So I suggested
that we meet in a closed session at the downtown First Presbyterian
Church, with no press or community members from either race there
to influence our actions. But Untreiner never responded to my request.
Rev. Gooden, Rev. Brooks, and I decided that appearing at the county
Health Department would be akin to walking into a lion's den, so we
chose to not be devoured for the pleasure of the white power structure.

The *News Journal* reported that Untreiner, state attorney Curtis
Golden, and two state legislatures appeared at the meeting and denounced
our decision to not appear. The headline on the twenty-second stated,
"Black leaders avoid meeting with sheriff" and blamed us for not cooperating with Untreiner. The meeting basically turned into the forum that
I suspected it would become, but we were not there to hear it. Untreiner
told those present that he had several responses to our concerns "but they
are not the answers these people want to hear." The next evening, we
responded to Untreiner's latest antic at our mass meeting.

Before our meeting occurred, however, a white man presented me
with an offer to withdraw from the local struggle.[70] On the day after
we were supposed to have met with Sheriff Untreiner and other law
enforcement officials, I received a telephone call from an influential
local white businessman. I thought it was strange when he asked me to
visit him at his place of business, Pensacola Hardware, because I knew
he opposed everything the black community tried to accomplish in the

area. Yet despite my suspicions, I went to the establishment. When I arrived, he told me that "some powerful friends" of his appointed him to "make me an offer." He said, "H. K., you have gone as far as you can go. You cannot do anything else, so you need to cool off your activities. I have been authorized to offer you an incentive to back out." I looked at him in amazement. He said, "Now, I am not asking you to sell out." I said, "Well, then what are you asking me to do? You are not asking me to sell out yet you are offering me some kind of incentive to abandon my people. That, to me, sounds like I am selling out." I did not think of taking the offer for a brief second. I told the man, "I cannot accept any deal because every morning I have to look at myself in the mirror. And I feel that when every young person in this community sees me, whether they know I sold out or not, I will feel like they will know what I have done." The man told me to consider my decision, but I walked out of the store. I later found out that no one else in my position received a similar offer. Some time following the experience, after I went through a lot of garbage for my efforts and spent time in prison, the same man who made the proposal saw me in town and remarked, "Eighteen thousand dollars does not look too bad now, does it?" For a moment, I thought that I should have taken the money. But when the proposition was first made, I had no idea how far the sheriff's department was willing to go to get rid of me. I found that out the next evening.

The crowd that assembled at Greater Mount Lily on February 23, the night after our aborted meeting with Untreiner and his crew, was one of the largest groups that gathered for a single mass meeting. The *News Journal* reported that only two hundred people were there, but they never were real good with numbers. They intentionally underestimated the number of folks that attended our events because they wanted to make it look like we had limited support from the black community. *News Journal* reporters usually cut our figures in half, but that night it seemed like we had four times as many in attendance as the papers said. I will never forget that evening's mass meeting because it was one of the only that ones Rev. Brooks missed. He was sick with the flu, and I asked him to stay home and regain his strength for future assemblies. Rev. Gooden appeared at the church, but I gave the main sermon that night and targeted the local press, in particular, for the role they played in stirring up white animosity toward the Pensacola movement. The paper quoted me as saying *News Journal* reporters "pounce upon every opportunity they get to bring attention to the fact there are people in the black community who disagree with Matthews, Gooden, and Leverette," despite the fact that "we speak for more black people than anyone else in the community." I also stated that Untreiner's failure to address our complaints did "more than anything in recent memory to unify Pensacola's black community." I concluded the meeting by leading the congregation to the Escambia County sheriff's department, as I had done nearly every night that month. Jim Edson's report of the evening's festivities continued to portray me as a violent person by stating that I told officers we "would meet force with force" from white officers, and "would take care of anyone that tried to stop" our activities. I never said anything of the sort. In addition, Edson claimed that we blocked all access to the department and refused to let deputies pass through barricades we formed. He also wrote that we spat on and made obscene gestures toward deputies and damaged police vehicles.[71] All of these statements were bald-faced lies. We were angry, but we were not stupid. I knew that any unlawful actions on our part would be counterproductive. I made sure to focus our outrage in a way that demanded justice, not vengeance. I knew that threats of that nature would get us nowhere fast with those people, so SCLC made a concerted effort to maintain a peaceful, relaxed atmosphere when officers were present. But the plan to silence all local black leaders had begun and nothing I did would postpone the devious plot. In fact, Edson stated in his notes that I led the so-called "assassination chant" once again and ended it by pointing at him and shouting, "And you too Jim Edson!" I did not know it at the time, but officers inside the county jail taped our demonstration that evening on an audio recorder.

Another interesting fact about Jim Edson's report of our activities that night is that he claimed Rev. Brooks, Rev. Leverette, and I led demonstrations on the county jail steps. Rev. Brooks did not participate in that rally in any capacity, because he was at home sick while we rallied at the jail. It is also interesting that Edson only listed the local people who led the protest. Although Rev. Gooden was there, Edson did not mention him as a leader that evening. Brooks, Leverette, and I were the main targets because local law enforcement wanted to silence those who lived in Escambia County. Especially me. They saw me as the lead dog; the one who stirred up everyone else. They had to shut us down because we lived in the area. And because I was the recognized leader of the Pensacola black community, the white power structure wanted to make an example of me. Gooden was easier for them to take care of because he lived outside of the county. If the going got tough, he could leave. They obviously did not know R. N. very well, but that is what they thought. Regardless, the sheriff's department's plan to permanently silence us was put into motion on February 24, 1975. It was an evening that I will never forget.

The night began as usual, except for Rev. Gooden's absence. He had to return home to Tallahassee for some reason, so Rev. Brooks and I led the assembly that night. We had our usual meeting at Greater Mount Lily Baptist and left the church at about 10:00 P.M. Several of us continued our usual practice of taking the demonstration to the county sheriff's department and jailhouse. Over 250 people gathered that night, which was one of the largest crowds to meet at the site, and a festive occasion once again characterized our activities. We were singing, praying, and laughing with each other. But something felt different. I had a strange suspicion that something was going to happen to us that night. I even remember telling Rev. Gooden on a prior occasion, "You know that your boy Curtis Golden is not going to just let us keep doing this without trying to shut us down. He is going to try and get us one of these days." Golden was the state's attorney for both Santa Rosa and Escambia County and consistently made negative statements about black leaders in the local papers. I had no idea that Golden planned to crush our movement that night.

The demonstrations began as soon as I arrived at the deputy's station. It was a peaceful, jubilant gathering, despite my misgivings. We did not block the roads or doors that led to the sheriff's department, contrary to what the deputies later said. We made sure there was a constant path opened through the crowd so that people who worked in the building could get through us to do their duties. Rev. Brooks, Rev. Leverette, Rev. Gooden, and I always made sure that those paths were maintained because the demonstrations often occurred when the evening shift changes occurred. We never intimidated those people, nor did we bother them. We just went about our usual routine of chanting, singing, and praying. Several members of our congregation carried their usual signs that said things like "Raines is a murderer" and "Do away with Douglas Raines." One little boy even carried one that stated, "Blackwell: Gone but not forgotten." Jim Edson told the child, "Boy, you've got the wrong sign. Hell, I forgot the nigger the next day." That was the kind of carelessness law enforcement displayed to us; it the kind of racism we constantly experienced from people who were supposed to protect our community.

After a few minutes of singing songs like "Every Time I Feel the Spirit Moving in My Heart I Will Pray," and "We Shall Overcome," I spoke to the group through a bullhorn and led them in prayer. The bullhorn was an important part of our demonstrations because I used it to organize our chants, get the crowd's attention, and things of that nature. After I led the prayer I made some motivational statements like "The sheriff's department has lied to blacks and we are tired of it!" I then led several of our usual chants like "One, two, three, four, five, we ain't going to take no jive," and "We're gonna stop, stop, stop the racist cops." I then announced, "Now we are going to do the 'two, four, six, eight' chant. And we are going to leave Governor Askew's name out because he has shown that he is sympathetic to our cause." I handed the horn over to Rev. Jimmie Lee Savage who led us all in proclaiming, "Two, four, six, eight, who shall we incarcerate? Untreiner, Raines, the whole damn bunch!" Our chanting was so loud that night that the prisoners housed inside the county jail sang along with us. After we recited the lyrics a few times, Jim Edson came out of the building to end our demonstration. He told us through a bullhorn that we had "disturbed the peace of night and the operations at this penal institution," were congregated unlawfully, and would be arrested in two minutes if we did not leave.

Interestingly enough, we had never added Jim Edson to our list of demands. He was never in the "Two, four, six, eight" chant, either. I do not know why we never included him in our demands; maybe we did not think he was worth it. But we did target Untreiner. We wanted him in prison and that is why we chanted, "Who shall we incarcerate? Untreiner, Raines." We wanted them both in jail because they were criminals. Doug Raines was a criminal because he killed Blackwell, and Untreiner was a criminal because he supported Doug Raines. Still, everyone was confused when Edson told us to leave the jail grounds because we had done the same thing several previous evenings and no one had said anything about it. Less than a minute later, though, the county riot squad waded into our crowd swinging their billy clubs. Chaos soon followed.[72]

Deputies used violence against movement activists for the very first time on February 24. The police action surprised many of us. In his report of the night's events, Edson claimed that B. J. Brooks told him, "Put us in jail, we is ready to go" after he ordered us to disperse, but this is simply untrue. Rev. Brooks was standing nowhere near Edson and responded to his order in the same confused way that the rest of us did. The officers had shown their frustrations at some of our previous meetings but they had not really done anything to us. They were totally frustrated and outnumbered, but they had never shown any inkling of violence towards us nor were hostile enough to make us think that they would do something so rash. But when they moved into our group in full riot gear, they did not just try to break up our gathering; they wanted to hurt folks. They greeted us with clubs and beat anyone who got in their way. People scattered in every direction when they realized what was going on. We expected that the arrests would come sooner or later, but I never expected such a display of blatant brutality. The violent acts deputies perpetrated were thoroughly ridiculous, and no black even tried to fight back. Untreiner later justified what happened by saying that we were a threat to his officers' safety.

The *Pensacola News Journal* also played a key role in the night's events. Untreiner and Curtis Golden told *News Journal* reporters that they had to help apprehend and arrest black protesters. Golden informed the journalists that they would be arrested if they refused the order. He also asked the reporters to cooperate with law enforcement officials in writing their accounts of the night's actions. Paper reporters complied and wrote, "There were no injuries reported to any of the crowd or the officers involved." But many of our people were hurt bad enough to receive treatment at area hospitals. One young man needed stitches after an officer hit him in the head with a nightstick, and two officers beat a seventeen-year-old as he tried to cross the street and escape the violence. Deputies even wrestled a young girl from her grandfather's arms and arrested the man. They eventually arrested thirty-four adults and thirteen juveniles for two misdemeanor charges: unlawful assembly and malicious trespassing. The *News Journal* published the names, addresses, and charges of each demonstrator police arrested. Everybody arrested for the two misdemeanors was released on a two thousand dollar bond. They pled innocent to the charges a week later at the county court.[73] When Rev. Brooks and I were released, the bond was twenty-two thousand dollars. A thousand dollars each for unlawful assembly and illegal trespassing, and a twenty thousand dollar bond for felony extortion.[74] I did not know until I bonded out the next morning that Rev. Brooks and I were charged with a felony. Even when I found out about the charge, I was not told what the exact felony was. I did not find until the next day that I was charged with extortion.

Rev. Brooks and I were in jail from the time of our arrest until the next morning. Needless to say, it was a very long night. Dr. Donald Spence, a dentist in Pensacola, signed our bonds. The arrest did not bother me that much; I was used to being in jail. The two misdemeanor charges did not even bother me. I even dismissed the felony extortion when I heard of it. I thought that the sheriff's department would never give up on trying to nail me with a lengthy jail sentence, and this was one more attempt to do so. The county had already tried to pin one felony charge on me for inciting a riot at Escambia High School and that did not stick. I initially felt the same way about the extortion charge. The felony charges came about because the state attorney, Curtis Golden, claimed that Rev. Brooks and I used threats in an attempt to force Sheriff

Untreiner to do something that was against his will, which was fire Doug Raines. Golden also claimed that several police witnesses heard me and Rev. Brooks lead songs that threatened the lives of Untreiner, Raines, and Governor Askew for not cooperating with our demands. They used the "Two, four, six, eight" chant as evidence, but claimed that we led the crowd to say "assassinate" instead of "incarcerate." Using physical threats against state employees was a felony charge, and that is what they claimed Rev. Brooks and I did. Everybody knew that the extortion charges were bogus, including the county officials who filed them. When I heard their reasoning behind the charges, I thought, "There is nothing to that" because I knew what the true chant was. I knew that neither Rev. Brooks nor I had done anything illegal. The only thing we wanted to say was that Doug Raines was a murderer and we were not going to rest until Untreiner removed him from the force.

But the more I thought about the felony charge, the more nervous I became. You see, I understood that I was a pain in the side of the local white power structure and had been for some time. I knew, too, that they wanted to silence me in any possible way. When they could not buy me off or silence me from defending my people, they wanted to literally get rid of me. They were hell-bent on silencing me and Rev. Brooks because we were the main leaders of the Pensacola black community. One thing that I learned during my time as an activist is that once the power structure decides to silence you, especially if you are a leader in a movement, they do not quit until they achieve their goals. When I finally understood the seriousness of the felony extortion charge, I remember becoming very numb and thought that they had finally gotten me.

The same officers who beat blacks down in front of the jail on the night we were arrested told the local papers the most blatant falsehoods. One deputy described our group as "hostile," "very threatening," and "frightening." Another who tried to leave department headquarters during the evening shift change said that we blocked all entrances so that no one could enter or exit the building. They even said we stood in front of department vehicles and refused to let them leave the parking lot. We knew better than to try something like that, because every black person there believed the officers would run us over if they had a reason. The papers also quoted officers who said we threatened, pushed, and spat on them. It was clear from the media reports that I was being blamed for the latest incident between blacks and law enforcement officials. Sheriff Untreiner claimed I told him, "If you try to stop us from demonstrating, there will be trouble." Jim Edson, unsurprisingly, told some of the biggest lies. He reported that I led the so-called "assassination" chant and told one deputy that I pointed at him and said, "Boy, we'll eliminate you too, if you don't straighten up." Edson also claimed that I told him, "The only way deputy cars will enter this parking lot is if we want them to come in." Furthermore, he said that many folks in the crowd possessed weapons and displayed them "in a rude, careless, angry, and threatening manner" to intimidate officers. Edson claimed that his deputies seized six clubs, six shotgun shells, three knives, and a bayonet from the group, but he never produced the alleged evidence. In fact, deputies arrested only four blacks for possessing small clubs and none of them recalled seeing any other items.[75]

I do not think that any person in our group ever showed any violence toward the jailors, particularly on the night we were arrested. But when you have a crowd of 250 to 300 people it is impossible to believe that no one will say something they had no business saying, or will not possess something they had no business possessing. I did, from time to time, see people in our groups carrying billy clubs, but we did not support that type of behavior. In fact, I chastised individuals I saw with anything that could have been perceived as a weapon. I realized that some blacks carried those small clubs because they did not trust the police and felt endangered, yet felt this was no excuse to possess anything that could harm another person. Rev. Gooden, Rev. Brooks, and I always made a point of telling our audiences, "We are going to our demonstrations and we are only taking ourselves and the Good Lord." We never supported violence, we never advocated violence, and we never suggested violence. But with that many people in the crowd, there were some who may have followed their own agendas. Within any movement, there will be people who are armed and it is impossible to tell who has concealed what. Dr. King, despite his reputation for advocating non-violent resistance, had some people with him who carried weapons. So I can not positively say without hesitation that no one at the sheriff's department on February 24 possessed some kind of weapon. But if there were, I never knew about it.

I surely did not egg those people on to commit violent acts against the deputies, which they accused me of doing. That was another flat out lie but it went along with their overall plan, which was to "get Matthews at any cost." To them, I was the one that caused the main problems and was the head troublemaker. I was viewed as a communist, a racist, and whatever other negative words that they wanted to call me. I was viewed by the power structure and many whites in Pensacola as everything that was bad. What those people never realized, and still do not understand, was that I fought for blacks and white folks alike. We supported just causes regardless of race, but the press and other whites never mentioned that because it did not support their theory of me as a radical black rabble-rouser. So the fact that SCLC and NAACP members demonstrated peacefully and remained non-violent really did not matter. We were still perceived as destructive by the media and the white community. This would not change after my felony arrest.

Almost immediately after Rev. Brooks and I posted bail on February 25, I began to plan more mass meetings and downtown demonstrations. I was not going to let this latest event dampen my resolve in any way because that was what the white power structure wanted to accomplish. I was not sure how Rev. Brooks, Rev. Gooden, or Rev. Leverette felt about the issue, but I was more encouraged than ever to keep fighting for civil rights in northwest Florida. I did know that a local judge lowered the bail for Brooks to seven thousand dollars but kept mine at twenty thousand. This further proved that I was the target white leaders wanted to demoralize. I later discovered that the NAACP paid Rev. Brooks's bail, but every penny of my bail came from my own pockets. After my release, the NAACP and SCLC held a joint press conference in Pensacola to address the felony charges. I promised to continue the campaign against Raines and Untreiner, and said, "There will be more protests and more people coming to join us in our struggle for racial equality." I also stated, "Black people are getting sick and tired of being misused and mistreated" in Escambia County, and said that "Sheriff Royal Untreiner's actions have only caused blacks to intensify their racial protests." Rev. Brooks and I also addressed the "assassination chant" we allegedly led and emphatically denied ever using such words.[76] Our arrests were nothing more than a silencing tactic, and it worked to a large degree. Black people were afraid. After they saw what those in power could do to the heads of the movement, people were afraid to take risks. I knew that our activities would continue and remained focused on Wendel Blackwell's death, but the movement now had a great personal meaning for me.

Soon after I bonded out of jail on the twenty-fifth, I discovered that the circuit court had issued a prior injunction against picketing on county property. The decision, which was obviously directed at movement activists, said that all demonstrators had to remain on the perimeter of county property, including but not limited to the jail grounds. We also had to maintain a minimum of ten feet between each person and not block access to any building. Violators faced a contempt of court charge. Deputies in full riot gear were ordered to guard county facilities and were told to arrest any protestor who violated the court's injunction.[77] It did not take long for me to realize that local blacks were now fighting for more than the removal of a corrupt sheriff's deputy; we were fighting an entire system for our basic rights as dignified human beings. But I promised that our protests would continue just as the law allowed. No piece of paper could stop me from doing what everyone has a right under the Constitution to do, which is assemble peacefully. Consequently, the racial situation in Pensacola grew more contentious as the days passed.

On the afternoon that I bonded out of the county jail, Rev. Brooks and I met with Rev. Gooden. He came from his Tallahassee home to the Florida panhandle after he heard about our arrests. We held a mass meeting that night and announced plans to have the largest march at that time in downtown Pensacola on February 27. Both Rev. Gooden and I publicly asked national and state NAACP officials, SCLC president Ralph Abernathy, and all whites interested in racial justice to join the march. We also returned to the county jail that night in a show of solidarity.

About five hundred of us appeared at the building and stood in silence. Curtis Golden came out of the building soon after we arrived and was surrounded by twelve riot control officers. He read the injunction the circuit court released earlier in the day and we peacefully dispersed. Over the next two days, Gooden, Brooks, and I planned for the upcoming demonstration. We wanted the event to be a peaceful and multiracial affair, but anticipated the worst from county law enforcement agents. I later found out that the sheriff's department was ready to use force against us if we gave them the opportunity. Royal Untreiner had every deputy and reserve officer on duty that afternoon and told Jim Edson to prepare for a battle. Untreiner even gave the riot squad small explosives that could kill anyone standing twenty yards from its detonation point and told officers to use them if necessary. I did not know the department was preparing for such a confrontation. If I had, I am not sure I would have asked each of the protesters to ignore the injunction against marching on county property, endure the impending arrests, and pack county jails.[78] Despite the potentially explosive situation, the march was a peaceful affair.

On February 27, nearly one thousand black and white citizens peacefully marched over a mile through downtown Pensacola. The deputies provoked no violent incidents. We honored the court injunction against assembling on county property and did not march to the courthouse. Rev. Gooden, Rev. Brooks, Rev. Leverette, and I led the group during the assembly. I spoke for nearly an hour through a bullhorn and we prayed, sang hymns, and thanked everyone in attendance for their peaceful activities, including the present deputies. In my address, I told those in attendance that we planned to "press for our constitutional rights against action we feel is unjust." I also reminded everyone, particularly the assembled press members, that "protests and demonstrations are our legal weapons to use against those seeking to oppress us and to attempt to deny us our freedom." Each speaker repeated demands for local leaders to fire and jail Douglas Raines. Brooks summarized the sentiment most succinctly by stating, "We want Deputy Doug Raines fired and in a chain gang." Gooden assured the crowd, "Violence is just around the corner" and "the whole world will find out what's going on here" in the near future. He also called the injunction against our protests unlawful and said if the American Constitution could not protect blacks, "we will destroy it and the system along with it." Some marchers noticed that a lot of white folks walked around in the crowd but did not participate in the event, and we figured they were undercover police. I later verified that about forty plainclothes officers mingled in the crowd during the march. The downtown rally lasted about two hours and no violent incidents transpired. But Sgt. Jim Edson made several statements prior to the event that infuriated the black community and encouraged us to add his name to the list of officers we wanted fired.[79]

On March 2, the *St. Petersburg Times* published several racist comments Sergeant Jim Edson made to one of their reporters just prior to our February 27 downtown march. A *Times* employee, Jane Daugherty, was in Pensacola to cover our demonstration and characterized it as an "old-fashioned civil rights protest." Most interestingly, though, Jim Edson thought Daugherty would share his negative opinion of blacks. Edson told her that his deputies prepared for the march by playing a game called "Selma." Edson said the game's only rule was, "You grab a club and hit a nigger." He even told the reporter, "Now I don't want you to think I'm a racist, I like black folks. In fact, I'd like to have two of them in my backyard for the dogs to play with. Niggers are better than Milk-Bones."[80] That was the attitude people in positions of leadership throughout Pensacola had demonstrated to blacks for years, and people thought we fabricated accusations concerning particular law enforcement authorities. But Edson possessed the ignorant assumption that all whites thought in his demented way, and he thought the white journalist from St. Petersburg would laugh at his comments like those in Pensacola did. He turned out to be quite wrong, and the *Times* published the quote. In addition, the article pointed out the many injustices local blacks endured and blamed the sheriff's department for doing nothing to improve the situation.

The *Times* piece used Edson's quote as evidence that white supremacy still characterized the Florida panhandle. The article gave a brief history of the racial unrest in Escambia County and proved very sympathetic to our plight. Daugherty even blamed county officials for the latest racial disturbances and said the main problem in our city was that "deputies know they can shoot blacks in Pensacola without fear of punishment." Yet the paper blamed more than just the deputies. It also called many other whites to task. For example, it castigated local whites for ignoring black protests and not demanding Raines's termination. The piece charged, "Each night, the shouts of angry protestors echo through a city more concerned with a major historic restoration project to commemorate its Spanish heritage and draw tourists" than racial equality. The *Times* also criticized our lovely newspaper for inflaming racial tensions by criticizing black activists and ignoring white brutality. In fact, the *Times* claimed that *News Journal* reporters "openly report to the sheriff's department after covering protests" and allowed deputies to edit their stories. The editor of the *News Journal,* Bill Gordon, admitted that his paper intentionally reported low black crowd estimates and refused to cover most black meetings, demonstrations, and news conferences because he did not want to "inflame the situation" between the races.

The *Times* also argued that the county Escambia-Pensacola Human Relations Commission was made up of "Uncle Toms," who bowed to white demands. It stated that the black commission members stood in total opposition to us, "the more militant ministers," who led the NAACP and SCLC. The *Times* concluded that local blacks "are committed to seeing justice served here" at any cost, which is what Rev. Brooks, Rev. Gooden, and I had been saying since the Blackwell shooting occurred.[81] Although the *St. Petersburg Times* correctly perceived what was going on in Pensacola and used Edson's comments as the most damning evidence of the strong white resistance to racial justice, the essay did little to change how whites felt about or responded to black demands. In fact, the way whites reacted to Edson's quotes further frustrated those of us involved in the local freedom movement.

Jim Edson's remarks infuriated the black community in Pensacola, and that is putting it mildly. It is one thing to express such racist beliefs privately; all blacks involved with our movement knew that was how he and many other whites in power thought. But it was something totally different to make such crass comments in the press. I was not surprised that Edson said what he did to the reporter. I was, however, surprised that the paper published such inflammatory rhetoric. It let us know that not all white reporters felt the same way that those in Pensacola felt, and that was encouraging. The *Times* article also supported my belief that the city was one of the most racist, hate-filled areas in the country when it came to acknowledging black humanity. Royal Untreiner's response to Edson's remarks strengthened the belief. Sheriff Untreiner adamantly defended his riot squad sergeant and said that the *Times* misquoted Edson. He later claimed that a civilian made the negative remarks, if anyone said them at all. Edson initially denied making the racist statements. A few days after the paper reported the remarks, though, Edson admitted that he made a comparison between Pensacola and Selma in a joking manner. He still maintained that he never made any racist remarks against blacks, despite substantial evidence to the contrary.

In fact, local radio news director Randall Hinton was present when Edson made his comments to Daugherty and denied under oath that the sergeant made the insulting comments. Yet a few days later, Hinton admitted during a recorded interview that Edson did make the comments. Hinton resigned from WBSR due to the lie and was charged with perjury by state attorney Curtis Golden. Despite Hinton's ordeal, Untreiner supported Edson's side of the story and continued to support him with no reservations. The sheriff proclaimed that Edson committed no criminal offense and "can not be suspended or reprimanded without cause." He also said that the sergeant "is entitled to security in his job while carrying out his law enforcement duties." Untreiner even wrote a letter that the *News Journal* published which said, "Jim Edson is one of my best officers and I take pride in the way he handles himself during a crisis." He insulted local blacks by stating that Edson "is worthy of praise."[82] An intriguing thing about the entire situation is that SCLC discovered the existence of a code in the "Sheriff's Department Deputy Handbook" that prohibited deputies from using racial slurs. The rule, which became part of the handbook in 1971, stated that violators faced suspension and possibly dismissal if they violated the regulation. I pointed this out to Royal Untreiner and the local media but, not surprisingly, they chose to ignore that particular ordinance. What did surprise us, however, was the reaction the *News Journal* had concerning Edson's quote.

On March 18, *Pensacola Journal* editors published its response to the Edson controversy. The paper admitted that it did not initially believe the *St. Petersburg Times* report because its reporters believed it "incredible" that "a deputy in a highly sensitive position would have the blindness to say such a thing in the presence of strangers, particularly news reporters." Yet the *News Journal* admitted that onlookers verified his quotes and acknowledged that Edson's comments "understandably incensed" black leaders. The paper finally brought up the same point we had been making for months by asking, "How can we expect blacks to maintain any confidence whatsoever in evenhanded justice when the man assigned to control these tense situations stands accused, at least by two witnesses, of uttering blatantly racist slurs?" It even criticized local law enforcement and asked, "Where is the integrity of the sheriff's department when this situation is allowed to stand uncorrected?" The *News Journal* editors ended the editorial by posing a simple question; "Are we, as a community, simply going to let this situation drift out of control?"[83] Again, this was nothing new to those who were involved in the black freedom struggle throughout the county. We had thought for quite some time that the situation had gotten out of hand. Anyone familiar with the area's racial history knew the situation had become critical when the *News Journal*, a pillar of white resistance in the community, publicly wondered what was going on in Pensacola.

The racial situation had become so serious that the Ku Klux Klan attempted a national rebirth in Escambia County that captured the attention of the national media. Soon after my felony arrest on February 24, I learned that the United Klans of America (UKA) planned an area recruiting drive in my honor. Their leader, or so-called Titan, was named C. E. Carroll. He should have given me an award or some kind of honor for all I did for his organization. Without me, he would not have had a group! I did more to boost Klan membership in Escambia County than any white person ever did! Carroll even singled me out as the main reason for all of the racial unrest in the area and thanked me for giving white folks a reason to hate blacks more than they already did. The UKA, therefore, designated me as their "public enemy number one." They held rallies, membership drives, marched through downtown Pensacola, and set up a telephone service they called the "Voice of the Klan" to spread their ignorant propaganda. On March 14, the *News Journal* reported a meeting that took place between Carroll and what he called twenty "cream of the crop" local whites who offered their services to Sheriff Royal Untreiner.[84] Knowing Untreiner as I did, he probably took them up on their proposal.

Two days later, the *New York Times* published a story that focused on the Klan's rebirth in the area. Although no one mentioned me by name in the story, the whites told the *Times* reporter that the only racial problem in Pensacola came because "blacks and communists," which we were frequently called during the crisis, constantly harassed police officers. Carroll told *Times* reporter Wayne King that, "One race or the other has to be assigned to be superior and that ought to be the white man."[85] The largest action the Klan staged in the area occurred on May 24 when about 135 UKA members followed their Imperial Wizard, Robert Shelton, through downtown Pensacola.[86]

The march occurred on the same morning that former Alabama governor George Wallace spoke at a ceremony at the county courthouse that honored area policemen. The Clownsmen dressed in their full regalia and marched through the downtown streets waving Confederate flags. The demonstration ended next to a downtown Confederate memorial in time for the group to join 3,500 other residents to hear Wallace speak. Later that night, the Klan held a membership drive at Pensacola Speedway. Shelton supposedly singled me out as their main target but had plenty of hatred to go around. Among others, Shelton blasted Ralph Abernathy, the NAACP, and the local school board for causing all of the racial unrest in northwest Florida. But Carroll thanked me personally and said I was one of his "best recruiters."[87] Although the local papers continued to report Klan activities and the nonsense they spouted about the local movement, *News Journal* writers advised whites to "reject the Klan, no matter how bitter some of the actions of black protest leaders have made" them. It did not matter to me, though, that the editors criticized the Klan. The fact that they discussed Klan activities in their pages and continued to blame blacks for fomenting racial hatred revealed where their true sentiments lay.

The *News Journal* and formal white supremacy organizations, however, were not the only elements area blacks continued to struggle against in the aftermath of my felony arrest. The sheriff's department remained committed to their goal of permanently silencing the black freedom struggle in Pensacola. Royal Untreiner demonstrated this by refusing to fire Doug Raines, which remained our primary demand throughout the ordeal, and by supporting Jim Edson after he made his racist comments to the *St. Petersburg Times*. Untreiner also tried to have additional charges filed against me through the state attorney general's office, and based his claim on a bogus deputy's report that said I encouraged black youths to attack unsuspecting whites. Nothing ever came of the request but it demonstrated how I remained the focal point of local white leaders, even after the February arrests. Furthermore, Untreiner asked the Escambia County Commission's Administrative Committee for financial assistance in early March so the department could purchase new riot control equipment. Rev. Brooks and I met with the group and asked them to not use tax money on items that deputies wanted solely to use against black protestors. We felt that revenue sharing should be used for all citizens, not for intimidating or brutalizing one segment of society. Yet they gave thirty thousand dollars to the sheriff's department to buy new riot squad gear and to pay the officer's overtime salaries. Most of that money was used solely for the purchase of what I called "black control equipment."[88] As the spring progressed, therefore, so too did our fight for racial justice.

Despite the best efforts of the sheriff's department, the Ku Klux Klan, the local media, and the state's attorney to end the black freedom struggle in Pensacola following the mass arrests at the county jail, the local NAACP and SCLC continued our civil rights activities throughout the spring of 1975. We organized selective buying campaigns and expanded our demands to include the terminations of Doug Raines, Royal Untreiner, and Jim Edson. The state NAACP even contacted us and promised their support. The Florida NAACP Board of Directors appealed to the national office for their assistance in our situation. The state branch promised to provide Rev. Brooks and me with legal aid and financial assistance during our impending felony trial.[89] In the meantime, SCLC organized protests in downtown Pensacola to protest the racial injustice that still plagued the city. We wanted the merchants and those who went downtown to insist that the sheriff's department acknowledge and address our grievances. We wanted to damage their business so they would pressure the sheriff's department to remove Raines and the other corrupt officers from duty.

The SCLC also planned marches at the county jail after my arrest. On March 1, for example, I led a protest across the street from the facility and made sure that our group complied with the injunction against gathering on county property. Despite the fact that we were peaceful and violated no law, deputies told us that we had to disperse or face arrest less than thirty minutes after our arrival. Such blatant resistance only encouraged us to continue our activities. Sometimes we just circled the jail and courthouse in our vehicles blowing our horns. The power structure had not passed any laws saying we could not do that, and I wanted to let our friends in the sheriff's department know that we were still around.[90] The most important thing, though, that the local NAACP and SCLC continued after the February arrests was the nightly mass meetings at local churches.

The mood of our mass meetings changed after the jailhouse arrests. They grew more serious in nature because the stakes had increased, and everyone involved in the movement realized it. From February 25 on, we were in a struggle with the white power structure for the very survival of the local movement. Some of us, in fact, were fighting quite literally for our freedom. I recorded several of the mass meetings we had in March, April, and May of 1975, and their contents reflect the somber atmosphere and sense of urgency that movement leaders and our audience shared.

Blacks march through downtown Pensacola in March 1975. Otha Leverette (second from front left), Matthews (third from front left and B. J. Brooks (fourth from left), lead the procession.

The meetings retained their revival-like feeling throughout that spring. In fact, our reliance upon God increased after the arrests because we realized that only He could deliver us from such a precarious situation. Many members of the black community, including myself, often referred to the gatherings as "spiritual meetings." The meetings still opened with religious hymns like "Leaning on the Everlasting Arms" and "Pass Me Not, O Gentle Savior." I even led the audience in singing, "He's Got the Whole World in His Hands," and replaced the "whole world" phrase with the names of Doug Raines, Royal Untreiner, Jim Edson, and Curtis Golden in each new refrain. We prayed and read Bible passages that pertained to our struggle against injustice. Our faith remained the primary theme of the meetings and formed the basis of the changes we wanted to see in Escambia County. I told the audience on numerous occasions that only God "will give us the ability to make freedom and justice a reality in Escambia County," for without Him, "none of us will survive."

I stressed that the real struggle in Pensacola was not between white and black, but between right and wrong. To me, it really was that simple. Righteousness faced evil because we lived in a city that—and dealt with men who—seemed to know nothing about God. We were all brothers because we had the same Father, but the power structure did not understand this. I frequently remind those who participated in the movement that ours was a spiritual struggle as much as it was a political and social struggle. God was on the side of right, and the only gains we made were accomplished because God Himself was involved in the movement. "The battle is going to be won," I told our followers, "with God and dedicated folks." The tapes that I have of those post-arrest mass meetings repeated the theme that "all blacks were united in a single garment of destiny." Every black in northwest Florida was connected because we were all in the same boat; all of us were treated as inferior to any white. We only had two things we could depend on, and that was each other and God. I often reiterated this point by telling those at the mass meetings on a nightly basis that "until all black folks are free, no black folks are free." Rev. Gooden echoed the themes and focused on those within the black community who worked against everything we were fighting to achieve.

Movement leaders were well aware that there had always been certain people in the black community who tried to tear down what we had worked so hard to build. The presence of those folks became more apparent after the February arrests. Some criticized us in the press while others criticized us from their pulpits. They told young blacks who participated in our activities, "Y'all ought to be ashamed of yourself for following people like Matthews." We were actually fighting two sets of enemies: one in the white community and one from within the black community. But not all whites should be lumped together. Some whites believed that our cause was right and just, even though they supported us in the background. Fighting the upper-class blacks along with the white supremacists, though, made us feel like we were struggling from within the lion's den itself. Rev. Gooden and I learned that a group of prominent black civic leaders met a number of times to discuss how to end our movement. NAACP and SCLC activities brought substantial amount of economic pressure on them from white businessmen, and we were bad for their businesses. Some people, particularly blacks in the so-called upper class, had the audacity to tell me that the church had no place interfering in the conflict between the police department and their critics. My reaction, which I voiced often at the meetings, was that "if the church is not the place for social activism, then where is the place?" It was clear that we faced problems from some of the same folks we tried to help, or had helped on previous occasions. Rev. Gooden addressed these people in one of the most emotional sermons that he gave during the 1975 mass meetings.

In a message he titled "The Problem of Danger," Gooden claimed that there were too many blacks in Pensacola who were not willing to stand shoulder-to-shoulder with their brothers in the current fight against racial injustice. He began the sermon by stating, "There is no way in the world for me to accept or stomach unrighteousness." Yet he noticed, "We've been scuffling down here for almost four months and it seems that the more we scuffle, the more we dig ourselves in a hole." Why did this seem to be happening? Because too many black people in Pensacola, Gooden proclaimed, "are running from danger." Those who protested at the county jail on the night of the arrests surely did not run from danger. In fact, Gooden and I believed that those who participated in the Pensacola movement during its darkest days deserved to be mentioned in the same books that mentioned people like Rosa Parks, Daisy Bates, Thurgood Marshall, and Rev. King. Our dedicated followers refused to run from danger, but there were simply too many blacks who remained silent or tried to stop our activities.

Rev. Gooden led a prayer every night for those "on the sidelines." We needed the help of the entire black community because Gooden saw that we "have a racist sheriff's department" in Escambia County that "pronounced genocide on all black people in this country." But too many local blacks were either scared or just did not care. This only contributed to the "seething unrest in Pensacola" that Gooden firmly believed "will erupt in violence." He predicted over and again "that the ultimate outcome of this struggle will be violence in the streets and there will be burnings, lootings, firebombings, shootings . . . I pray to God that if it happens, it

B. J. Brooks speaks to the crowd at a downtown demonstration in 1975. Matthews is on his right.

doesn't happen to the masses, but to the classes." If someone had to die by "racist executions," as we both believed would happen, Gooden said that he hoped "it happens to one of our class niggers" because "they ain't got sense enough to realize what's been going on about our struggle." They failed to understand that we were fighting just as much for their rights as we were for our own. But they accepted white mistreatment and those of us involved in the movement viewed them as cowards. They were just as much a problem to us as racist whites; at least we knew where people like Raines and Untreiner stood. As Rev. Gooden put it in his sermon on danger, "No matter how much love or righteousness you have, there is a point where you stand up and don't let anybody else run over you. That's the point that we are now in Pensacola."

One of the hardest things for Rev. Gooden and I to stomach during the movement were the numbers of influential blacks within Pensacola

who conspired with the white power structure against us. I have since
forgiven all of those who did and even understand why they made the
decisions that they did; they had to feed their families, just like I did.
They simply put their family first, and I have to respect that, to a certain
degree. But in 1975, a different situation existed for blacks. We preached
about loving our enemies, and those we had in mind were individuals
such as Doug Raines and Jim Edson. Rev. Gooden liked to call Edson
"a big bloated up goat" who brags about "putting niggers in their place"
and had Royal Untreiner's permission to "shoot you and get away with
it." But we always maintained that "if we put enough pressure on this
county, Royal Untreiner himself will fire Doug Raines." We also believed
that God could and would change people. As Rev. Gooden stated, "The
only way that the white man and the black man will be able to walk
together is through Jesus" because "we're still living in one of the most
racist societies in the whole world." "Love," we often declared, "is the
most dangerous weapon in the world."

It was, though, a little harder to understand why so many blacks
were not supporting our struggle. They were even tougher to love than
the whites who wanted us dead. We called them everything from "Uncle
Toms" to "hand-picked establishment niggers that accept what the white
man says." We were extremely hurt by and angry at those who down-
graded us after the arrests because Rev. Brooks and I needed their help
more than ever.

Our trial was scheduled to begin in July, and Gooden promised us
there would be one thousand people marching in Pensacola on the day
of our trial. He called it "righteous justice" and asked the mass meeting
congregations, "How do we influence that courtroom unless we're raising
some hell in the streets. If we call our demonstrations off, what happens
to" Brooks and me? Gooden jokingly told the audience that when we
the freedom struggle in Pensacola finally ended, all of the "class niggers"
would probably move to Alabama out of shame for not supporting us!
We realized quite clearly, therefore, that it was not only several whites that
needed to be changed; a lot of black folks needed it too. I often reminded
those at the meeting that while "we may not be what you want" as move-

ment leaders, "we are all you've got right now." As time passed and my felony trial grew closer, our meetings became much more intense.

There was a definite change in the mood of our mass meetings as the spring of 1975 progressed. The atmosphere became much more serious because the felony trials approached. I also became more disappointed and discouraged as the movement continued. I was disappointed because attendance declined and many people abandoned the struggle at its most crucial stage. I was disappointed that the national organizations which had promised to help me in times of dire need were nowhere to be found. But I was most disappointed that the criminals whose actions had inspired our mass movement still held their jobs and lived their lives like nothing had happened. They deserved to be locked up in prison but walked the streets as free men, and many people did not seem to give a damn. So as the mass meetings continued my rhetoric probably seemed inflammatory to many who did not understand the frustration I experienced at that particular time. My unhappiness showed at a number of meetings that I spoke at weeks before my trial began. For instance, I told the congregation that despite the fact that "the crackers in this city are waging a war of fear," I still promised to "get things done in this city." I also stated that "I love fighting white folks" who constantly tried to deny my people their basic dignity. The fact that the police used "class niggers" to undermine our efforts showed that they were desperate, but an animal is most dangerous when it is wounded. I reminded the crowds that these policemen were "sophisticated crackers" when it came to silencing blacks and they would do anything possible to break the movement. I told the story of one unnamed "cracker who had the audacity to ask me what I would do if he burned a cross in my yard." I responded, "If I caught you burning a cross in my yard, I would leave you there for evidence." My warning "did not just go for that white boy. That went for any black boy who decides to burn a cross in my yard." I reassured those who remained in the struggle that their efforts were not in vain because "one black person has more power than five hundred white folks in Pensacola. If you don't believe it, go to north end [of town] and buy a house. Within twenty-four hours, there would be 'for sale' signs all over that neighborhood." I despise the fact that so many blacks have an inferiority complex concerning our worth to society. Then, as well as now, I stressed that "it is time that black folks in this city need to realize that we are somebody." I thought that one of the best ways for our people to understand their true value was to hear it from an outsider. So I asked Marzine Emmett to speak at one of our gatherings before my trial commenced.

Emmett was a postal worker from Mobile, Alabama who was involved with a local civil rights organization from that city called Neighborhood Organized Workers, or NOW. Mobile, like Pensacola, was in the midst of a heated struggle with the white power structure. I had even traveled to Mobile on several occasions to work with NOW volunteers in some of their demonstrations. NOW differed from the NAACP and SCLC, though. Their leaders were more radical than we were in Pensacola, and their supporters seemed more diligent in using all necessary force in obtaining equality. This message came through in the speech Marzine gave in Pensacola. He opened by introducing himself and stating, "I think about raising hell with the honky every time I see him." He cited Nat Turner, "a bad nigger," as his hero and role model. He explained that during the Mobile movement whites killed his brother, destroyed his car, and shot at his pregnant wife. He had also lost several jobs. Two of his best friends, local leaders of the black community in Mobile, received lengthy prison terms for their involvement in the local civil rights movement. Emmett revealed his solution to the problem of white racism by stating that "you better get you some guns" because "one thing a honky respects is violence." He told us, "I'm just as peaceful as you let me be, and I'm just as violent as that honky wants me to be."

Yet he pointed out one thing that Rev. Gooden and I had noticed since the movement began, and that was the fact that some blacks within the community tried to undermine our work. In fact, Emmett looked in the crowd and said, "There's somebody out there" that "the white man downtown sent here. Somebody here," he promised, "is going to get hurt" for selling out their brother. To emphasize his point, Emmett pulled a small pistol out of his pocket, showed it to the crowd, and proclaimed, "These things were made for more than lighting cigarettes. Now I am not preaching violence, but if I ever found out that was a black man that was going to those white people and telling them what was going on, I'd take care of them." He concluded his message by stating, "The most important thing is that you stick together." Yet he assured us, "You are going to have to clean your own back yard" with what he termed "necessary violence." Although I did not agree with the tactics Emmett advocated, I understood his main points and felt his anger. If we continued to deal with the Escambia County sheriff's department and Pensacola white power structure in the same manner that we used for the previous six months, the movement would die. But violence was not the answer and our tactics changed very little in the final demonstrations Brooks, Gooden, and I organized before the felony trials began. Still, my sense of frustration increased as time passed that spring.

It became abundantly clear between my arrests and felony trial that local whites continued to see me as "public enemy number one" in Pensacola. My phone number was unlisted in the city phone book, but I still received death threats and harassing phone calls. That is one reason why my phone number is still unlisted. Even to this day I am never sure who may call me or what they may have to say to me or my family. During the Escambia County movement, several folks called and said things to me like, "Nigger, get out of town or die," "We will kill you if you don't quit your activities," and "You better stop marching for your own good." All of the people who called me and threatened me were nothing more than cowards because no one ever left a name with their threat. A lot of the phone calls, I am still convinced, came from Afro-Americans.

Due to the large number of death threats I received during the ordeal, I had several men from the black community who offered their services as my personal bodyguards. Numerous armed men always guarded the church entrances during our mass meetings and, after the arrests, several carried firearms inside the building. Volunteers even guarded my home each night after someone threw a brick through the living room window and vandalized my property. I remember that a man named Michael Jackson, who is still an activist in Pensacola, watched my house like a farmer protects his henhouse. Pensacola was never a safe haven for me,

but I never acted like I was afraid. Like a recent commercial stated, "Never
let them see you sweat." I often told people that "I do not have enough
sense to be scared," but it was a lie. I was a little scared throughout most
of the movement and at times, I actually feared for my life. The period
before my trial was one of those times, as the calls and threats increased
as the court date got closer. But as the big day neared, so too did my
feeling of isolation.

One reason that I felt abandoned was because the SCLC and
NAACP gave me no help before the trial began. Each organization
publicly championed my cause and I certainly wanted their help, but it
was not forthcoming before the trial. I never directly asked the SCLC or
NAACP for assistance, financial or otherwise, but I did speak with Ralph

SCLC President Ralph Abernathy with Matthews, December 1975.

Abernathy after the arrests and let him know what was going on. Each organization, particularly the SCLC, lost an opportunity for national exposure. They could have made a very public stand for my innocence and stuck with me throughout the ordeal, but they did not. The national organizations let me down, and let the local citizens involved in the Pensacola movement down.

In addition, my family proved a source of tension during the turbulent period. My first wife eventually divorced me because she could not take the pressure of living with a controversial public leader. It was just too much for her to handle. She told me several times at the movement's peak that she hated being left alone. After my arrest, the threats on our lives took their toll. I remember telling her to view Coretta Scott King as an example, but she argued that their three children kept her company. We, on the other hand, had only one child and he had left the house by that year. The stress involved with the movement proved more than she could bear. In a certain way, she tried to get me to give up my activism. She did support what I was doing, particularly after the arrests, and I understand her reasons why. When my civil rights activities first started, she was deeply involved in the movement. As I became more involved with SCLC, though, the danger increased and I was often away from home traveling throughout the region. Consequently, she often was the one who received the threats while I was gone, and she pressured me to withdraw from SCLC affairs. Yet I refused, and became isolated in my own home. Those feelings of abandonment, however, were nothing compared to what I endured after the trial ended.

8

A Legal Lynching

The felony extortion trials of Rev. B. J. Brooks and I were scheduled to start on July 9, 1975. In the meantime, several things occurred that began the downfall of the civil rights movement in Pensacola. Despite the fact that our struggle would be all but over in less than six months, the SCLC and NAACP continued to protest the racism that existed in Escambia County at the time. In March, for instance, we continued to boycott downtown stores in hopes of influencing white-owned businesses to pressure the sheriff's department to fire their corrupt officers. We used the Easter buying season as a way to magnify our concerns. I am not sure if the proprietors ever tried to persuade police leaders to meet our demands, but movement leaders did their part to keep blacks out of the stores we boycotted. Newberry's Department Store, for instance, was one of our main targets because it was a large store that depended heavily upon black patronage. Yet despite our efforts to boycott certain establishments, some blacks continued to shop there. They knew the SCLC and NAACP had asked everyone to stay out of those stores and they knew why we wanted them to shop elsewhere, but they ignored our requests.

The way I dealt with the problem was simple; I carried a camera with me downtown and took pictures of any black person who entered a boycotted store. When I snapped shots of those who entered the stores, they nearly came unglued. They asked me nervously, "Rev. Matthews, why did you do that?" They knew exactly why I did it; the black community was boycotting that particular store and they betrayed us by continuing to shop there. Some even said, "Please don't show that picture to anybody." I told them that if they did not mind shopping in places that we boycotted, they surely would not mind other blacks seeing them enter the stores. Those people knew what would happen to them if anyone knew they were undermining our efforts, so they begged me to not develop the photos. Needless to say, they honored our boycotts through the rest of the Easter holiday. Many individuals needed a little persuasion to join our movement, but they eventually came around to our side of the fence. We particularly needed their help after what happened to B. J. Brooks.

Rev. Brooks preached at Greater Mount Lilly Baptist Church on the weekends, but worked full-time for the Florida Department of Transportation during the week. On March 27, the agency suspended him from his job without pay for "conduct unbecoming a Department of Transportation employee." There was no doubt in anyone's mind that the department made their decision because of the bogus felony charges the sheriff's department levied against each of us. The DOT claimed that a state law existed that banned anyone accused of a felony from state employment, but they never produced any evidence that proved their claim. What is certain is that the department conducted no investigation into the charges. The NAACP and SCLC quickly came to the defense of Rev. Brooks. On the afternoon that Brooks found out about his suspension, Rev. Gooden and I organized a press conference where we addressed the latest attempt to cripple the Pensacola movement.

At the public forum, Rev. Gooden, Rev. Brooks, and I questioned many aspects of the suspension. We wondered how he could be suspended without being presented with any evidence of his guilt. He had no trial. The state denied him due process which, the last time I checked, was illegal. The SCLC and NAACP argued that, as Rev. Gooden put it, "a double standard of justice exists in this county." Rev. Brooks had received no trial and had not been found guilty of committing a crime, but he still lost his weekly income. We pointed out that certain Escambia County commissioners had been indicted for crimes by a grand jury but never lost a day's pay from their jobs. We also argued that neither Raines nor Edson had been removed from their jobs, and they were accused of doing much more harm to the community than any black person. Brooks owned a small service station, but it did not do enough business to replace the two hundred dollars each week he lost with his DOT suspension. As he put it, "This is practically my whole livelihood they're playing around with." It was pure racism on the part of the Department of Justice and we had no problem levying that accusation. We also questioned why the department waited a month after our arrests to suspend him.

The DOT decision came at a time when racial tensions were at their highest in Pensacola, which is really saying something. The suspension only fanned the flames of hatred between whites and blacks in our area, and both the NAACP and SCLC promised to take Rev. Brooks's case to court. Rev. Gooden announced, "We'll have a suit against the state and expose racism for what it is" in northwest Florida. Despite the best efforts of the white power structure to silence black leaders, we publicly promised that "the protest movement in Pensacola isn't about to die." However, the DOT suspension had a dramatic impact upon B. J. Brooks and created a significant rift among the black leadership in Escambia County.

In response to the economic coercion brought by the state of Florida upon Brooks, he distanced himself from Rev. Gooden and I after his March suspension. He appealed the decision to the Escambia County Career Service Commission less than two weeks after he received it and pulled away from the movement soon thereafter. He stopped coming to the mass meetings and did not appear at the downtown rallies. The suspension from his job caused him to withdraw all support from SCLC endeavors. He even began to say disparaging things about me and Gooden in the press. For example, Brooks told the *Pensacola News Journal* that his organization would take no further part in the Pensacola protest marches and demonstrations because "there were some things going on behind the scenes that the NAACP cannot support." He argued that Rev. Gooden and I, against his wishes, "want to blow this thing up" in Pensacola, which would destroy the NAACP's peaceful image if it remained active in the movement.[91] A few weeks after his suspension Brooks proclaimed, "I can no longer support the ideas and philosophies of the present leadership of the protest," and stated that neither I, Rev. Gooden, nor Rev. Leverette "have the interest of our people at heart." In fact, he called our tactics "underhanded," whatever that meant.

Despite my suspicions to the contrary, Brooks said that his DOT suspension had nothing to do with his decisions to split from SCLC. He claimed that we encouraged blacks "to break the law" and "castigate citizens for non-involvement." Brooks remained president of the local NAACP and promised the group would continue fighting for civil rights in northwest Florida. He pledged that his organization, unlike the SCLC, would challenge racial injustice only through the judicial system. He also promised to never again publicly petition for racial equality in Escambia County.[92] B. J. Brooks's choice to abandon the movement at a critical juncture caused a permanent rift in our friendship. He did not change that much towards me personally, but we never again worked together for a common cause. I remained angry and bitter concerning his action for many years. Over time, however, I have really come to understand why Brooks made the decision that he did.

B. J. Brooks had a family that depend on him for their livelihood. He had a well-paying state job and had a wife and children to provide for; I did not have those same responsibilities. I was working for no one outside of my part-time position at St. Mark AME Zion Church. In addition, my congregation continued to support me. His congregation was not as supportive, from what he told me. He felt the heat and he was a man who wanted to look out for his family. As he told the *Pensacola Journal*, his suspension "causes undo suffering for my family."[93] I did not always agree with him for doing some things and not doing other things, and he did not always agree with what I did or did not do. But we were very close for quite some time during the 1960s and 1970s. I do not think that he ever really sold me or the local movement out, but he definitely toned his rhetoric down. He just tapered off, as far as movement activities were concerned, and eventually it got to the point where his activity was non-existent. He withdrew gradually before his job crisis, but the process accelerated after the suspension to the point that he even denounced what we did. Brooks told the press that we walked a fine line between nonviolent direct action protest and radical activism.

He told me personally that he felt that SCLC tactics were too rash. I am convinced that the NAACP gave him an ultimatum to denounce me and limit his activities only to what the state office approved in advance, or they would no longer support him. He especially needed the organization to fund his trial defense when the DOT suspended him. The NAACP later issued Gooden the same deal, but he did not accept it. Brooks's family situation, therefore, is the reason he heeded the NAACP's advice to split with me and the Escambia County SCLC.

Another ironic aspect of Brooks's suspension was that the DOT announced its decision a day after he, Rev. Gooden, and I met with federal and local representatives to discuss a solution to the racial unrest in Escambia County. On March 26, the Justice Department's Community Relations Division met with leaders from the black and white community. It was the first time since Blackwell's death shooting that the sheriff's department formally met with us to discuss the incident. Two representatives from the federal government met with me, Rev. Brooks, Rev. Gooden, and Royal Untreiner. The Justice Department promised to "work toward a final agreement" to end racial conflict in Pensacola, but they fought an uphill battle because of the white power structure's non-repentant attitude. The *Pensacola Journal* wrote an editorial concerning the meetings and commended the federal government for trying "to bridge the communication gap" between the sheriff's department and the black community. They noted quite correctly, though, that the situation had reached a near-irreconcilable point. The article argued, "If an agreement is not reached and one or both sides come away from the table unsatisfied, it may lead to a hardening of attitudes on the part of both whites and blacks not privy to discussion." It also noted that while blacks were "doing much of the marching and protesting," area whites were "just as adamant in their position as" SCLC and NAACP members.[94] Royal Untreiner remained the primary reason that we never reached a resolution in the crisis.

The Justice Department sessions failed for a variety of reasons. First, the white leaders wanted to assemble on their turf and under their terms. Brooks, Gooden, and I compromised on that point somewhat, but Un-

treiner wanted more. Our main demand remained the termination of
Doug Raines, but Untreiner refused to take any action against him. For
that reason, the meetings solved nothing. Untreiner only wanted to talk
with us if he could dominate the session and tell us how he was going to
handle the situation, and we refused to listen to his orders. For instance,
Untreiner demanded that I cancel all SCLC meetings, demonstrations, and
marches during the deliberations, but I adamantly refused to do so.

Because the meetings failed to resolve any issue between each side,
Justice Department representatives grew frustrated and left town after
only a few sessions. The federal lack of action did not surprise me. I had
previous experiences with the Justice Department during the Atlanta Five
investigations and they did nothing for local blacks then, either. I felt
that the Justice Department only wanted to stabilize the racial situation
in Pensacola and would do so at the expense of the black community. In
short, Gooden and I believed the agency would do whatever the federal
government told them to. Privately, the Justice Department spokesmen
sympathized with our plight against the sheriff's department but were not
given the authority to force Untreiner to do anything he did not agree to
do. We had, therefore, little confidence in the Justice Department, the
FBI, or any federal agency. The government demonstrated to us on more
than one occasion that we could not trust them. And as my extortion trial
approached, I had lost confidence in nearly everyone. Still, Gooden and
I continued the SCLC and NAACP's public campaign for racial justice
by organizing a downtown demonstration on Good Friday, 1975.

On March 29, Rev. Gooden and I led over four hundred folks in a
downtown march to commemorate the holiday. Many whites joined us
for that demonstration, which took place across the street from the county
courthouse. Both Gooden and I spoke to the crowd. Gooden reminded
us, "This is the only court house in the United States of America where
we are not allowed to hold a rally" and led us in chanting, "I may be
black, but I am somebody." I carried an American flag during the rally
to remind everyone in attendance that the U.S. Constitution guaranteed
our right to protest racial injustice in this country. As Rev. Gooden stated,
"This flag is our flag and anywhere you see that flag flying you belong."

I also began the rally by leading everyone in the Pledge of Allegiance. I carried the flag and recited the pledge partially in response to the mounting allegations that I was a radical militant. I can not count how many times I was called unpatriotic or a communist during our campaigns. The flag represented that I fully believed in this county's commitment to preserve equality for all citizens. Pensacola blacks never wanted to tear our country down. We merely wanted to share in the same benefits of American citizenship that whites in this nation possessed. We wanted to end the dual system of justice that existed not only in Escambia County, but in the nation as a whole.

I have always stressed that social activism is does not indicate that someone is unpatriotic. On the contrary, constructive, legal protest demonstrates that the person or people involved love this country and want to perfect it. I often used the analogy of an airplane to explain this point. Assume that you board the world's most luxurious airplane and sit in the first-class section. The take-off is smooth and the flight is pleasant. You are served a delicious five-course meal on expensive china, eat it with the finest silver, and enjoy a glass of fine wine with the dinner. The movies, music, and other amenities provided are enjoyable and satisfying. But then the captain comes over the intercom and announces that the landing gear does not work. Do the passengers ignore this one problem and focus on the flight's numerous positive attributes? Of course not. That one issue overrides the rest of the privileges available. To many blacks, therefore, the landing gear in America does not work. It was true in 1975 and it is still true today, in many respects. I love this country fully, but the racism is a problem that must be dealt with immediately. And pointing out this fact does not make me any less of an American. This is one theme I addressed during the 1975 Good Friday rally.

During the protest, Rev. Gooden and I announced that our Easter boycott had spread from the downtown area during the weekend. Rev. Gooden stated that for the next three days, "There will be no black buying in Pensacola at all. We're going to ask black people to not go to no job, no motel, no restaurant, NOTHING." In addition, we repeated our demands that county leaders fire Raines, Untreiner, and Edson. Those

terms never changed; we always insisted that those officers had to go for
the black community in northwest Florida to be satisfied. Rev. Gooden
summarized this at the meeting by stating, "Law enforcement in this town
stinks. It stinks from high heaven to low hell. And black people will not
be satisfied until we remove the stink from Pensacola." We praised the
city police, with whom we were very pleased, because they maintained
their credibility with us by not resorting to the terroristic actions that
county deputies used. I also voiced our continued support for Rev. Brooks,
even though he did not to participate in the Good Friday protest. I even
asked Governor Reuben Askew to personally overturn the Department
of Transportation's suspension of Brooks as a show of good faith to the
black community. Rev. Gooden told the crowd that if Brooks "can be
suspended, it means he is guilty until proven innocent and that is not
the way" American justice "is supposed to work." Yet the theme that
both Rev. Gooden and I emphasized during the rally was that the local
movement was not going away. "For Pensacola," I promised, "it looks
like a long, hot summer, and I do mean a hot one."[95] Our demonstration across from the county courthouse ended after about an hour, but
it reconvened later that night at Greater Mount Lilly Baptist Church.

I announced at the evening service that Governor Reuben Askew
planned to be in Pensacola later in the week for a Chamber of Commerce
dinner. Rev. Gooden and I decided that NAACP and SCLC members
would meet the governor at the Pensacola airport. I told the crowd, which
the *Pensacola Journal* printed the next day, that "at a time when black
people are being killed, murdered, and jailed on trumped up charges,
beaten in the process of arrest, that the chief officer of this state certainly
ought to speak out against these acts." The response from the crowd was
overwhelmingly supportive of the plan, and about fifty of us gathered
at the airport on April 2. What I never considered was that Governor
Askew might land elsewhere, which he did. I later discovered that his
plane landed at a private airstrip somewhere else in the county. I was
already frustrated with the way the local movement had progressed since
our arrests, and my anger boiled over when Askew failed to appear at
the airport. At the time I called the decision to land at another location

"a deliberate avoidance-of-blacks tactic." However, I now do not think that the incident was planned because Askew had expressed interest in our cause since it began. Some of his advisors may have known that we planned to be there, but I believe that the governor would have at least met with us while he was in town.

Rev. Otha Leverette was more critical of Governor Askew than I was. He, too, thought Askew was ducking us intentionally and wrote a letter to the *Pensacola Journal* that said as much. Rev. Leverette stated that the NAACP "opposes Governor Askew's non commitment [*sic*] and in not acting forthrightly in solving the present racial crisis in Escambia County." He claimed that the governor had ignored his campaign promise to represent all races, feared the racist white power structure in his hometown, and called his latest inaction "an outrageous act of cowardice." Leverette ended the letter by requesting Askew's aid in ending racism in Pensacola and stated, "He can do no less."[96] While appeals for assistance with our struggling movement continued, the legal issues facing Rev. Brooks and I also progressed.

On April 17, B. J. Brooks and I each filed "not guilty" pleas with the county court. At the hearing I told the white circuit court judge, Kirke Beall, that "white racist political pressure" led to the felony charges levied against Brooks and I. I also said the SCLC and NAACP "plan to do a little marching" because local leaders had "performed an abortion on black justice before it had a chance to be born."[97] My speech did little to endear me to Beall, especially when Brooks refused to make any comments at the hearing. Still, I wanted the judge, Brooks, and everyone else in Pensacola to know that I would not give up fighting for local blacks, regardless of the consequences I would have to pay for it. I possessed a relentlessness that had grown stronger since my arrest, and that attitude caused me to say many brash things. I later paid for the many strong, although true, statements I made. Rev. Brooks and I initially shared an attorney that the state NAACP provided. His name was Ed Duffee, and he had previously represented local blacks in their suit against the Confederate images at Escambia High School. He agreed to take our case and remained my attorney throughout the felony trial, which proved to be a huge mistake. By the time I realized that I needed another attorney, though, it was too late.

Thirteen days after Brooks and I pled not guilty to the extortion counts we were charged with after our February arrests, twenty-three individuals arrested with me that night went on trial in county court for misdemeanor counts of trespassing and unlawful assembly. Rev. Brooks, Rev. Leverette, and I were tried separately for the same charges. The trial indicated what was in store for us in the coming weeks. The jury in the misdemeanor cases consisted of six whites and one black. Twenty deputies testified against those arrested that night and claimed that we threatened and spat on them, blocked the entrance into and exit from the jail, shouted numerous obscenities at them, and had a variety of weapons in our possession on the night of the arrests. Only three defendants testified on the behalf of the black defendants, but it would not have mattered if more took the stand. The jury found everyone guilty of trespassing and declared seventeen blacks guilty of unlawful assembly. Ed Duffee appealed the verdicts, and the judge postponed sentencing until a higher court reviewed the decisions.[98] The trial further whittled away at some black citizens' commitments to obtaining racial justice in our community. More began to wonder if the struggle was worth what they would have to pay for their participation. As the spring of 1975 progressed, therefore, the civil rights movement in Pensacola needed all of the help it could get. The situation became dire when the NAACP relieved Rev. R. N. Gooden of all duties within the organization.

On May 2, the NAACP fired Gooden as the state field director for Florida. The state president, Charles Cherry, said that the organization dismissed Gooden because he "led too many demonstrations in Pensacola," which were "counter to the methods preferred" by the NAACP. According to Cherry, Gooden also demonstrated an "inability to negotiate some kind of settlement" between Escambia County blacks and local law enforcement. He continued, "We have been involved for four months and feel that the approach that has been used from January until now is ineffective." The NAACP, Cherry maintained, must "use more negotiation and less demonstrations" in their quest for racial justice. In conclusion,

Cherry proclaimed his belief that Gooden had "defected to the Southern Christian Leadership Conference." Gooden and I organized a press conference at St. John Devine Church later that evening where Gooden protested his removal. He was incensed because NAACP bylaws stated that the organization could not remove the state field director without a majority vote of all branch members, and an election was never held. Gooden also stated the NAACP made the decision without presenting him with any evidence that he had violated organization standards, or giving him a formal hearing to address the charges. I spoke at the press conference and denied any SCLC recruitment of Gooden. I did not have to convince him to participate in any activities my organization planned and we never gave him any funds for his work; he participated in the Escambia County struggles and brought in the state NAACP on his own volition. As I told the audience that night, "The SCLC has by no means tried to divide the leadership in this community in order to build itself." The NAACP simply used the claim to pull out of the Pensacola struggle.

The strategy worked. The day the NAACP dismissed him from duty, Gooden returned to Tallahassee to spend more time with his church and ministry. Soon after the organization sold out the Pensacola movement, I contacted the national SCLC and asked Ralph Abernathy for his personal support in the struggle. He promised to come in and help, but he did nothing. The NAACP had abandoned the local movement at its most critical juncture, and the national SCLC was not far behind. I had been totally discarded by each group and neither my misdemeanor nor felony trials had started. My feelings of desperation and loneliness only increased when they finally began.[99]

On May 7, an all-white jury found me guilty of unlawful assembly and malicious trespassing. County Court Judge Walter Langergren gave me sixty days in prison on each count, which I had to serve concurrently. My attorney, Ed Duffee, filed an appeal and I posted a one thousand dollar bond. The judge originally denied my bond, but the circuit court overruled Langergren. I was thoroughly convinced that I was going to jail. The plan against me was laid out; I would be found guilty of the two misdemeanors, serve the maximum prison sentence, and have my bail denied. I had to turn myself into the county jail by 5:00 P.M. on Wednesday, May 8, and had packed my toothbrush and toothpaste in preparation for imprisonment when I discovered that the circuit judge overturned my denial of bail ruling. The call came twelve minutes before the deadline arrived. Langergren denied my bond for two reasons. First, he said that I had a felony charge pending against me and was, therefore, a flight risk. Second, he said that the court was convinced that I would continue to make public announcements that would "cause anxiety and unrest in the community." In other words, I was told, "Don't protest, don't exercise freedoms guaranteed to you, keep your mouth shut when injustices are done, and accept whatever happens to you in both the community and in court."[100] I escaped the full wrath of the white-controlled local justice system this time, but would not be so lucky when the next legal proceedings concluded.

On June 9, 1975, Judge Kirke M. Beall began B. J. Brooks and my felony trials. The NAACP stood behind Brooks completely, but ignored me. The organization promised to take his case to the United States Supreme Court if necessary, but it never made such guarantees on my behalf. Despite the fact that Brooks had distanced himself publicly from me in the weeks leading to the trial, we agreed with the allegations levied against us. Brooks told *News Journal* reporters that the "trumped up" felony charges were "ridiculous."[101] He, like I, believed the trial was nothing more than a thinly-veiled case of political persecution. Local white leaders had been trying to discredit and silence movement leaders, particularly me, for years. This was their best chance to do away with Matthews and Brooks, and they took full advantage of the situation. Simply put, Judge Beall did not give us a fair trial. The proceedings got off to a rocky start with the selection of our jury, and provided a hint of what was to come.

State attorney Curtis Golden and his assistant, Barry Baroset, were the attorneys for the prosecution. Golden was present throughout the proceedings but Baroset asked most of the questions. Ed Duffee was the attorney the NAACP appointed to represent me and Rev. Brooks.

In my opinion, Duffee was incompetent. He was not familiar with the racial atmosphere in Escambia County and did not take the case against us seriously. It seemed like an open and shut case in our favor, but he did not understand how bad the Pensacola white power struggle wanted me silenced. He did not prepare for the trial adequately and remained entirely too laid back during the ordeal.

Duffee's lack of readiness first became evident during jury selection, which hinted that the trial was probably not going to go our way. Baroset and Duffee questioned thirty-seven potential jurors before our trial began. All but six jury pool members were white. One of the first questions our lawyer asked the group was, "Are there any of you all not aware of what's been going on here in Pensacola insofar as Rev. Brooks and Rev. Matthews are concerned?" Only two raised their hands, and both of them were young white women who attended college out of the state during the previous seven months. Duffee seemed a little surprised that everyone who lived in Pensacola had heard of us, but I was not. Anyone who resided in Escambia County during the previous nine months had heard my name. The local papers put me on their front pages nearly every day since the Atlanta Five investigations. Local radio and television stations also reported movement activities on their news broadcasts every time they had a chance, and H. K. Matthews was public enemy number one in the eyes of whites. Only a person who was totally ignorant or whose head was buried in the sand since the year began, therefore, could not have heard about our plight during that period. Duffee even restated his question and asked, "In other words, every time this agitation has been going on or you've heard something about it, the names of the people involved has always been Brooks and Matthews, or Brooks or Matthews, or one or the other, is that right?"[102] Everyone of the potential jurors sitting in the courtroom except the two ladies nodded their heads in agreement.

One juror even made his feelings about Brooks and I known before the selection process occurred. His name was Oscar Moss, and I remember him clearly to this very day. Moss first distinguished himself from the others in attendance by admitting that he associated "socially" with Curtis Golden. He also admitted that he knew Jim Edson on a personal level. That raised red flags in my mind right away. No one else in the group knew both men, or at least admitted it, so I thought very early in the selection process that Moss could not make the final jury. Baroset later asked if anyone had a preconceived idea concerning the guilt or innocence of me and Rev. Brooks, and Moss stated that he had "a personal opinion" concerning our guilt. Duffee later asked him to clarify his opinion and Moss replied, "My opinion is just based on the fact that there's been a lot of agitation [in Pensacola], and it just seems as though these two people are usually involved in it." But he did not stop there. He proclaimed that he had a negative experience downtown during one of our demonstrations and alleged that "at least fifty black people" surrounded and threatened him. Later during the jury selection process, Moss tried to get out of duty by stating that he was involved in several community projects and had appointments scheduled for June 9 and 10, the days our trial were scheduled to take place.[103]

His prejudicial statements and attempts to evade jury duty did not matter, because Oscar Moss was selected as a juror in my felony trial. He should have been struck from serving almost immediately during questioning, but he was seated anyway. It became clear before my trial even began, then, that it really did not matter what Brooks, Duffee, or I said or did during the proceedings. The prosecution would use everything possible, including placing someone like Oscar Moss on the jury, to get rid of me. The jury consisted of five men and one woman, all of whom were white, and one white alternate. The two young women who had not heard of me or Brooks did not make the final jury, while Moss did.

Another factor that worked against me and Rev. Brooks during our trial was the total ineptitude and unpreparedness of our attorney. For example, the only protest Duffee lodged concerning the jury stated that he had "no individual challenges, per se, but" objected in general that each juror had knowledge of our arrests "and some have discussed some of the circumstances" with others. That jury should not have heard our case and Duffee did not fight its selection. His incompetence revealed itself in other critical ways before opening arguments began. Duffee filed a change of venue motion because of the "undue publicity to activities and circumstances surrounding the charges filed against" us. He argued, quite correctly, that a "fair and impartial trial can not be had in this county" because the jurors could not forget all that they had admittedly heard, seen, and read about us in the press before our trial began. Because they were saturated with negative information concerning Brooks and me shortly before and after our felony arrests, an impartial verdict was impossible. Duffee made the valid argument that "this prospective jury possibly knows more about what the State has charged these defendants with than perhaps the defendants." The jury definitely knew more about us and the racial atmosphere that existed in Pensacola than Duffee did, and the trial should not have been held in Escambia County. But Duffee gave the change of venue papers to the court on the morning of June 9. By law, he had to submit them at least ten days before the trial began. Duffee's careless mistake gave Judge Beall a legal reason to deny the change of venue plea.[104] In addition, Beall stated that Duffee failed to present evidence that the local press had made incriminating or prejudicial comments about me and Brooks. This further angered me, because previous steps were taken to deny us a fair hearing in Escambia County.

The defense collected petitions from several local blacks that requested a change of venue for our trial, and Duffee presented them to Beall. Rev. K. C. Bass, for instance, wrote that "the massive, unfair, and prejudicial comments by the news media concerning Matthews" and "the political nature of the case" made a fair trial impossible. Rev. Harvey Jones also argued, "The issues involved in the case are racial in nature" and claimed, "If one has casually read an Escambia County newspaper within the last six months, there can be no denying that Reverends Brooks and Matthews and all that they stand for is anathema to the vast majority of the citizens of" Pensacola. I personally gave Duffee numerous *News Journal* clippings and tape recordings of news reports that demonstrated white hostility toward me in particular, but he forgot to bring them to court as evidence. Beall concluded that the affidavits alone did not prove that the area media was biased against me or Brooks. Not only, then, did I face the fury of the white power structure in Pensacola during the trail, but my attorney was not adequately equipped to defend me against their charges.[105]

Opening arguments in the case began on June 9, 1975. Barry Baro-set spoke first and outlined the state's charge against me and Brooks. He stated that each of us did "verbally, and maliciously, threaten injury to the persons of Sheriff Royal Untreiner, Deputy Doug Raines, and numerous other deputies, with intent thereby to compel the persons so threatened against their will to compel the suspension or resignation of Deputy Sheriff Doug Raines." The prosecution traced the evolution of our movement from the Blackwell shooting to the mass meetings of early 1975. They did not spend much time on the Blackwell incident because Baroset pointed out that the jury already understood the circumstances surrounding our movement. He did remind the jury, though, that a grand jury found that Raines used justifiable homicide in the shooting, and that he faced no disciplinary consequences of his action.

The prosecution focused their case on the downtown demonstrations SCLC and the NAACP organized from January 24 through mid-February. The state charged that our protests grew more violent and intimidating by February 19, while deputies "stood there restrained like London soldiers that you see in movies." Baroset even ridiculed our protests in his opening statement. He said that we marched around county buildings during our protests because we probably thought it would "make the courthouse fall down." The jury got a good laugh out of the comment.

The prosecution also maintained that on the nineteenth we made our first "assassination" chant. In the nights before our arrests on the twenty-fourth, Baroset alleged that we brought weapons to the demonstra-tions, threatened deputies, spat on them, moved police barricades, and "totally abused and intimidated the officers." The state maintained that we controlled the crowd and everyone in it acted under our authority. In conclusion, Baroset said that "Matthews used the group as a tool" to force Untreiner to suspend an "exonerated" man against his will.[106]

I found it quite interesting that although two men were on trial, the prosecution focused their wrath and most serious allegations against me. The prosecution's first witness singled me out as the individual responsible for all of the racial unrest in Pensacola. Jim Edson's multitude of lies was the primary reason that I endured so many later hardships. His testimony, in short, sent me to jail.

Edson was the prosecution's first and most important witness. He was the person who got to tell his story first and it was an uphill climb for me and Brooks from then on. But the deputies who took the stand after Edson revealed several contradictions and flat out lies in their testimonies. Edson was the most important witness, though, because he laid out our demonstrations' time line and first described the atmosphere that surrounded the gatherings as they progressed. The first problem that I noticed was that Edson could not speak from the witness stand without reading from the police reports that he filed each night during our rallies. In fact, he answered Baroset's questions by basically reading his reports line by line. Duffee objected to Edson's dependence upon the notes, but Judge Beall let him get away with it. Everyone else had to rely on their memories, but Edson got to read from papers he had falsified before the trial even began. He started his indictment against me and Brooks with the February 14 demonstration. On that night, he said, our actions became threatening. Interestingly enough, deputies who testified later stated that during that same date "a pep rally, cheer-type situation" characterized our rallies. One even commented on our politeness and said that we greeted him every night and addressed him by name. Still, Edson stated that on the fourteenth of February numerous blacks under my command congregated on the jail grounds, blocked all traffic coming in and out of the building, and would not let anyone pass through the crowd unmolested.[107]

Jim Edson singled me out for his most serious allegations. He testified that each night "Matthews had his bullhorn and seemed to be the evident leader or the spokesman for the group, and Mr. Brooks was in his accompaniment." He later repeated the claim and stated I "carried the megaphone, the portable bullhorn, and he used it exclusively." That was another lie the officers could not get straight, as another deputy later revealed. Regardless, Edson did his best to paint a negative picture of our activities. By February 19, he claimed that our crowds had grown larger, louder, and more demanding. It was the on the nineteenth when he claimed that we conducted the first so-called "assassination" chant. The sheriff claimed he stood two feet behind me when I climbed the stairs of the county jail's front porch and sang through the bullhorn, "Two, four, six, eight, who shall we assassinate? Doug Raines, Doug Raines, Sheriff Untreiner, Askew, and the whole punch of you pigs." Edson stated, "They turned around and pointed their fingers at us" and repeated the chant three more times. For good measure, Edson later claimed that "I heard my name mentioned in the chant . . . 'and especially you, Jim Edson.'"[108] Not only did Jim Edson lie about the chant's words and who led it, but he also lied about the demonstration's atmosphere in his lengthy testimony.

Deputy Edson testified that when he heard the threatening chant, "I felt quite nervous at the time. I felt I hadn't done anything to provoke this group. I couldn't figure out why my name would be included in the assassination chant." He stated that on that same night he witnessed a number of black men slap two feet-long clubs in their palms while they stood three inches from officer's noses. Edson claimed that we scared his deputies. Female dispatchers even refused to come in to work that night because of our presence. The laughable aspect of that scene is the deputies arrested no one for these alleged actions. Edson claimed he ordered no arrests because he did not "want to try to provoke the situation."[109] Every black in Escambia County knew that if they even looked at a deputy wrong, they would go to jail. This is one of the things I reminded the activists of every time we went to the courthouse to march: "Do not take anything downtown that can be even perceived as a weapon because those crackers are looking for a reason to break us up!" At my felony trial, though, Edson painted a much different picture. We were threatening. We were dangerous. We even scared sheriff's deputies to the point where they were afraid to arrest us, despite the fact that we promised assassinations. The whole scene is ludicrous, but Edson swore under oath that this was what happened at his jailhouse. We were so dangerous that he allowed us to meet the next evening so he could get our threats on tape.

On February 20, Edson asked Deputy Dan Collins to bring a tape recorder with him to work. They made two recordings that night; one was from the floorboard of a parked cruiser and the other was from the front steps of the jailhouse. The first time I heard that the sheriff's department had a recording of our chants was in court that afternoon, and it was a big relief. I knew that we had not made any "assassination" threats and believed the tape would prove it. I may have been too optimistic, but I truly thought the recording would exonerate us. Edson was determined, though, that we would not be acquitted. On the same night that they made the tapes, he claimed that I became more violent and ordered the crowd to move the barricades that the sheriff's department put up at four locations leading to the jail. Edson ordered the barriers erected to keep blacks from supposedly blocking the building's entrances and exists, but I was now accused of having them torn down. He ordered his deputies that "those barricades were not to be removed," but I reportedly told the crowd, "We're going to go to those barricades; we're going to remove those barricades, and if anyone tries to interfere with us, we will remove them, too; we will meet force with force." Edson testified that I did, in fact, move the barricades and directed others to block all entrances to department headquarters. Despite my open disobedience, I was again spared arrest. The sergeant even exonerated B. J. Brooks to a point, whom he said asked other blacks to keep the paths open. Interestingly enough, Deputy Bill Sandifer testified later that day that no black person, including me, ever tried to move the barricades.[110]

Another falsehood that Edson continuously made was that Brooks was at the jailhouse every night. Brooks was at home sick with the flu on February 20 and 21. They were the only rallies he missed during nearly the entire movement. But his name still appeared in the officer's notes and testimony concerning the night's events. Jim Edson and the Escambia County sheriff's department was already going out of its way to portray me as the trouble-making leader of the group, while Brooks was the "good Negro." That dual characterization later played a larger role in the trial than I ever thought it would. Yet I was the main target, and Edson made this clear as his questioning continued.

Edson testified that we grew even more hostile between the twenty-first and our arrests on the twenty-fourth. Other deputies later made similar claims in their testimonies. On the twenty-first, Edson reported that I once again moved barricades that deputies had erected. Our presence and refusal to move, Edson maintained, prevented an ambulance from taking an injured prisoner to the hospital. Edson said that the only way deputy cruisers broke through the demonstrators who clogged the entrances was if the officers physically pushed us back with their hands. Then we vandalized their cars and spit on them.

The more he talked, the more outrageous his lies became. I really could not believe the words that were came out of his mouth. Edson even testified that one of the audience members announced, "We are going down there in the rich white neighborhood to the sheriff's house." He then called Royal Untreiner and Doug Raines to warn them of possible danger. Later that night, Edson said someone told him that three cars parked across from his driveway with six black men in them. Edson claimed that numbers of armed friends guarded his home for six week, and someone telephoned death threats to his home, cut his phone lines, and threw flammable materials at his house. Of course, this was all ridiculous hearsay and the prosecution offered no evidence that any of those things happened or that it had anything to do with me or Brooks, but our attorney let him ramble on. Our February 24 arrests, Edson argued, were a necessary last resort. The black crowds grew increasingly violent and they had to do something to stop us. As he stated, "I thought maybe they would try to scare me into resigning or do harm to my property or to my family."[111]

The five other members of the Escambia County sheriff's department who testified against me and Brooks basically repeated the themes Edson first told, but there were inconsistencies with some key details. For example, Bill Sandifer stated that the word "assassinate" was not used in a chant until February 19, and that our gatherings did not produce a "more hostile, frightening-type situation" until the twenty-third. Both were much later than Edson previously claimed. Still, those details were lost on the jury after Sandifer testified that the crowd threatened him with weapons on the twenty-first. He claimed on that night that blacks displayed golf clubs "in a threatening manner" and one black man "kept his right hand in his front pocket, never removing it, giving me the feeling that possibly there was something concealed in there as a weapon." Similarly, Deputy Curtis Mitchell said he saw a lead-wrapped stick in the crowd that frightened him, although he later testified that he and other deputies had "no need to carry a gun" while they patrolled our crowd. Deputy Joe Cardwell said that we blocked every driveway leading to the county jail, refused to let department vehicles leave the premises, and blew our automobile horns so often that those inside the building could not talk over the noise.

The one element that each of the testimonies had in common, though, was that they targeted me as the group's leader. Sandifer stated that after I led the "assassination" chant on the twenty-third, I turned and said, "That goes for you, too, Jim Edson." Sandifer also claimed that I shook my fist within an inch of his face and said "oink, oink, oink" in an attempt to provoke a riot. He declared that several blacks in the crowd told him "they knew where we lived and would go to our homes." Cardwell said that after I led the "assassination" chant on the twentieth I told him, "Boy, we'll eliminate you, too, if you don't straighten up." He also claimed that I often called the deputies "sons-of-a-bitches."[112] When the first day of our felony case ended, therefore, it was clear that the sheriff's department was hell-bent on holding me responsible for every lie they concocted concerning all black activity at the downtown jail. The testimonies grew more interesting the following day.

B. J. Brooks and my felony trials continued on June 10. The most climatic moment of the case came when Deputy Dan Collins took the stand. He made the two recordings that the prosecution claimed proved beyond a shadow of a doubt that we not only made the assassination chant several times, but that I led it. Collins testified that Edson ordered him to make the tapes on February 20. The first tape lasted twenty-eight minutes, and he made it with a "shotgun microphone extension" that he held out of a car window three feet from the crowd. We made four chants on that recording: "We're gonna stop, stop the racist cops of Florida," "I am somebody," "Ain't going to let nobody turn me around," and

"Two, four, six, eight." The second tape lasted twelve minutes and Collins claimed that he made it on the front porch of the jail, but that was incorrect. We stood there the whole time and never saw anyone holding a recording extension. Regardless, we made four chants on that recording as well: "I feel sanctified," "Stand up for the black folks," "When you're hot, you're hot," and "Two, four six, eight." Collins could not identify any leader of the songs except the "Two, four, six, eight" chant, and he said I led it. Seven different chants, and he could only identify the leader of one. Conveniently enough, it was the so-called "assassination" chant and I led it. He also said that I used the word "assassinate" each time when conducting the chant. Yet later in his testimony he stated, "Most of those chants, to the best of my knowledge, were spontaneous. I don't know that anyone led them. There was a group of young men in the center, kind of towards the front, that started a lot of these chants." In other words, "No one person led the chants." He even testified that "I don't recall Rev. Matthews using a bullhorn" on the night tapes were made, which totally contradicted both his and Jim Edson's testimony.[113] Edson said that I led the chants through a horn. Collins said that I led the assassination chant but did not possess a horn. Then he said that no one in particular led the chants. When the lies started backfiring, Barry Baroset decided that it was time to play the tapes for the jury.

Ed Duffee's reaction to the use of the tape as evidence further revealed his incompetence to everyone in the courtroom. Duffee objected to their use and stated that he knew nothing of their existence. However, the assistant state attorney provided proof that he sent paperwork to Duffee during the discovery process that cited the tapes as evidence, and Duffee had let the May 6 deadline to file a Motion to Suppress the materials pass. In other words, Duffee was told about tapes but took no action concerning them. But I wanted the tapes to be played because I knew they would reveal the truth about that night. And sure enough, they revealed a happy atmosphere with a lot of singing. We heard each chant, including the one that I was on trial for leading. My voice never appeared on either of the tapes, but it was clear who led the "Two, four, six, eight" chant: Rev. Jimmie Lee Savage, a close friend of mine and fellow freedom worker. Not only did I not lead any of the chants, but it was clear that the word we used in the "Two, four, six, eight" chant was "incarcerate." The word "assassinate" simply did not appear. The *News Journal* reporter who was in the audience said the tapes "revealed festive activity at the jail with joking, singing, and praying" by blacks. He thought that the chant asked "Who shall we castigate," and remarked that those in the court could barely hear the demonstrators say anything in unison. Those comments came from the representative of a paper that did everything in its power to cripple the black freedom struggle in Pensacola and discredit its leaders, and he thought the tapes cleared Brooks and I of any wrongdoing.[114] After the recordings finished playing, I thought "Thank God. That exonerates me right there." The tapes clearly proved that I neither led the chant nor uttered the word "assassinate." The prosecution knew they were on the ropes, too. Their key evidence could not clearly portray me and Brooks as dangerous radicals, so their next two witnesses had to do the job. Royal Untreiner and Doug Raines were up for the task.

Sheriff Untreiner testified against us after Dan Collins exited the stand. Untreiner did his best to depict me and Brooks as violent criminals who wanted to use black people as weapons against him and his deputies. He stated that blacks threatened to burn down his house, rape his wife, and shoot him while he worked at the station. He told the court that he had never experienced anything like this in his twenty-two years as an FBI agent or seven years as a sheriff, and that he feared for his life on a daily basis. Untreiner said he was forced to take drastic measures to protect himself from local blacks. For instance, he claimed to have "bullet-proof glass on the windows of my office" and said he "put in a security device at my own home." Deputies watched his home at night. He removed his reserved parking sign at deputy headquarters so we would not know which car he owned, and he used several vehicles each day in case we discovered what he drove. He also maintained that he never went out in public unless an armed deputy drove him in an unmarked automobile. Untreiner was so scared of us that he even placed informants in our gatherings at Greater Mount Lilly Baptist Church to record the sermons we gave. He testified that our speeches were "very inflammatory, and they were very hostile towards the sheriff and towards Raines and even the governor." His statement confirmed my suspicion that the department had paid informants who spied on us for the local white power structure. Finally, with no other alternative, Untreiner said he contacted state attorney Curtis Golden and they planned our arrests for the February 24.[115] The sheriff was there the night his deputies beat us down, placed us in handcuffs, and made the bogus felony charges.

The problem with Untreiner's testimony is that none of it connected directly to the charges of extortion that were levied against Brooks and I. He produced no evidence that we tried to extort him to do anything against his will. He knew that the Pensacola black community wanted Doug Raines fired. That was our main goal. Yet he never fired Raines. How, then, did Brooks and I extort anything from Untreiner? He never, for any reason, met our demands. And if we were so dangerous beginning on February 14, why were we not arrested then? Furthermore, why did deputies wait four days to arrest us after they made the recording that supposedly proved that we wanted to assassinate the sheriff, a deputy, and the governor? The prosecution did not focus on what had happened; their attorneys focused on what could have happened. We were threatening. We sponsored a reign of terror against the department. They all feared for their very lives and could do nothing about it. We had to be stopped before race relations grew worse in the panhandle. Untreiner's case was further weakened because he testified that he never had personal contact with either me or Brooks. In his words, we refused to meet with him. He left out the Justice Department's mediation and the fact he canceled earlier sessions with us. Finally, Untreiner never accused us of being the people who made threatening phone calls to his home, prowling his neighborhood at night, or ordering anyone to do so. At the very worst, he revealed a personal paranoia concerning black people. He could not tie any of his fears to threats we supposedly made, yet still tried to hold me, particularly, responsible for all negative black activities he could imagine. Douglas Raines followed the same pattern in his testimony.

The prosecution used Doug Raines to do nothing more than illicit more sympathy from an already friendly jury. He traced the Blackwell incident and the course of events that followed from his point of view. He reminded the jury that he shot Blackwell in self-defense and a grand jury agreed. He said that the verdict did not satisfy me or Brooks, so we led a campaign to have him fired. Untreiner removed him from the field and gave him a desk assignment at the jail for his own safety. He testified that we had taken a position from him that he dearly loved. In the meantime, someone cut his phone lines and vandalized his home. He lived in such fear, he maintained, that he changed his phone number several times and moved his family from the home he lived in. Yet he never had any direct, personal contact with me or Brooks. He said very little about us per se, but blamed everything that had presumably happened to him on B. J. Brooks and H. K. Matthews. When his testimony concluded, the prosecution rested. I wanted Duffee to go on the attack. I thought he should point out the contradictions the deputies raised in their statements, discuss the racial hatred that permeated the county sheriff's department, and contest the characterization of Brooks and me as violent, radical rabble-rousers. Most importantly, I wanted to testify on my own behalf at the trial. But Duffee refused my request and only called two witnesses to defend us. The first person to testify on our behalf was a dubious selection, to say the least. Duffee opened his case by recalling Jim Edson to the stand.

I never understood why our attorney put Edson back in the witness chair. It benefitted our case in no way. Duffee did not ask Edson any original questions or bring up his contradictory statements. Everything Duffee asked had been brought up in Edson's earlier testimony. In fact, Duffee asked many of the same questions twice. It just gave Edson a chance to repeat his earlier themes and add more to his story of pure terror. He reiterated a department-wide fear of me, Brooks, and the demonstrations. Edson even ridiculed one of our chants by saying that it stated, "I may be black, I may be on welfare, I may be on food stamps, but I'm black." The only thing that Edson mentioned that no one previously had was the presence of Rev. R. N. Gooden at the jailhouse demonstrations. Even then, Edson said he only saw Gooden at the gatherings "one time."[116] The omission of R. N. Gooden from all previous testimonies was an interesting aspect of the trial that further convinced me that I was the sheriff's department's main target throughout the ordeal. Most deputies went out of their way to say that I led the groups of protesters at all times. They portrayed Brooks as a misguided accomplice, of sorts, and a few mentioned that Rev. Otha Leverette attended some of the assemblies. However, only Edson mentioned the presence of Rev. Gooden, even though he was at the department every time we gathered there after the mass meetings.

Gooden led as many songs, chants, and prayers as anyone present. The *News Journal* even described him repeatedly as one of the primary leaders of the nightly meetings at the department while they occurred. The reason his name did not surface more often during the trial is that I was the local scapegoat for all angry whites in the area. Gooden could go back to Tallahassee, and eventually did. I, on the other hand, was a local boy who was supposed to act better than I did. I stirred up trouble in my hometown and had to pay for what most whites and some blacks perceived as transgressions against racial harmony in the area. I spoke out against racism in Escambia County and I was the person who had to pay the price for questioning the status quo, not R. N. Gooden or anyone else. So his name only surfaced once throughout the trial because he was not their target.

After Edson finished his second diatribe against me, Brooks, and the local movement, Duffee actually called someone to the stand that helped our case. Rev. Jimmie Lee Savage, the pastor of New Providence Baptist Church, corrected one of the prosecution's main points. He maintained that he was the one who initiated and conducted the "Two, four, six, eight" chant, "a standard chant civil rights groups have used all across the country," that I was accused of leading. According to Savage, "My main role at the jail was to help in controlling the audience, getting their attention if necessary." He would announce "Quiet please," or "May I have your attention" before he launched into the "one particular chant that I would always preface and lead." He remembered conducting the chant because it was "the only one that I really led." The only question he ever asked in the chant, he testified, was "Who shall we incarcerate?" Savage denied using any other words in his tune and proclaimed, "The first time I heard the word 'assassinate' in connection with this demonstration was the day after the massive arrests of February the twenty-fourth." He also stated that no one, including me and Brooks, ever led that particular chant, that I never ordered any barricades removed, and that he never saw any weapons in the peaceful crowds. Savage's testimony should have guaranteed our innocence. The prosecution accused us of leading a chant that threatened the lives of public servants in an attempt to extort Untreiner to fire Raines against his will. Savage declared that he both led the chant in question and that he never used the word "assassinate."[117] His admission should have rendered all charges against Brooks and I null and void. But it was the word of a black preacher against the words of the county sheriff and six of his deputies. Still, the prosecution made a proposal to Duffee before closing arguments began that revealed the weakness of their case and their uncertainty that the jury would return a guilty verdict against us.

When all testimonies in our trial ended, Barry Baroset asked the court to drop our extortion charge to "attempted extortion." This revealed their desperation to pin something on me and Brooks. The trial had not gone as smoothly as they wanted, so the state wanted to lessen the charges to ensure a conviction of some type. Duffee, however, refused to accept the lesser charges and Judge Beall agreed. In closing statements, Baroset repeated that Brooks and I threatened to use the crowd as a weapon to intimidate Untreiner into firing Doug Raines. He portrayed us as renegades who took the law into our own hands, while deputies "exercised great restraint and discretion to avoid any confrontation." Duffee stressed that neither of us led the chants, that we never used the word "assassinate," and that local blacks were only exercising our freedoms of expression and assembly on county property. "All we had," Duffee argued, "was a freedom of expression, pep rally type atmosphere" at the jail each night.[118] Before the jury retired for deliberations, Beall gave them final instructions. His words broadened the likelihood of a guilty verdict against me and Brooks.

The judge explained that the state did not have to prove that we committed any crime on February 20, the night Deputy Collins made his recordings, or February 24, the night of the arrests. Instead, "if the evidence established beyond a reasonable doubt that the crime was committed sometime within two years immediately prior to the filing of the information [April 28, 1975]" we could be found guilty of extortion.[119] Not only, then, were Brooks and I held accountable for all local black protests that had taken place since Blackwell's murder, but we were held accountable for all local black protests that had occurred since the spring of 1973. Not coincidentally, that was the same time when the situation at Escambia High School exploded. I led those activities as well. Beall, the sheriff's department, and the white power structure in Pensacola, therefore, saw the felony trial as their best chance to silence me and did everything possible to help the jury reach a verdict they wanted. Despite the odds I faced against walking out of the courtroom a free man, the jury's verdict still shocked me.

On the afternoon of June 10, the jury found both me and Brooks guilty of extortion by threat after they deliberated for forty-five minutes. The maximum penalty for the second degree felony conviction was fifteen years in state prison. Beall delayed our sentencing until July 24 because he wanted to conduct an inquiry into our backgrounds.[120] In the meantime, Duffee appealed the verdict and we were released on a twenty thousand dollar bond. The decision thoroughly surprised me because I believed that the evidence had proven our innocence. My worst fears were now realized: I was at the mercy of a local system that was used to persecute me because I demanded justice and equality for African-Americans. I was not sure what my sentence would be and did not care. I had promised black folks that I would fight to my death for their rights as American citizens and planned to continue the struggle. Besides, I did not believe that any appeals court would uphold the unjust verdicts when they looked at all of the available evidence. So I, naturally, displayed my frustration and ran my big mouth off to reporters before I left the building. I told *News Journal* reporters that the verdict was "justice, Escambia County style" and "the penalty you pay for being black in this community." The tapes, I maintained, "clearly showed that what they say we did never happened." On the basis of that evidence, which I deemed "a joke," I predicted that "my conviction will be overturned and I will probably never serve any jail sentence." It was an unwise statement, but I wanted to show the white community that I did not fear their penalties. "Somewhere in the state," I declared, "there are people who would sit on an honest jury and listen to evidence proving my innocence." B. J. Brooks, on the other hand, remained quiet and criticized no one after his conviction. A month later, the Florida Department of Transportation fired Brooks from his position with them.[121]

On July 9, the county circuit court tried Brooks for the unlawful assembly and malicious trespassing charges that we were arrested for on February 24. I was found guilty of both charges earlier, but Brooks was tried separately. He and Rev. Otha Leverette were scheduled to face the jury together, but Judge Langergren granted his appeal for a separate trial at the last minute. After my felony conviction, I fired Ed Duffee and hired Paul Shimek as my attorney, but Duffee still represented B. J. Brooks. On the day of Brooks's misdemeanor trial, Duffee failed to appear in court. Brooks later found that his attorney had confused the trial date. Not surprisingly, Ed Duffee was investigated and subsequently disbarred by the Florida Supreme Court in March 1977 for defrauding a client.

Nevertheless, Brooks waived his right to postpone the misdemeanor trial and threw himself upon the mercy of the judge and his all-white jury. It represented his official surrender to the local power structure. He repeatedly told the jury, "I have faith in you" and "I believe that you know every citizen has the right to peaceful protest." Three deputies even testified on his behalf and said that Brooks never used foul language, threatened anyone, or tried to incite violence during the demonstrations. Needless to say, none of them previously testified on my behalf. Brooks's conciliatory tactics did not work, though, because the jury found him guilty of both charges. On May 1, the court found seventeen other blacks guilty of the same misdemeanor charges. They were given short probations or fined about two hundred dollars each. The largest fine was only four hundred dollars. Brooks and I, however, faced 120 days in jail and a thousand dollar fine.[122]

The misdemeanor convictions were just as unfounded as the felony conviction. It was one of the final nails the sheriff's department used to close the coffin on the local black freedom struggle. Brooks was in full retreat before the felony trial began. I did not have enough sense, though, to keep my mouth shut, even after the second conviction. The leaders of the white community hoped that the two trials would shut me down, but they only inflamed my desire to see justice served. Despite the verdicts, I promised to continue organizing demonstrations and fighting for the full equality of my people. What I failed to comprehend was the degree of power the court system had over me.

I knew that I was basically alone in leading the Pensacola civil rights movement after June 10, but I still worked to organize the local black community. For instance, I contacted Ralph Abernathy and asked the national SCLC to come to Pensacola. I needed assistance in sustaining our struggle and hoped that national exposure would reveal to the nation the injustices that characterized northwest Florida. Abernathy was excited about the opportunity to intervene and promised me, "We'll be there within a week." I held a press conference after Brooks's misdemeanor trial on July 9 and announced SCLC intentions. I stated that because of the recent biased convictions against me and Brooks, SCLC "will be cranking up our activities to include more peaceful protest demonstrations and picketing in Escambia County." I promised that the white conspiracy to silence me and cripple the struggle "is simply not going to work because I will ignore the threats, intimidation, physical violence, and whatever else is being done to stamp out the black demonstrations. We are going to reestablish our cries for equal justice." Pickets, I promised, would resume at the county jail the next day. I also announced that "Ralph Abernathy is coming to town," and "Pensacola is going to have the biggest demonstration it had ever seen."

I scheduled the SCLC march for July 12 and asked blacks from around the United States to come to Pensacola and participate in the protest parade. Our main goal remained "equal treatment for all people and especially the removal of sheriff's deputy Doug Raines" from his position. The evening *Pensacola News* reported what I said at the press conference and at about 7:30 P.M. that night, deputies came to my house and arrested me once again.[123]

I was preparing to speak at St. Mark AME Zion Church concerning SCLC's latest plans when two deputies knocked on my door with an arrest warrant. The officers took me into custody in my own living room because they said that I had violated the conditions of my bond agreement. The next evening, I went before Kirke Beall for a hearing. Judge Beall informed me that he revoked my bond because I continued to plan marches, boycotts, and demonstrations in Escambia County. Three reporters testified against me. One even played a tape of the previous day's press conference where I revealed SCLC intentions, while another presented the previous day's *Pensacola News* article against me as evidence. Beall said that my statements necessitated arrest. He told the paper, "I would have to be a damned fool to allow Matthews freedom while he continued the same activities he was convicted of."

His statement revealed that I was convicted not because I used force to extort something from anyone, but because I organized civil rights demonstrations in the area. I was allowed to finally take the stand in my own defense and maintained that I had done nothing wrong either before or after the felony trial. I added that my activism would continue while racial injustice existed in Escambia County and the SCLC would obey the law and honor every injunction issued against us. It was defiant, but my fate was already determined. So I decided to remain unrepentant to the end, and Beall rewarded me by putting me behind bars until my felony sentencing. He did so because I was "a threat to the community." I was terribly disappointed in the decision and told the reporters in attendance, "I thought there was some justice around, but I found out there isn't, especially when it comes to me."

My attorney, Paul Shimek, stated that my bond could not be revoked because Beall had not formally found me guilty. Florida state law declared that the judge must formally pronounce the defendant guilty after the jury reached such a verdict, and Beall had not yet made that declaration. At my hearing, though, Beall promptly declared me guilty of extortion and officially revoked my bond. Shimek appealed the decision to the First District Court of Appeals in Tallahassee but the body dismissed the motion two days later. Shimek called the "frivolous" ruling a "clear judicial error" and promised to appeal the decision to the state Supreme Court. Yet my incarceration served one of the court's purposes: it temporarily terminated our plans to picket the county jail. Otha Leverette canceled all SCLC demonstrations after Beall revoked my bond. Leverette stated that my ordeal "lets us know we live in a racist community."[124] We had known this for years, but my imprisonment further verified the racial hatred that saturated northwest Florida.

After Beall pronounced my guilt and revoked my bond at the July 10 hearing, deputies immediately marched me to a holding cell in the county jail. While I was at trial, one of the officers who arrested me told an inmate that "I wish Matthews would have tried to run when we went to arrest him, so I could have shot him." Those comments confirmed that I could possibly die for my civil rights activities. I did not think that I had to worry about that, though, while I was in the county jail. There were people there who had been sentenced a month or two earlier and were still waiting for a transfer to the state penitentiary. I was certain that I would be out before long and would surely not go to the Raiford State Prison. Much to my surprise, though, deputies woke me up between two and three o'clock that morning and said that I was going to Lake Butler for processing into Raiford. They obviously did not want my time ticking down in the county cell when I could enjoy the state's finest accommodations at its most notorious prison. You see, an inmate's time served began to count down as soon as they were sentenced. Even if I spent a week in the county jail awaiting transport, it was a week that was taken off of my time. It was also seven days that I did not have to spend at Raiford. As usual, though, I was given special treatment. The judge wanted to get me to the big house so that I could spend most of my time there.

I was transported to Lake Butler in a county squad car by the same two deputies who arrested me at my home on July 9. When I was escorted out of my cell that morning, the deputies handcuffed me to a young white boy. I thought it was odd that we were the only ones being transported to the state facility. Usually, the county would send several inmates to the state facility together at one time on a bus. In fact, the *News Journal* said that nineteen people were taken to Lake Butler with me, but that was a lie. On my transfer, it was only me and a prisoner I had never seen before, and we were placed together in the back seat of a county cruiser. We stopped three times on the way from Pensacola to Lake Butler, and each time both deputies got out of the car and left us unattended. I will never forget the first stop, which occurred somewhere just across the Tallahachee River. We stopped at a service station and both deputies went inside. They were nowhere in sight and, strangely enough, the back door on the driver's side was ajar. I sat on the passenger side and do not know how or when the door got in that position. In fact, I did not notice it until the white boy I was handcuffed to made a startling proposition. He pointed out the door's position and said to me, "Let's run and get away from here." I replied, "You can take off running if you want, but if you go you will have to drag me behind you. I am not going anywhere." I remembered what the deputy had previously said about shooting me and knew that I needed to say in my seat. I also knew that the judge would have added time to my sentence if I attempted an escape. I thought to myself that "I am not very safe in these handcuffs and in state custody, but I am safer here than I would be if I tried to escape."

The thought of getting away during the transfer never, ever crossed my mind. That would have made me a criminal, which I was not. During the last stop before we got to Lake Butler, while the deputies were both out of the vehicle, the youth who was being transferred with me confessed that the officers told him to try and talk me into running. I did not have time to ask a lot of questions, but he made it clear that I was being set up by the officers. I suspect that they were going to shoot me and say that I initiated the escape. That was the kind of fun I was having. I never again saw the person I was handcuffed to during the trip to Lake Butler. I concluded that he went back to Escambia County with the deputies. The entire ordeal provided further evidence that every section of the justice system felt nothing for me but pure hatred. I was convicted of a felony on bogus charges, had my bond revoked for exercising my constitutional rights of assembly and free speech, was transported to the state facility mere hours after being sent to the county jail, and had my death planned out. I did not know how long I would be held in state custody and did not know who would support me back home when I was released. I did find out that Ralph Abernathy canceled SCLC's support of the July 12 rally in Pensacola the day after Beall revoked my bond, so I was also unsure of the local movement's state. I truly felt like the world was crumbling around me. I did not want to admit it to myself then, but I realized that our unified struggle for racial equality in Escambia County was coming to an end.

9

THE FALL

The time I spent at Lake Butler processing center awaiting transfer to Raiford as inmate number 047832 was pure hell. The only positive thing that I can say about my time in the Florida penal system was that I never served in Raiford State Penitentiary. I can only thank God that I never actually hit "the rock," as inmates called it.

When I first arrived at Lake Butler, guards put me in the minimum security quarters. After one day at the prison, I was walking on the recreation yard when a guard approached me with new orders. He said that he had to move me to the maximum security section of the prison. I asked why and he said, "I really do not know. My supervisor just told me to put you in maximum security." He escorted me to an even rougher part of the facility and placed me in a cell with three other inmates. The cell was six by eight by ten feet in size and was designed to hold two prisoners. We literally lived in feces because the toilet did not work and no one was in a hurry to fix it. Prisoners convicted of murder and rape had more privileges at Lake Butler than I did. Some time after I was placed under maximum security, the guard returned to my new cell and told me that I was transferred there because of the nature of my crime. I had threatened to assassinate the sheriff and the governor and was, therefore, a dangerous inmate capable of organizing prisoners and encouraging violent behavior.

I could only imagine how bad it was at Raiford based on the near inhumane conditions that existed at Lake Butler. The worst problem there was the overcrowded conditions. Overcrowding was the root of nearly all the trouble I witnessed. The guards were understaffed and they tried to manipulate the situation for their own benefits. The more observant prisoners watched the guards orchestrate certain conditions in hopes of sparking riots. It did not matter if the problems were between prisoners and the guards or between prisoners themselves, the facility employees wanted to create unrest in order to call attention to the fact that they needed more workers on the grounds. I saw a lot of things in prison that I never want to witness again. I saw prisoners get beaten down by guards and other prisoners. I saw routine stabbings among inmates. I heard numerous stories of how some people were raped in their bunks. Incarceration was a terrible feeling. I do not care if it was the Escambia County jail, the Lake Butler processing center, or Raiford, it was all prison. My freedom was taken away and I could do nothing about it. It only made it worse that I was locked up in a place reserved for the state's most vicious criminals for something I did not do.

My stay at Lake Butler could have been much worse, but some inmates in the prison knew who I was before I arrived. The racial unrest I was involved with in Pensacola made national and state news, and some prisoners had heard of my struggles. My reputation spread rapidly throughout the compound after I arrived and the conditions of my incarceration became known. The prisoners protected me while I was in maximum security because they understood why I was there. Some of them were victimized by a racist justice system too, so they comprehended my situation and knew I was an innocent man. They did not let anybody get close to me who may have had bad intentions.

The guards knew I was protected, so they went out of their way to let me know my place while I remained under their control. For example, when I was being checked into the prison, officers checked all possessions that the Escambia County sheriff's department transferred with me. One thing that I foolishly carried to the jail was a scrapbook of newspaper articles, pictures, and personal letters pertaining to my activism. The officers at Lake Butler tore it up in front of my eyes and laughed while they did it. On another occasion, I sat in the cafeteria when a corrections officers shouted "Reverend" across the room. I automatically turned around and saw that he was talking to someone else, but the guard noticed my reaction. He yelled out, "I am not talking to you. You are not a reverend; you're a convict." My experience at Lake Butler was humiliating, but the workers there wanted it to be even worse. They wanted to dehumanize me and strip me of my basic dignity. My faith is the only thing that sustained me during my time in state custody.

I felt throughout my time in prison that God was always with me. I never had any doubt about His presence. I often sat in my overcrowded cell all night without sleeping, just thinking about my predicament. One night I heard something inside me say "Lift up your head," and I lifted my head up. I remembered a passage in Psalms that read, "Open the everlasting doors and the king of glory shall come in." I asked, "Who is this?" The answer was clear and came from a hymn I knew: "King of glory, the Lord strong and mighty, and the Lord mighty in battle, He is the king of glory." After that night, I never again questioned the purpose of my situation. I strongly believe that God put me on earth to do what I did, and He put me at Lake Butler to experience what I experienced. He brought me through the trials and tribulations to give me a greater appreciation for Him. He kept me going during my trial and throughout my incarcerations. He brought me out of several situations where people wanted to hurt me, but I survived. Despite my public activities and the fact that they enraged several people in the community, both black and white, I did not have anything happen to me that brought physical danger. There is a reason for that and it was not luck or coincidence. What protected me from bodily harm was Divine Providence.

During my time in prison, I grew closer to God and came to realize that I did not ever want to let Him down because I failed to do what He intended for me to do. I tried to get bitter about my situation, but could not. It would have been a waste of time anyway, because bitterness is like acid; they eat away the container. Hatred is not productive for anyone, and I am living proof of it. I will go to my grave doing God's will, regardless of the consequences I will endure for it. I guess I am too old to quit now even if I wanted to! Still, it was my faith in God and the realization that I had to suffer personally for a greater cause that sustained me at Lake Butler. Through God's will, I only stayed in state custody for thirty days before the First District Court of Appeals released me on an appeals bond. In the meantime, the felony sentences for me and B. J. Brooks were announced.

On July 17, 1975, Judge Kirke Beall sentenced B. J. Brooks to five years' probation with the stipulation that he "not conduct or participate in any public demonstration in the state" during his term. In contrast, he gave me five years in state prison "at hard labor." Beall defended the decision by stating that during his presentence investigation he found "nothing adverse" in Brooks's past, and that those he interviewed had "very favorable" things to say about Brooks's character. On the other hand, everyone he supposedly talked to "who had any dealings with this man businesswise or otherwise had nothing good to say about him." The interesting thing about the investigation was that Beall refused to make his findings public. He did not give the results of his presentence investigation to the press or our attorneys and he warned Ed Duffee and Paul Shimek against criticizing his judgements to the press. He made these orders for good reason. The interviews that Beall claimed were a part of my presentence investigation never took place.

Furthermore, the prosecuting attorneys made no suggestion concerning my sentence. They evidently thought that conviction was enough to silence me and did not think it necessary to send me to prison for any amount of time. Beall obviously did not agree. Both Shimek and Duffee appealed the sentences after Beall announced them. Reporters from the *Pensacola News Journal* called me while I was imprisoned to get my reaction to the verdicts, and I was determined to remain defiant despite my situation. I told the writer that my punishment was "no surprise" because "the judge has a personal vendetta against me." For good measure, I even declared that "I will get out of jail pretty quickly."[125]

The severity of the sentence against me, therefore, was no surprise. The lenient punishment B. J. Brooks received only reinforced the fact that I, and no one else, was the main target of the white power structure. I was the one they wanted and they would have given anything or cooperated with anybody to get me. They had been after me for years because I was a vocal activist, and they finally got me in 1975. I posed

Matthews (center) upon his first release from prison, July 30, 1975. Otha Leverette is to his left.

the biggest threat to them and they were determined to get me out of their way. I was wanted dead or alive and many people did not care how I was silenced. I felt this hatred from many ordinary citizens, Escambia County deputies, the sheriff, local judges, and jailors at Lake Butler, but experienced all of their resentment most clearly when Judge Beall sentenced me and Brooks.

Everyone who followed our activities, arrests, and trials over the previous months noticed both the discrepancies between the sentences of me and Brooks and the harshness of my punishment. Even the *Pensacola Journal* wrote an editorial concerning the penalties and asked "Why was Matthews treated differently from Brooks?" In a July 18 article, the paper declared my five-year prison term "an exceptionally harsh penalty for someone who is, in reality, guilty of not much more than an excess of rhetoric." They knew that the judgement was a way that the court system could persecute me, whom the editorial said "has long been a thorn bush obstructing the long and gingerly-trod road to racial harmony." It also urged Judge Beall to release his presentence investigation findings to the public so that local residents could determine "whether justice has prevailed, or whether one more black man who has become a nuisance has been trod upon and kicked aside" by the white power structure.

I already knew the answer to that query and that is why Beall refused to make the results of his investigation public. It would have shown that I was made the scapegoat for all the racist frustrations whites had toward blacks in Escambia County. Brooks was not the target, so Beall suspended his sentence and gave him five years of probation. He was a likable Negro to white folks because he had demonstrated that he would do what those with power wanted him to do. He had distanced himself from me and the movement at that point and promised to never become involved in public protests again. So Brooks was rewarded with a light sentence, and eventually got his job back with the Florida Department of Transportation. He returned to work on August 8, 1976 and received all of the wages he lost during his suspension with interest added to it. In the meantime, I could not even get bail without a struggle and ended up being the only person involved in the local civil rights movement to have the privilege of spending time behind bars.[126]

On July 24, Judge Beall rejected a bail request from my attorney for the five-year sentence because he stated I possessed "an utter and total disregard for law and the legal process and, more particularly, law enforcement officers." Five days later, the First District Court of Appeal in Tallahassee granted me a twenty thousand dollar bond until it heard the appeal of my extortion conviction. On August 2, I posted bond and left Lake Butler with the full knowledge that I could possibly return.[127] I returned to Pensacola that night and attended a mass meeting at St. John Devine Baptist Church that Rev. Gooden and Rev. Leverette organized. The church was packed and the reception was great. It was one of the most electrifying meetings I have ever attended. I delivered the keynote address and received standing ovations before, during, and after my speech. I remember reading my sentence and release forms, which I had in my pocket, to the crowd. I also held up my wrist to show everyone the prison band I still wore. I told the audience that I was proud of the bracelet because "I got it fighting for my folks." It may sound dumb to be proud of a prison badge, but it was because of the way that had I earned it. I told the crowd that I did not want the struggle to die and that I would "fight until Hell freezes over for the rights of my people . . . As long as there is breath in my body, I shall continue to fight for the rights of black folks." I pledged to continue organizing marches, boycotts, and demonstrations against racism in northwest Florida and promised to get the national SCLC and Ralph Abernathy more involved in the Pensacola struggle. The people initially responded very well to my pleas, but the local black leadership had become fragmented.

Everything the black community had worked for during the previous decade rapidly collapsed after my release from prison and return to Pensacola. The organizations in Pensacola, the SCLC and NAACP, pulled out of the struggle for racial justice. Their members soon followed their example. Activities tapered off because white leaders had made an example out of me. The SCLC and NAACP had been frightened off, to an extent, because of my prison sentence. They were not as supportive as they should have been because I had been sent to jail on bogus charges. Consequently, they did not want to touch me with a ten foot pole. Commitment is something that not everyone has. I found out that people will do things for the common good as long as doing things for the common good does not cause them any hardship. Yet when it reaches the point where sacrifices must be made, most people are simply not willing to do it. I happened to be the one that was stupid enough to have a firm belief that my purpose on earth was to champion the underdog. I did not set out to do that, but it happened. I told everyone who questioned my risks, including my own family, "If I refuse to help people I am not doing what God has ordained me to do, and I am then letting God down." The last thing I wanted to do was let God down, because without Him there is absolutely no way that I would have come out of the situations I had been in. I also did not want to let the people down in Pensacola who had stood by me throughout my trial and incarceration, so I had to keep fighting racism. There were many, though, who turned their backs on me.

The NAACP took advantage of my situation when it benefitted them, but they did nothing to help me when I most needed it. On June 30, when the organization discussed my ordeal at its annual convention in Washington, D.C., NAACP lead attorney Nathan Jones called my conviction "a shocking abuse of the criminal system" and said, "This situation should shock the conscience of not only this community, but of the entire nation." Jones even pledged, "The full resources of the NAACP would be thrown into the effort to have the convictions reversed." He stated that I was "not a criminal, is deeply rooted in this community, and the public interest does not require his incarceration." The NAACP promised to assist with my legal fees and used my ordeal to raise money for their organization, but they never gave me one cent. They helped Rev. Brooks with his legal fees, but chose not to pay even a portion of my expenses. The national, state, and local NAACP simply did not want to risk the consequences of supporting H. K. Matthews. So they paid lip service to my cause when it paid dividends for them, but washed their hands clean of me soon thereafter. On September 12, NAACP Executive Director Roy Wilkins came to Pensacola and held a press conference vowing to continue the group's support of B. J. Brooks "as long as it takes." He made no mention, though, of my struggle.[128]

I now understand the decision that the local NAACP made concerning me. Rev. Brooks had been threatened, his family had been threatened, the state NAACP had instructed him to back off, and he was under obligation to obey. When he followed their demands, some people, including me, thought he did it to save his own hide. I now think he did it to save his family and protect his livelihood. Brooks worked for the national and Florida NAACP and they told him to leave it alone, so I can not criticize Rev. Brooks. He did what he had to do. The same thing goes for Rev. Gooden. The state office tried to make him abandon the Pensacola movement and he refused, so they cut all ties with him. And the national office supported the state branch, so they share the responsibility of neglecting my case. Regardless of who made the final decision, I was without the local NAACP even before I entered Lake Butler. After my release, Brooks told me that the organization could not support me because our tactics were too different. I guess their main goal was to not offend the good white folks. The NAACP, though, was not the only organization that relinquished my cause when I returned to Pensacola. The SCLC also proved to be of little help after I got out of Lake Butler.

Tyrone Brooks, one of the SCLC field representatives, came to Pensacola after my prison stay and made several promises concerning what the organization would do for me. He pledged that the national branch would support me financially and would continue our mass meetings and downtown demonstrations. He even said that Ralph Abernathy was personally interested in my ordeal and wanted to visit Pensacola to organize more protests. But the assistance never came.

In fact, the Escambia County branch of SCLC elected a new president after my conviction, Fred L. Henderson. I helped Fred obtain a promotion at Monsanto some years ago that had been denied due to his race, so I thought he would stand by me. On December 9, 1975, however, Henderson severed the local SCLC relationship with me and said that "Matthews is not authorized to speak, collect, or solicit funds for this organization." Henderson proclaimed that the nine hundred member SCLC branch "was designed to be a peaceful, nonviolent organization and this is still our aim," but I made statements "which do not reflect the official position of the organization."[129] Henderson justified his decision by portraying me as a radical malcontent which had corrupted a peaceful group. The national branch repudiated Henderson's decision and confirmed my role as northwest Florida coordinator, but he tried to make it appear that I was dropped by the national branch. It was an interesting situation; I was supported by the national agency and remained a regional leader within SCLC, but the county branch had ostracized me. In reality, the national SCLC supported me in words alone. They, like the NAACP, promised to provide my legal defense and help with my rapidly deteriorating financial situation. Yet they provided nothing. Unlike the NAACP, however, the SCLC organized an official fund-raising campaign using my name and experiences.

In 1978 the SCLC, Andrew Young in particular, pointed out that the United States had a number of political prisoners in its jails. My story was used as the main example to back up Young's argument, and SCLC named me the nation's "number one political prisoner" at its August 1978 annual meeting. SCLC president Joseph Lowery called me "a guy who was in jail because of an unfair, unjust system" and promised SCLC would ask the U.S. Justice Department to investigate "the criminal system that can produce this outrage." National SCLC spokesman Hosea Williams told members, "Matthews was persecuted on a trumped-up charge because he spoke" against racism in Pensacola and concluded, "It's absolutely amazing such a thing could happen." I even appeared at the annual convention in Anniston, Alabama to accept an award.

I remember that meeting both due to my award and because Redd Foxx, who was there as an entertainer, gave me a twenty-five hundred dollar check to help with my legal expenses. The SCLC as a group, though, gave me nothing. Yet they used my case in their annual fund-raising drive later that year. The group mailed letters to members asking for donations to help with their fight against racism in America. They cited my case as an example that "the criminal justice system is still being used against us." SCLC used my sentence of "five years for singing a popular marching chant" to solicit organization funds. Interestingly enough, I never received any money from SCLC. In fact, the only way I even knew about the letter and membership drive was because an SCLC member I knew gave me a copy of the letter that the group sent him.[130] The point that SCLC used my name to raise money that I never saw bothered me, but it was not the worst part of my experience with that group after my trial. The most tragic part of SCLC's abandonment of my cause is that they lost a prime opportunity to make a more direct, positive difference in the lives of blacks throughout the nation.

My trial, incarceration, and subsequent legal battles presented an opportunity for SCLC to reestablish itself as a leading civil rights organization in the United States. Some within the organization would claim that it never lost that role, but after Dr. King's death, SCLC faced an identity crisis. The group no longer had its founder, leader, or spokesman, and its national direction was unclear. SCLC served an important purpose on the local level in many areas, such as northwest Florida, but its importance on the national level was cloudy at best. Ralph Abernathy did little to clarify the SCLC's role in the 1970s American black freedom structure. He did not have the intelligence, charisma, or skill to lead a national organization, and it showed. Ralph went from city to city trying to make a name for himself and, in the process, SCLC suffered. The organization could have helped both me and the local movement. The media had noticed the Pensacola struggle and would have provided Abernathy and our group the national publicity they both needed. In addition, the Escambia County crisis resembled a conflict from the 1960s, which SCLC had experience with. The main problem in northwest Florida was the existence of racist whites who held political power. The local SCLC was already using nonviolent passive resistance tactics, and the national office could have joined and strengthened our movement. At the very least, they could have brought national attention to the legal lynching that I endured and provided my legal defense. In addition, SCLC intervention could have helped Pensacola blacks tremendously. It would have brought exposure, participants, and cohesion to the local movement, all of which we needed at one time or another. With outside pressure, Doug Raines, Jim Edson, and Royal Untreiner would have probably all lost their jobs, which remained our primary demand. Instead, the SCLC and the NAACP lost a prime opportunity to strengthen their organizations and positively influence our movement. Despite the fact that the organizations failed to support me at a critical juncture in the Escambia County struggle, I still worked for the national SCLC in 1976 through 1977, and even expanded my activities into Mississippi.

Shortly after both my initial release from prison and the Anniston conventions, Ralph Abernathy asked me to represent the SCLC in Jackson County, Mississippi. The organization had become involved in the area because a young black man was accused of raping and killing a white woman in Moss Point, which was located on the state's coast. I had the opportunity to work with James Orange, who met us in the city. James was the big fellow with the horn-rimmed glasses who walked beside the horse-drawn carriage that carried Dr. King's body during his funeral. Regardless, SCLC was interested in the area because of the heightened racial tensions that surrounded what seemed an unjust murder accusation. We discovered during our investigation that the female's body revealed no signs of sexual molestation. The rape charges also came five days after she was killed. Many whites and blacks did not believe that the black man accused of the crime did it. SCLC discovered that the murdered woman preferred the company of black men, frequented a predominantly black club called the High Chaperral, and was romantically linked to the black accused of killing her. A vast majority of individuals we interviewed suspected that her husband was involved in the crime, but we found no concrete evidence to support the claim.

Yet the evidence that implicated the black was just as sparse, so SCLC organized daily demonstrations outside of the local prison and marched from Moss Point to the county courthouse in Pascagoula every evening for approximately a three-month period. Some nights we even camped out on the courthouse lawn to make our presence known. I did not think that my activities in Mississippi differed tremendously from what I did in Escambia County, but whites in the Magnolia State responded with more direct resistance. Racism was more blatant in Mississippi than anywhere else I have ever worked. In Pensacola, feelings of black inferiority were more subtle, which made it worse in many ways. At least in Mississippi, we knew where whites stood on the race issue. Two incidents, in particular, illuminate this point.

During my travels to Jackson County, I often rode with a fellow SCLC member from Pensacola named Wendell McCray. The organization did not allow me to travel alone or take my own vehicle, even when I worked outside of Escambia County. As we left Pascagoula after one of our initial area campaigns, we noticed that something blocked the road a few hundred yards in the distance. We noticed, as we drew closer, that approximately ten members of the Ku Klux Klan, in full regalia, had formed a human chain in the middle of the highway and were motioning for us to stop. When I told my son about this episode some years later, he asked me what most folks ask at the same point: "Did you stop?" My response is always, "I am still alive, ain't I?" I fully believe that bad things would have happened if we would have stopped our vehicle, so I floored the accelerator when I realized who blocked our path. Those Kluxers got off the pavement real fast when they realized that our vehicle had sped up! That should have been an indication to stay out of Mississippi, but I returned and encountered an even more dangerous situation at a local motel.

Most of the times when I went to Jackson County, I stayed with a SCLC member in Pascagoula named Leon Wells. The Klan even telephoned Leon several times and threatened to kill us both if I kept returning to the area. But Leon was a very brave and a determined advocate of black equality who ignored the intimidation tactics. On one occasion, though, for a reason that I can not recall, I had to stay in a Pascagoula motel. During that particular journey, I was accompanied by three members of the Escambia County SCLC, including Tony McRae, Sr. We checked into our rooms and went to them in our automobile. As was our custom, the men checked the rooms for suspicious signs while I waited in the car. All of us noticed that the curtains to one room were not completely shut. McRae looked in and saw an older white man sitting on the bed with a shotgun in his lap. I saw my companions run back from the window to our car at a brisk rate. I said, "What's wrong with you all? You look like you saw a ghost." They then told me what they saw. I never saw the person and did not have to in order to believe their story. I do not know why the person was in the room, but our assumption was that the hotel was not a place where I needed to be. The reaction of the front desk clerk made us even more suspicious. We went to the lobby, returned the key, and told him we did not wish to stay at his establishment. He began stammering and stuttering and demanded to know why we wanted to leave. He promised to fix any problems if we just waited in our room. His attitude convinced us that he knew about the man who waited in our room. We suspected that the man was probably a Klan member who wanted to intimidate us, or even worse. But the Lord does not let unexpected events occur if His people are trying to do His will.

Despite my brushes with tragedy, I traveled from Pensacola to southeast Mississippi on several occasions as a spokesman for the SCLC during the episode. The organization finally withdrew me from the region when a jury found the accused man guilt of murder and rape. I still have no idea why our efforts failed to make headway against racism in Jackson County. It could have been because racism was more firmly entrenched there, or because we were outsiders and not members of a local organization. Regardless of the reason, my relatively limited activities on the Mississippi coast revealed that I remained active within the SCLC despite its abandonment of my situation in Escambia County. The organization's failure to support me hurt, but it did not trouble me as much as the rejection I encountered from many within Pensacola's black populace.

The community treated me fine after I returned from prison, and many pledged to continue our struggle for racial justice. The community was upset because they knew that I was imprisoned for unjust reasons. Although I still planned demonstrations and organized mass meetings in Pensacola to protest local racism, the movement lost its momentum and never regained it. I understood that this was a consequence of my incarceration. When someone is made an example of, when they are picked up and sent to the state penitentiary, sentenced to five years for doing what should come naturally to anyone who is sick of oppression and want their rights guaranteed, people get scared. In Pensacola, folks did not want to be part of anything potentially dangerous because they did not want to risk happening to them what happened to me. I guess that is human nature. But that still did not keep some from making a lot of money off of my name. A few enterprising blacks organized the "Matthews Legal Defense Fund" and raised thousands of dollars in my name, but I never saw a dime of it. Others gave lawn parties in my honor and gathered appreciation offerings for me. The events were often organized by individuals who had no tie to any civil rights organization. Those who gave did so sincerely and understood why I served time. They knew I went to prison because I fought for them. There are a lot of people in Pensacola today who still appreciate my efforts. Some of them tried to help with my financial struggles in 1975 and 1976, but they were misled by groups who took their money by using my name. I guess the thieves who raised the funds kept them, because I never received a penny.

Regardless of the reason, though, the black community slowly dropped both the causes of me and Wendel Blackwell after my conviction. I felt especially bad for Elaine R. Blackwell, the widow of Wendel. She was involved in all of the protests and mass meetings that we held on her husband's behalf, but no one wanted to risk their livelihoods by taking up her cause after my imprisonment. In early 1976, she filed a lawsuit against Escambia County Sheriff Royal Untreiner, Deputy Doug Raines, and the department's insurance provider for the wrongful death of Wendel Blackwell. It was nearly a year after the murder, and she was in debt because of her husband's medical and funeral costs and lack of financial support. Yet on November 14, 1977, Escambia County Judge Jack H. Greenhut dismissed the suit because he claimed no evidence demonstrated that Raines was negligent in the shooting. In fact, Greenhut ordered Elaine Blackwell to pay the defense's court costs.[131] I felt partially responsible for the decision because our actions failed to bring financial relief for the Blackwell family. My suffering simply sucked all steam out of the local movement. But I do not hold the black community fully responsible for their actions. They were led by people who stood in the pulpits on Sundays.

Some of the local African-American preachers stood in their pulpits after my return to Pensacola and declared, "This movement had gone far enough" and "You need to leave this alone." When such respected figures in the black community told their congregations to do or not do something, the people would listen. If they decided to ignore the preachers they had to make the decision on their own, which was difficult to do. I continued to stress the need for direct action against racism, but I was nearly alone. Rev. Brooks had withdrawn NAACP support from the struggle and Rev. Gooden had left Pensacola. Most Afro-American ministers in Escambia County said that the local struggle had reached its limit and was all but over, and their church members listened. Rev. Otha Leverette was one of the only people who stood at my side during my entire tenure in Pensacola. He was with me whenever we mobilized the community. He was also the only one between me, him, and Brooks not found guilty of committing the two misdemeanors police arrested us for. Leverette had two hung juries before the charges were finally dropped. The local SCLC tried to force him to denounce my activities, so Rev. Leverette resigned his post as the group's county chairman.[132] In short, he played a unique role in the Pensacola movement. Every important social movement needs someone that everyone else thought was crazy, and Otha Leverette played that role for us. He was loud and boisterous, but he was effective. He used all type of tactics to convince people of his craziness. Whatever came out of his mouth just came out. He did not care what he said or who he said it to.

On the morning before one of his trials, I heard WCOA news report that Leverette was scheduled to appear in court that day for a hearing. I called him and asked if he was aware of his appointment and, naturally, he had no idea. So he showed up late for the hearing and Judge Walter Langergren said something that Leverette did not like. Leverette responded by shouting, for all in the court to hear, "Judge, your honor, I'll beat that goddamn robe off of your ass!" Langergren said, "Get him out of here, get him out of here," and two deputies took him to the county jail. I went to bail him out and Leverette was pacing up and down the hall saying to no one in particular, "Lock me up Goddammit, lock me up." The deputies said, "Reverend, we are not going to lock you up. You have a mental problem." He responded, "Hell, I ain't crazy," and we left. Those were some of the things that he did to take the attention off of me. He understood that I had sacrificed for the greater good of humanity. I clearly remember that as we drove to yet another legal hearing, Leverette looked at me and stated, "You know that you should be dead, don't you?" A majority of local whites believed that he had no sense, but his actions were very calculated because he fully understood what we faced in our struggle for human dignity. The press made it seem like I was totally alone, that it was just me out there barking at the moon and raising hell by myself with no support from anyone, but that was untrue. Many of my supporters were forced into silence, but they still agreed with my stance concerning injustice in Escambia County. Otha Leverette was one such person. He and Rev. Brooks were my two closest companions during the Pensacola struggle, but Leverette stood by me throughout my time in northwest Florida. Others, though, abandoned the cause.

When I realized that the local movement was dying after my imprisonment, I became very upset and grew angry at the people that I believed had deserted our struggle. Over time, though, I have thought about the period a lot and prayed about it even more. One day, not very long ago, the question came to me, "H. K., if you were in their shoes and you were not totally committed to a cause, what would you have done?" It is similar to the popular question, "What Would Jesus Do?" You must try to put yourself in another person's position before you respond to a situation and judge them for not acting the exact way you believe they should. It is still hard for me to buy any excuses for ignoring the mistreatment of others, because of what I have been through. My family has been threatened. I have spent time in state custody. I have been offered money to keep my mouth shut and declined it. My commitment, though, was stronger than others, and not everyone could put the welfare of others before the welfare of their families. But it is like the song says, "There's something within that holdeth the rain, there's something within that vanishes the pain, there's something within I can't explain, all that I know is that there is something within." That is what kept me going and still sustains me today, that "something within." My advanced age indicates that I should have retired from civil rights activity several years ago, but I believe that I am destined to fight for the downtrodden until I die. I will never retire from championing justice. I subscribed a long time ago to the Bible verse that states that the spirit of the Lord is upon me, and He has anointed me to preach deliverance to the poor and set the captives free. That is my life in a nutshell, and I can not get mad and remain upset with people who are not as dedicated in their quest for universal justice as I am. They may be anointed by God to do something that I am not equipped to do. I have become so frustrated at times that I have said, "I am not doing anything for anyone else again. Nothing is going to trigger me to put myself in harm's way once more." But I am lying to myself, because I go right back into the struggle when the spirit leads me. As time has passed, therefore, my anger toward what happened to the Pensacola movement has reduced and my understanding has increased. The true enemy was not my own folks, but the atmosphere of pure hatred that existed in northwest Florida at the time toward anyone who questioned the status quo. The sheriff's department slowed our movement by harassing those who participated in events they did not like, and the justice system crushed the struggle by distributing harsh punishments to its foremost spokesman.

On August 4, Circuit Judge Woodrow Melvin renewed an injunction against anyone who demonstrated on county property. The judge praised Sheriff Royal Untreiner for "his patience" and for "trying to avert mass arrests" during our previous activities. He made his decision solely to limit black demonstrations and picketing. It worked. The next day, County Judge Walter Langergren denied B. J. Brooks's appeal of his misdemeanor trespassing and assembly charges and fined him five hundred dollars. Brooks told him that he could not pay the charges, so Langergren placed him in the county jail. A short time later Langergren released Brooks and the NAACP paid his fine on August 11. In return, the trespassing charge was suspended.[133] The court obviously thought that Brooks had learned his lesson. I was more hard-headed though, and the justice system continued to be anything but just for me.

On December 11, Escambia County Circuit Judge M. C. Blanchard denied a rehearing request for my misdemeanor convictions and gave me a sixty-day sentence for the two misdemeanors. I spent my time in the county jail. My attorney, Paul Shimek, appealed the decision and used a new strategy to prevent me from spending more time behind bars than I did. Shimek told the court that "Matthews achieved a full realization that he could not repeat his previous acts" of protest and "has distanced himself from all the demonstrations and movements being continued by the organizations of which he is a member." I was not aware that my attorney had resorted to a conciliatory tactic. I never made such proclamations and did not ask him to use the strategy, but at the time I really did not care what he said or did to get me out of jail. I simply did not want to spend more time in the county's custody than I had to. In arguing for my early release, Shimek also cited my exemplary behavior during the previous thirty-three days in state custody. He concluded his plea by stating, "The Christmas blessing of peace and good will to all men makes this request especially appropriate." On December 24, Judge Walter Langergren gave me what he called "an early Christmas present." He released me from jail and reduced my penalty to "time served."[134] The next day, a bail bondsman who later became an AME Zion minister named Bill Marshall secured my release. The tribulations that surrounded my misdemeanor convictions were finally over, but my five-year felony sentence still awaited appeal.

Paul Shimek and I believed that 1976 would bring renewed hope to my struggle against the justice system, and he continued to fight my felony conviction in the new year. On January 20, Shimek filed a motion for a second extortion trial for me and Brooks. Shimek based the request on newly-discovered evidence that he said exonerated us of any criminal activity. Over a month earlier, Shimek hired an electronics expert to analyze the audio tape that the deputies used against us in court. It was the most important evidence for the prosecution because they testified that I led the "Two, four, six, eight" chants and repeatedly used the word "assassinate." Vince Ponciano, the owner of an electronics store in Pensacola, conducted a series of detailed examinations of each tape's contents. He concluded that my voice was not on the tape and that the word "assassinate" was never uttered. The term protestors used in the chant, Ponciano said, was "incarcerate." He blamed a misinterpretation of the words on an inferior tape player that the prosecution used in court. Shimek said that the expert's report exonerated me and Brooks of our felony convictions and promised to pursue perjury charges against the officers who testified against us in court. Unsurprisingly, Beall denied each motion on March 1, 1976.[135] It did not matter to him what was said or who said it. All he wanted was to silence H. K. Matthews and teach him a lesson. I remained the sole target and no new evidence or expert reports would change that, regardless of their conclusion.

While my legal situation progressed through the court system, my financial condition steadily deteriorated. I had a lot of trouble finding employment when I got out of Lake Butler. I sought jobs from black and white employers in Pensacola. I asked the owner of Magnolia Nursing Home, a former federal judge, to give me a job mopping floors. He said, "I just can not hire any more workers now." I went to Bill Marshall, my bail bondsman who was the principal of Spencer-Bibb Elementary School and asked him to give me a job as a janitor, but he refused. He told me, "Matt, you know it would not look good if I hired you because everyone knows that we are friends. I can not give you work because of our relationship." I told him, "What difference does it make if we are friends or not? I need to make some money. I have to provide for my family. I need to eat." But I was basically white-balled in Pensacola.

The only work I had after my release was as minister of St. Mark AME Zion Church in Pensacola. I lost many things due to my struggle, but I never lost my congregation. It had a small membership when I arrived and had a small one when I left, but my parishioner's support never waned. The district bishop that I reported to in the church hierarchy was Alfred G. Dunston of Philadelphia, Pennsylvania. He supported my activities and wanted to help my financial predicament, so he transferred me to Evergreen, Alabama. The new position brought a little more money than my Pensacola pastorate. Rev. Dunston also thought it would be wise to get me out of the city, and I was ready to spend some time outside of Escambia County. I wanted to keep fighting racial injustice in Pensacola, but it seemed that I was the only one who wanted to do so. Only Rev. Leverette was willing to assume leadership of the local movement, and no established civil rights group supported him. The indifference blacks demonstrated was one reason that I split my time between Pensacola and Evergreen. Soon after I accepted the Alabama position, I made my feelings known at a local press conference.

I held a press conference in March 1976 to announce that I was severing all ties with the civil rights movement in Escambia County so that I could focus my activities on Evergreen and Conecuh County, Alabama. Yet I also organized the conference to get some things off my chest and clarify the facts concerning my ordeal. I made a copy of the conference's audio tape for my personal collection so no one could distort the last formal message I had for the community. I stressed two things at that press conference. The first was that the local black community had abandoned me despite all of the things that I had done for them in the past. I began the proceedings by laying out everything that I had accomplished for the downtrodden in northwest Florida. I cited what SCLC and NAACP had done for black voting, employment, and integrating public facilities. I also mentioned that Black History Month existed in county schools due primarily to my efforts. Since my arrests, though, many local people and civil rights organizations had abandoned me. Even though many blacks had benefitted from my efforts, they "turn their noses up at me" and "are running off at the mouth" about me deserving incarceration. They forgot, I reminded them, that "in some areas I am solely responsible for them being where they are." They had "mistreated the one person who has risked more than any single individual in this town to fight for black folks." I had "gained the wrath of the entire racist element in the white community who feel that any sassy or uppity black should be done away with," but I was dealing with "blacks who are more interested in being pacified and pleasing the white establishment than they are in achieving racial justice and equality." I even read a poem for those who "kicked me while I'm down and are giving me hell." It began, "In speaking of person's faults, pray don't forget your own; remember those in homes of glass, should never throw a stone." That poem, I said, was "for all the good colored folks in this community who have torn me down." I was disheartened, hurt, and angry, and all of those elements surfaced during the press conference.

My frustration bubbled over in front of those cameras and tape recorders. I told everyone who would listen, "I'm a little sick and tired of warped minds blaming me for everything that happens in this city. It's reached the point that if Santa Claus doesn't come, if the Easter Bunny gets delayed, if white bigots tear up Escambia High School while white deputies stand around and watch, then blame H. K. Matthews." I stated, "If this one little black boy can upset a city that much, then he must be a hell of a fellow." I even made a proposition for local officials. Instead of criticizing me, the city should build a statue in his honor for unifying everyone in town. "If I can cause that much trouble, recognize it," I urged. "Name two or three streets after H. K. Matthews." Furthermore, I deemed the American "Pledge of Allegiance" a lie. I declared that because of my experiences I could no longer "repeat that part of the pledge of allegiance that says 'liberty and justice for all' because it did not apply to me."[136] Despite my anger and feeling of betrayal, the second theme that I emphasized at the conference concerned personal commitment. I stressed that I had not and would never cease my activities, regardless of where I worked.

I repeatedly argued that "I never, regardless of my personal circumstances, stooped to the point that I have sold my people down the river," despite the fact that "of all of the people who were arrested during the struggle, only I had the distinct privilege of having to serve a jail sentence." I also promised, "Nothing short of death will stop me from fighting for the rights of black people who want me to fight for them." Again, I felt this way because God ordained me to stand up to injustice. There was simply not enough pressure to stop me from fighting for right, despite the bitter experiences I had in Pensacola. I told the audience that I would continue the struggle against racism because "I am not going to allow myself to be kicked and walked on by bigots." God was on my side, and I could not let Him down. I proclaimed that, "The God I serve is a good God. I've got a God on my side that can do everything but fail." I concluded the press conference by declaring, "Pensacola, as far as I'm concerned, is the most racist and backwards city in this whole country . . . Never again," I promised, "will I go to the lengths of getting myself thrown in prison for people who just don't give a damn."[137] It was a shame that I gave so much for folks in northwest Florida and had to leave the state to make even a paltry living. But I never deserted the Pensacola movement. It deserted me.

There were three churches in Evergreen that I took over because their previous minister, a man named Rev. Pete Andrews, was promoted to presiding elder within the AME Zion church. The three vacancies brought me more income than I made at St. Mark AME Zion Church in Pensacola, so I enthusiastically accepted the position. In the last weeks of 1975, therefore, I was transferred to Evergreen but continued to live in Pensacola. I pastored Belleville Faulk AME Zion on the first Sunday of each month, Mount Zion AME Zion Church on the second and fourth Sunday, and Old Field AME Zion Church on the third Sunday. I stayed in Pensacola during the week unless one of my churches needed me. I left every Friday afternoon for Evergreen and returned on Sunday night. I usually stayed with one of my church members on the weekends. My wife remained in Pensacola because that was her home. She never considered relocating to Evergreen and did not like the arrangements I accepted but she lived with them, at least for a little while.

One thing I noticed early in Evergreen was that their racial situation was even worse than it was in Escambia County. Segregation was still a way of life for everyone who lived in that city. Neighborhoods were segregated, as were public facilities. There were no signs that declared that blacks were not allowed in the buildings, but there may as well have been. Blacks had no positions of meaningful employment in the city. Those who worked in Evergreen were either farmers or performed menial tasks for white folks. Furthermore, most blacks were not on the voting rolls and whites discouraged those who were registered. The whites who lived in Evergreen did not see anything wrong with this scenario. Everything was fine with them because local blacks knew their place and seemed happy in it, which was below all white people. When I transferred to the Evergreen churches, therefore, I knew I had to challenge the backwards way of life. On March 7, 1976, I organized the Conecuh County SCLC to change the status quo and publicize the fact that blacks in Evergreen were treated as subjects, not citizens. It is safe to say that the bond between me and the SCLC was never as tight after the imprisonment as before. Still, I thought it was important that Evergreen had an SCLC branch. I never doubted whether or not I should initiate civil rights activities in the city, because Evergreen was an area where blacks feared whites. There were a few die-hard young people who were determined to pursue their rights, so I picked up in Evergreen where I left off at in Pensacola.

My reputation had preceded me in that part of Alabama. Even before I started the SCLC, some influential whites in the area had besieged my presiding elder in an effort to have me shipped out of Evergreen. The elder, who lived in the city and formerly served as minister of the three churches where I worked, was Rev. Pete Andrews. He tried to pacify local whites and evidently promised them that he would curtail my activities. He did everything he could under the AME Zion conference rules to stifle my endeavors. But his pleas fell on deaf ears and I continued to organize local blacks. One of the largest activities I organized in Evergreen occurred on July 4, 1976, our nation's bicentennial. The SCLC held "Suffrage Day," in which I requested that all blacks not participate in activities that the city had organized. "Suffrage Day" protested our nation's failure to guarantee equal rights for all citizens, and Evergreen blacks supported the demonstration wholeheartedly. The next year, SCLC persuaded Mayor O. B. Tuggle to proclaim January 15 as Martin Luther King, Jr., Day in Evergreen. It was the first time Dr. King's birthday was either recognized or celebrated as a holiday in Conecuh County. While much of my attention was focused on events outside of Florida, the situation in Pensacola deteriorated for blacks.

The racial atmosphere in Pensacola had worsened to such a degree that the Ku Klux Klan appeared in Escambia County once again in the spring of 1976. On March 6, the Imperial Wizard of the UKA, Robert Shelton, led a Klan parade and membership rally in Milton, which lies approximately twenty miles east of Pensacola. Over 120 unmasked Klansmen from Alabama, Mississippi, Georgia, and Florida marched through downtown Milton waving Confederate flags and passing out white supremacist literature to the crowd. At a membership rally later that day, Shelton announced that the Pensacola Klavern was one of his organization's most active chapters and was a model for other racist groups in America. He chose Escambia County to hold the demonstration because it was a Klan stronghold and he wanted "to let people know we're being reactivated" throughout the South from the panhandle.[138] While the Klan chose the area to attempt yet another national rebirth, the courts stonewalled my attempt to obtain another trial for my felony charges.

On April 26, the First Circuit Court of Appeals denied new extortion trials for me and Rev. Brooks. The court accepted expert analysis from the electronics expert that Paul Shimek hired, but they still upheld our convictions. The majority opinion stated, "It is the opinion of this Court that whether the words spoken or chanted were 'assassinate,' 'castrate,' or 'incarcerate,' they are still coercive threats" that we led. To add insult to the decision, the court displayed sympathy for the present deputies and commended those "who had these words shouted directly into their faces with fingers pointed in their faces." The court concluded that regardless of our choice of words, Brooks and I "maliciously threatened" officers "with injury."[139] Exactly three months later, the same court denied the appeal of my extortion conviction. The unanimous ruling concluded that during the February 1975 jailhouse demonstrations, I repeatedly threatened Royal Untreiner, Doug Raines, and several other officers with death to intimidate and force them into accepting my demands. The court claimed our gatherings were armed and violent, which proved that I "consciously embraced fear of bodily harm as an instrument of enforcing otherwise lawful demands" and "was sufficient to convict him of extortion." Furthermore, the court cleared B. J. Brooks from any responsibility in the matter. They stated that he played no leadership role in the demonstrations, did not lead the assassination threats, and made sure that traffic at the jail flowed without complications during our assemblies. Despite the praise the court gave Brooks, it still upheld his misdemeanor convictions on August 10, 1976. He continued to play the role local whites wanted him to play by stating, "I now see clearly the numerous errors I committed" during the previous year. The *Pensacola Journal* reported that the NAACP spent about fourteen thousand dollars protesting Brooks's misdemeanor conviction alone.[140] The year only became more frustrating and disheartening for me as it progressed.

Sheriff Royal Untreiner used my name as part of his campaign for re-election in the fall of 1976. He bragged that he single-handedly ran me out of Escambia County and sent me to prison. For instance, the local paper reported that Untreiner told a crowd, "My calming influence restored racial harmony" in the county during the year and that tensions between whites and blacks "practically disappeared" since Rev. Gooden and I left Pensacola "and transferred their racial agitation to other places." Untreiner even claimed that area black leaders supported his re-election campaign. He said that Rev. Leverette had apologized for his previous protest activities and blamed me for leading him astray. It was all a lie. He could not, and did not, force me out of the movement. And Leverette, of all people, did not apologize to him for anything. In fact, Leverette told local reporters, "Led astray? Led astray where . . . ain't nobody led me astray." He also denied one of Untreiner's main claims and stated, "No racial tensions have been calmed in this county. Why, it's worse than it's ever been." It did not surprise me that some Uncle Toms supported Untreiner's campaign. They had always existed in Pensacola and worked against what SCLC tried to accomplish. The Escambia-Pensacola Human Relations Commission chairman Eugene Brown, for example, was one person who constantly denounced my activities. He said that Untreiner "has tried to help the black community in every way possible, but he didn't get the cooperation for some black leaders."[141] Much to my chagrin, Untreiner won the election. While Royal Untreiner was rewarded for terrorizing innocent people, lying under oath in court, and sending an innocent person to prison, I continued to pay the price for standing up to racial oppression.

On September 9, 1976, the First District Court of Appeals rejected an appeal for a rehearing of my felony conviction. Paul Shimek took the decision to the Florida Supreme Court, but Escambia County Circuit Court Judge Kirke Beall had the chance to send me to prison once again and took full advantage of it. He ordered me to turn myself in by the twentieth and denied my bail request. Shimek contacted Sheriff Royal Untreiner and asked for a two-day extension. Surprisingly, he granted my request. On September 22, as promised, I walked into the Escambia County jail fully prepared to return to Lake Butler. I was hurting on the inside and was scared to death. I knew this time that they finally had me. This was my final stand, so to speak. I was going to prison and nothing could be done to stop it. I feared for my physical safety and was not sure that I would get out of my predicament alive. Still, I was determined to remain defiant to the very end. I did not want my tormentors to believe that they had affected me as much as they had. I was not going to let them know how I really felt, and I hid my pain well. I never have been one to allow people to see the effect things have on me. I remained my usual self, despite of their expectations. I was upbeat not because of, but in spite of my situation. I wanted my surrender, therefore, to resemble a festive occasion for me, and I believe it did. Several of my church members from Evergreen accompanied me to Pensacola and some local people, including Otha Leverette, met me at the jail. I greeted *News Journal* reporters with a big smile and a raised clenched fist. I even rubbed my stomach and told the jail guards, "I hope I'm in time for supper."[142] But the lightheartedness was all an act. The second imprisonment was one of the most devastating points of my life because I believed I would serve the full five-year sentence. I had already been in state custody and did not want to return. I knew what awaited me at Lake Butler, so the second incarceration was the lowest, most helpless point in my life.

There were a few differences between my first and second imprison-ment. First of all, on my second trip to Lake Butler I read in the *Pensacola News Journal* that my wife had filed for divorce. She later told me that she wanted the divorce because I could no longer support her financially, and she was correct. I did not have a regular full-time job and I was on my way to prison once more. There was no prior indication that she planned to divorce me, so the decision and its timing completely sur-prised me. Another difference between my two incarcerations was that no one tried to get me to escape with them on the second occasion. The fact that my death was not planned in advance again was a relief. Also, I was not placed in maximum security my second go-around and I had privileges given to me that I did not have during my first stay. I was still fully accepted and protected by the inmates in the facility, so my situa-tion could have been a lot worse.

To pass the time during my second stay, I organized a Bible study group that met every evening around a sawdust pile on the recreation grounds. Prison administrators approved the meetings because the prisoners demanded it, and I was an ordained minister. One of the most interesting things that I witnessed in prison occurred because of our worship service. The guard who watched over our proceedings initially watched from a distance with a shotgun in his hands. As the

Appeal denied, Matthews surrenders to police, October 22, 1976.

days progressed, he moved closer and closer to our group. He eventually took part in services with us and sang, prayed, and worshipped beside prisoners. That guard became another member of our group because he realized that we had not gathered to plan an escape or start trouble. We assembled every evening because we wanted to worship our Lord, just like we had always proclaimed. That guard was an exception, though, at Lake Butler. Most of the officers there treated me like a common criminal or worse because of my status among the inmates. But those prisoners promised to never let anything happen to me. In fact, most of them repeatedly told me, "You are not a criminal, you are a political prisoner." They, like I, accepted the fact that I had been wrongly imprisoned and never belonged behind bars. They realized that I had not done anything to legitimize my imprisonment. I had not broken any written laws. My only transgression against the Pensacola white power structure was that I was born black and would accept nothing less than first class citizenship. The prisoners at Lake Butler knew this, and their encouragement sustained me through many difficult times. I will never forget the way they responded the night I was finally released.

Prison guards at Lake Butler had a brutal reputation during my incarceration. They were known for beating prisoners with their clubs for the smallest transgressions. Sometimes they beat inmates because they had too much influence within the prison population, so I always worried that they would target me. They would often get the prisoners out of their cells in the middle of the night, take them to a room, and have their way with them. On the morning of November 22, at about 2:00 or 3:00 A.M., I was awakened by the opening of my cell door. The guard said, "Come with me. Someone needs to see you." I was scared to death and thought that my time had arrived. I was convinced that the guards were going to remind me where I was. Much to my relief, I met a bail bondsman from Tallahassee who told me that a judge had granted my bail. I was a free man after serving thirty days in the processing center during my second stage of imprisonment. When I returned to my cell, every one of the prisoners on my block were awake and awaiting my arrival. Some were sitting on their beds facing the cell, others were standing. But they were all waiting for me to come back to the cell. I told them that I had received bail and my cellmate told me, "It is a good thing, because if those guards would have hurt you we would have torn this prison down." I fully believed that the prisoners would have rioted if the guards harmed me. But the Lord watched over me during both of my tenures at the compound. Only through His grace did I get through those episodes unscathed. Mentally and emotionally, though, I was a wreck.[143]

I was determined to remain in Pensacola after my second stay at Lake Butler. First of all, I needed to make a living and Pensacola had more employment opportunities than anywhere else in the region. I still preached in Evergreen, but there was nothing there that could provide a livelihood. I also decided to stay in Pensacola because I was stubborn. Pensacola was my home, and I did not want to give people the satisfaction of thinking that they chased me out of town. I still had that defiant streak and retained it at the expense of my own well-being, because it was nearly impossible to find work during the week. I simply could not get a job because I was a convicted felon. I had been labeled as anti-white, which was the farthest thing from the truth. I had been labeled as one that would jump to every cause that black people were involved in, regardless of the situation, but the label was not true. I was the one with the big mouth and an arrogant attitude that had been involved in so much conflict. None of those stereotypes were true, but they all stuck with me. Some exist to this day in Escambia County, Florida. After my time behind bars, therefore, I was an untouchable person in Pensacola; nobody would do anything to help me because of my reputation. I had lost almost everything that I ever possessed because of the stance I took for black people in northwest Florida. I had lost my home, I lost my family, I temporarily lost my freedom, and no one seemed to care. I had hit rock bottom. I lived in a boarding house with all of my personal belongings. I stayed there off and on for almost two years. The only things I retained was my dignity and my faith, and neither of those paid the bills. What made me even more angry was that some local lawyers told me, "H. K., you sure got the shaft, the legal system did you wrong." I responded, "Why are you telling me that now? You knew that I was getting the shaft all along, and many of you refused to represent me. Where were you when I was railroaded, and what did you do about it?" I did not appreciate people who told me that they knew I was victimized when my ordeal ended. They stood by and watched it happen, which made them just as guilty as the deputies, judges, and juries that sent me away. I realized that it would be hard to remain in northwest Florida, but I had no other options.

In the first weeks of 1977, I thought I had finally caught a break concerning a job. I applied for employment through the Pensacola Community Action Program (CAP) in February of that year. I went to the CAP because the agency located temporary employment for destitute citizens. To receive assistance from the organization, I had to sign a statement stating that I had earned less than twenty-eight thousand dollars in 1976 and remained "in a critical financial situation." On February 9, the CAP hired me to work for the Escambia-Pensacola Human Relations Commission. The job paid minimum wage and was planned to only last two weeks, but it would have provided me with some much-needed funds. My task was to compile a list of minority-owned businesses in the county. Even though it was menial work with menial pay, my appointment angered many local officials, including Pensacola mayor pro tem John Frenkel, Jr. He threatened to resign as chairman of the CAP and cut its funding if I was allowed to keep working. On February 14, program director Willie Junior fired me. He made up some excuse about a residency requirement that I violated, even though he knew I lived in Pensacola when he hired me. The reason I was fired is as clear today as it was then. I lost my job because of my past activities and because of the

Rev. Matthews registering to vote after his release from the Florida State Penitentiary, 1976.

negative perception many in the area had toward me.[144]

It was a lonely period between my second release from Lake Butler and my permanent exodus from Pensacola. During that time, I really felt empty. I felt deserted and betrayed. I believed that I had given up too much for people who did not care about what my sacrifices had done to me personally. Several negative thoughts periodically clouded my mind. Was it all worth it? Would I do it again? Why did I do it? Why did people say to me, "Matthews, shouldn't you have known better?" These were the same people that I fought for, the folks that I put my life on the line for, and when I got in trouble, they said, "You really should not have gone that far." I had a lot of mixed feelings about my experiences as a civil rights leader after the second incarceration. After much solitude, contemplation, and prayer, I realized that I had not given too much for justice. I was in the right, even though others had wronged me. I came to the realization that I was convicted for a reason. The imprisonment made me a stronger man, and those convictions made me more appreciative of human beings. I would not be the man I am today without those experiences. But my continuous rejection by those who lived in Escambia County had a negative impact upon me. By the fall of 1977, I was near both spiritual and financial bankruptcy and suffered another great blow.

I was transferred from my churches in Evergreen to Brewton, Alabama, in October 1977. Presiding elder Rev. Pete Andrews had wanted to get me out of Evergreen for some time, but Bishop Dunston would not allow it. Andrews tried to have me transferred after my second incarceration but transfers could not take place within the AME Zion church until the annual conference occurred, and the one for that year had passed. However, Rev. Andrews approached me at the 1977 conference and asked, "Do you want to go back to your churches in Evergreen?" I said yes, and he replied, with a grin on his face, "Well, you ain't going." Bishop Dunston had transferred me to Brewton, Alabama, which was about thirty miles south of Evergreen. I understand why Bishop Dunston made his decision. Rev. Andrews had presented him with evidence that the Ku Klux Klan had threatened my life in Evergreen, so the bishop moved me for my own safety. The Klan threats were a reality. My life was threatened so many times in Evergreen that the Federal Bureau of Investigation watched over me when I was in Alabama, which I did not know at the time.[145] In October 1977, therefore, I began a new job in Brewton. I continued to live in a Pensacola boarding house and commuted to my new church, because the Escambia-Pensacola Human Relations Commission rehired me later that year.

The Escambia-Pensacola Human Relations Commission hired me again when a new director took control of the agency. Alan Hebert, who was the administrator when the commission first fired me, was replaced by a black female named Toni Brooks. I do not recall if I contacted her or she called me, but I was given another job with the organization. The commission hired me to investigate job discrimination claims in the county. The position was originally supposed to last a year, but Brooks preserved my job for eighteen months. I worked there and lived between Pensacola and Brewton until my employment with the commission ended. Another situation that I was previously involved with heated up during my legal and personal problems, but I was powerless to do anything about it. It concerned the racist symbols at Escambia High School.

The Confederate icons at Escambia High continued to be a source of black frustration as my ordeal progressed, but my attention was focused elsewhere and I could not give my full attention to fighting the insulting symbols. Judge Winston Arnow declared the Confederate flag, "Dixie" fight song, and the Johnny Reb mascot "racial irritants" in his 1973 decision. He recommended that the county school board abolish the symbols, but the body took the cowardly way out and decided to let the students vote on the "Rebel" name. Rev. Leverette and I were still involved in the dispute at that point, and we argued that a majority vote meant certain victory for Rebel supporters because blacks constituted a minority of EHS students. The school board decided that the "Rebels" name needed to pass by a two-thirds majority vote, or the school would keep the "Raiders" mascot the board gave EHS. The vote took place on February 4, 1976, and "Rebels" fell 116 votes short of the majority it needed to remain the school's symbol. The morning after the vote occurred, white students raised hell on the campus. They provoked a riot that lasted almost an hour. Black students were locked inside the gymnasium for protection. The white mob smashed windows, started fires, and beat innocent black bystanders. In addition, gunfire wounded four people before county deputies finally stopped the riot.[146] Before the day ended, state representative Smokey Peaden and state senator W. D. Childers became involved in the controversy once again.

Peaden and Childers promised white parents that the "Rebel" name would not be abolished at the school. Whites had their spokesmen, but the black community had no one to stand up for their children. The local SCLC and NAACP previously cut ties with me and there was no one with enough backbone in their groups to do anything about the EHS affair. Even if I would have involved myself in the situation, I had no outside support and may have divided the black community, which was the last thing I wanted to do. So I deliberately kept a low profile during the entire ordeal, even though it was a situation that was near and dear to my heart. Before my extortion trial I told some of my closest associates, "If I die, quit, or go to jail, Pensacola race relations will go back to the level they were at during the 1950s." That may have sounded like bragging, but it was the truth. Whites did not like me, but they respected me. If they did not perceive me as a threat, I never would have gone to jail.

During the EHS riot and its aftermath, then, I was not in the picture. Consequently, Peaden and Childers rallied whites and waved Rebel flags all over Escambia County. They wanted nothing less than the full reinstatement of the Confederate icons at EHS, even though they knew how blacks felt about the symbols. The dispute intensified white hatred and disrespect of blacks throughout the area. White leaders thought they had gotten rid of me and were determined to settle for nothing less than total victory in this situation. When the pro-Confederate masses did not get exactly what they wanted, they acted like spoiled little children. It did not matter that the symbols further divided a community and led to riots and violence. They wanted to preserve their heritage, which was based on white supremacy. On March 17, 1976, the school board changed the EHS nickname to "Patriots" in the spirit of America's bicentennial, but the patriotic move failed to satisfy white students, parents, and local residents. W. D. Childers responded to the change by introducing a bill in the state senate that proposed a county-wide vote on the EHS images. Governor Askew threatened to veto any such bill, and it never made it out of committee. The matter finally ended on September 7, 1977, when new EHS principal Eugene Key arranged a final mascot vote for school students. Key excluded all previous mascots from the vote, so the Confederate issue finally ended. "Gators" won the vote and remains the EHS mascot to this day.[147] But the damage had been done. The races were further divided in northwest Florida and the black community had no cohesion or spokesperson. Not only did the symbols situation in Pensacola deteriorate, but the Ku Klux Klan reinforced their standing in northwest Florida while my activities remained limited to southern Alabama.

On July 5, 1977, Gulf Coast Knights of the KKK asked county school board superintendent Charlie Stokes for permission to use Escambia High School's gymnasium so they could hold another public assembly and membership rally. Incredibly, Stokes granted the request. The Klan organized a forum for July 26 at EHS where Grand Wizard David Duke was scheduled to address the audience and moderate the racist film "The Birth of a Nation." The school board later moved the meeting to a local elementary school, but the Klan still held their assembly. To make matters worse, the Klan actively supported a candidate in a county school board election because he pledged to restore the racist imagery at EHS.[148] The Klan's presence and symbols debate went unchallenged because no one in Pensacola was willing to stand up to the numerous bigots in the area. As the racial atmosphere continued to deteriorate for blacks in Escambia County, my legal ordeal finally came to an end.

On July 27, 1978, the Florida Supreme Court heard the appeal of my extortion conviction. I thought that I had a good chance of being exonerated. In his brief to the court, Paul Shimek clearly laid out his argument. He stated that the extortion conviction violated my first amendment right of free speech and the resulting sentence violated my eighth amendment protection against cruel and unusual punishment.

Shimek focused on the biased conditions that permeated my first trial. He stated that the proceedings never decisively concluded that I threatened anyone. He criticized Oscar Moss's inclusion on the jury, despite the fact that the man admitted being prejudiced against me and Brooks before the trial began. Shimek also painstakingly picked apart each deputy's testimony against me by highlighting the inconsistencies that characterized their statements. Finally, my attorney pointed out that Rev. J. L. Savage admitted that he, not I, was the person who led the chant in question. Shimek argued that the proceedings against me provided "positive evidence of abuse by police, prosecutor, jury, and trial court . . . against an unpopular man leading an unpopular cause."[149] I hoped that the state Supreme Court would finally deliver justice for me. Their decision was a great disappointment. The body upheld my guilt and five-year prison sentence with a four-to-two vote.

One judge on the court, though, clearly understood what was going on in Pensacola. His name was Judge Joseph Hatchett and he happened to be the only black justice on the court. He also wrote the judgement's longest opinion and voted to reverse the conviction. Hatchett argued, "The record implies that the police merely used these spoken words in order to arrest the leaders of the demonstration on charges more serious than the misdemeanor of disorderly conduct." He maintained that Escambia County officers did not believe that our cheers threatened them because they made no arrests for five days after the alleged chants began. The state had to prove Untreiner "reasonably feared imminent violence against his life if he did not concede to the protestor's demand," which he did not demonstrate during any of our demonstrations. Hatchett also pointed out that police arrested no one for weapons possession during the protest and claimed the "absence of any firearms among the demonstrators is significant" because it proved that I "did not urge the crowd to take up weapons and kill local police officers." He also argued that the district court's reversal of the extortion charge against Brooks proved relevant in my case. Hatchett called "Brooks's secondary leadership role and efforts to keep the demonstration peaceful," arguments which led to his exoneration, "irrelevant as a defense" because the chant still threatened officers. In other words, if the courts exonerated Brooks for that reason, they needed to do the same for me.

The judge argued that our group may have trespassed or participated in disorderly conduct, but committed no other crime. He even defended my activities by maintaining that the Constitution allows "uninhibited, robust, and wide-open" public debate and "political hyperbole" that "may well include vehement, caustic, and sometimes unpleasantly sharp attack on government and public officials." He correctly observed, "The greatest fear on the part of the sheriff was the growing size of each night's demonstration, and the greater effectiveness that such demonstrations were having on the operations of the sheriff's office and the community." Judge Hatchett concluded his opinion by stating, "Only by allowing our citizens to voice their political opposition to the fullest extent possible can we encourage the use of the open political forum and inhibit the growing tendency of clandestine violent attacks as a means of political change."[150] The judge made the same legal arguments that I had made since my arrests. Yet his points, like mine, fell on deaf ears.

Shimek filed a petition asking the Florida Supreme Court to rehear the case and wanted to take the state verdict to the United States Supreme Court, but I wanted the ordeal to end. I was physically, financially, and emotionally drained, so I asked Governor Reuben Askew for a pardon, despite its implication of guilt. Askew told me to advertise the request, and I did in the July 15 *Pensacola Voice*. Askew still denied the pardon because he wanted me to take the case to the nation's highest court so that it would set a precedent for future cases that threatened freedom of speech.[151] On November 28, 1978, the Florida Supreme Court denied my attorney's rehearing request. I was in Brewton when I found out that my appeal had been turned down. I knew that this meant I was going back to Lake Butler and possibly Raiford. I personally called Reuben Askew that evening and expressed my concerns. He told me, "H. K., go home, go to bed, and do not worry about the court's decision. You are not going back to prison." I did not know what he had planned, but I found out about two weeks later.

On December 13, 1978, Governor Askew recommended to the state

Clemency Board that my sentence be commuted to the sixty-three days I had already served in prison. It was the last meeting Askew conducted as governor of Florida. Despite a letter from Sheriff Royal Untreiner that called Askew's motion "a gross miscarriage of justice" and the protests of Agriculture Commissioner Doyle Conner, the cabinet voted seven-to-zero to approve the decision. The governor did not grant me a full pardon because he did not want to impair any future appeals to the United States Supreme Court. Nevertheless, Askew attributed his decision to his dedication to free speech and told the press, "This country must be large enough to entertain dissent." He called all of the decisions rendered against me "bad law" and defended my right to protest by stating, "I know that it's not a popular thing to lead an unpopular cause." The governor told me and the rest of the cabinet during the meeting, "I have the privilege of knowing you, whereas these members of the Cabinet do not, and I don't think anyone could have ever convinced me that you ever would ever say that in regard to me." Interestingly enough, two of the people that wrote letters which supported the governor's ruling were Pensacola Police Chief James Davis and State Senator W. D. Childers. Askew even paid me a great compliment by comparing me to Martin Luther King, Jr., in the amount of harassment and persecution that I endured over the previous years.

I appreciate Governor Askew's willingness to defend me and make the decision that he did. Askew has always exemplified a sense of fair play and justice, even before he became governor, so his decision to commute my sentence was in line with his character. But the fact that it was one of the last decisions he made as governor was not lost on me. My arrest, trial, imprisonment, and release, therefore, were all motivated by the politics of race.

My response to the commutation was simple: "I will go to my grave saying I'm not guilty" of any crime. I also responded positively to having the civil rights that I lost upon my felony conviction restored. I could vote again, which meant everything. I could not own a firearm, but that was okay. My prayers and the prayers of others were much stronger and much more potent than any weapon. On the day I received notification that my rights had been restored, I traveled to the Escambia County Supervisor of Elections office and registered to vote. I joked that I may even run for sheriff, which some whites probably did not consider very humorous. The *Pensacola Journal*, like me, remained defiant to the end. It endorsed the sentence reduction reluctantly and declared, "Suppose the case had involved hooded Klansmen surrounding the jail and threatening to 'assassinate' a black deputy who had slain a white suspect: Would it still amount to 'free speech'?" Another state paper, though, defended the decision. The *St. Petersburg Times* called my sentence commutation "almost mandatory" because the "grossly excessive" original sentence and my "incompetent" defense attorney made the previous "situation impossible" to overcome. The United States Supreme Court dismissed my case on a technicality and never heard it, so Florida Governor Bob Graham pardoned me in 1979.[152] The pardon thrilled me, but it was not something I thought about every day up to that point. By 1979, I had already began a new life for myself in Brewton, Alabama.

10

VICTORY

The move from Escambia County, Florida, to Escambia County, Alabama, was a major turning point in my life. It was in southern Alabama that I experienced victory after such a tremendous fall in Pensacola, but it did not seem that a triumph would occur when I arrived in my new church home. I was rejected in Brewton before I even arrived. Some local residents, including a few members of my congregation at Zion Fountain AME Zion Church, thought that a trouble-making malcontent was coming to town to wreak havoc.

The only thing Brewton residents knew about me was what they had seen on television and had read in the newspapers, so they thought the absolute worst about H. K. Matthews. I understood, therefore, why the congregation that I inherited was so hesitant about my initial arrival. But they eventually got to know me for who I am, and grew to both respect and love me. In fact, I have several staunch defenders in Brewton today who wanted to run me out of town as soon as I unpacked my belongings. I never tried to change their minds about me or alter my actions in any way to prove them wrong. I was just myself, and what everyone learned about me is that they got exactly what they saw. I am genuine, and I want people to judge me based on what they know from a first-hand perspective. When my parishioners at Zion Fountain realized that I was not the monster some made me out to be, but that I was an honest and sincere individual, we became as close as relatives. My church congregation, however, was only one new family that I built in Brewton.

Only a few weeks after I transferred from Evergreen and began my ministry at Zion Fountain, I visited a church member after a Sunday morning service who was recuperating from an illness at the Brewton hospital. As soon as I got off the elevator, I saw a pretty lady standing near the doors. I had never seen her before but she asked, "They have not killed you yet?" I laughed and replied, "No ma'am, I am still alive." We began talking and I found out that her name was Bobbie Ann Avant. She was a nursing assistant who worked at the hospital and had lived in Brewton for most of her life. She knew who I was because she had followed my ordeal through the local media. We began dating soon after meeting on that special Sunday.

Knowing Bobbie was the highest point of my life at that period. She was a friendly face and a friendly voice at a time when they were few and far between. We married on May 7, 1979 at her home in Brewton. We did not have a church wedding because it was the second marriage for both of us. Neither I nor Bobbie wanted a big, formal church wedding, so we married in a living room with three witnesses in attendance. Not only did I have a new wife, but I also inherited a daughter. Her name is Tisha Drayon Smith and I have never referred to her as or thought of her as a step-daughter. I have always considered her to be my daughter, and I have never treated her as or thought of her to be anything other than my own blood. Our family expanded soon after we married. In 1980, Christopher Jonathan Matthews came into the lives of me, Bobbie, and Tisha. My new family was the pinnacle of a personal renewal in Brewton.

I really believe that I started a new life in Escambia County, Alabama. I had put the misery I endured due to my experiences in Pensacola behind me, and it felt extraordinary. I came to Brewton with nothing and was given the best reward I have had on this earth. I was unemployed and broke, financially and otherwise. When I met Bobbie, I had no full-time job. I drew unemployment for a while and eventually found work as a substitute teacher. The superintendent of county schools, a man named Harry Weaver, sympathized with my plight and gave me a job making twenty dollars a day. I was glad to have any kind of work, and taught many days at W. S. Neal Middle School. To this day, I have a lot of respect for both Mr. Weaver and Mr. Eugene Stallworth, the principal at

Neal, who stuck their necks out for me when they did not have to. Yet the pay was modest and I questioned whether or not it made economic sense for me and Bobbie to marry. But she told me, "We will make it even if we have to eat bread and drink water." She stood beside me for who I was and what I believed in. We both had faith that God would work everything out, and He did. I was, and still am, eternally grateful for someone like Bobbie who married me when I had nothing materially to offer her and has stayed by my side ever since. I had left Pensacola and all of the negative things that happened to me there behind, but I had not forgotten about what God placed me on this earth to do, which was to stand up for those who had no political or social voice. I continued to do God's will in Alabama, but the circumstances there diverged from the situation that existed in northwest Florida.

There was very little civil rights activism that occurred in Brewton before I arrived in town. The problems that blacks encountered in Escambia County, Alabama, differed in many ways from those blacks experienced in Escambia County, Florida. For example, Glenn Holt, the Brewton Police Chief when I moved to the city, was committed to fairness for all citizens. He was a friend to both the black and to the poor, which did not make him the most popular person in Brewton. Yet he always acknowledged my concerns and seemed to rectify all major complaints. The fact that local police leaders listened to black voices and responded sensitively to our concerns made the relationship between law enforcement officers and ordinary citizens much better than it was in Pensacola.

Another difference between Pensacola and Brewton was that no vehicle for black activism existed in Brewton. There was no organization in the city that actively pursued civil rights for oppressed citizens. In my estimation, some Brewton blacks possessed more of a "back-woods" kind of mentality than even what I encountered in Evergreen. They accepted second class citizenship and rarely questioned the political status quo. They had endured unequal treatment their entire lives and had learned to live with it. It seemed that nothing could organize or excite the Brewton population when it came to fighting for their rights. Two groups existed in the area that supposedly defended black interests, but the county branches of the NAACP and the Alabama Democratic Conference (ADC) had complacent leaders and passive members. I did what I could under the circumstances to address oppressive situations, but no one was willing to directly or actively confront racism in Brewton.

I contemplated starting a SCLC branch in Brewton, but found no one who expressed an interest in joining the group. I learned a long time ago that a one-man band is no good unless it is in a nightclub, so I abandoned all aspirations of bringing the organization to my new hometown. Local complacency kept the SCLC out of Escambia County, Alabama. Besides, I had gone out on the limb enough for SCLC and the organization had help cut the limb out from under me. I had pledged to never again risk my safety and freedom for people who did not seem to care about their own rights, so I did not want to replicate in Brewton what had happened in Pensacola.

My wife also did not want me to become involved in Brewton with an organization that would offer no assistance. Bobbie knew Brewton very well and understood that a new civil rights group, particular one led by an "outsider" with my reputation, would create a tremendous white backlash against local blacks. She also insisted that I limit my activities because of my health and well-being. She had seen what being repeatedly hung out to dry by others had done to me emotionally, and she thought it was best if I totally withdrew from activism. I completely appreciated her concern. Throughout my experiences in the movement, very few people have demonstrated concern for me as a person. Yet I do not agree that I could be happier or better off by stepping completely out of the picture. I feel that I would be ignoring God's calling for me, so I can not cease my struggles on the behalf of others. But I decided to compromise somewhat by first trying to work within the two organizations that existed in Brewton.

The Alabama Democratic Conference was the only organized alliance that existed for those who wanted to become politically active in Escambia County. It was a state organization that had a local branch in Brewton. It gave political endorsements, supposedly addressed local conditions, and publicized legislative decisions that impacted our area,

but did little when it came to making substantiative changes for minorities. It was, however, a multi-racial organization that did not focus on
racial equality per se, but African-Americans comprised a majority of
the group's membership. Although they discussed black mistreatment
from time to time at ADC meetings, the group rarely questioned the
social status quo. I even withdrew from the ADC because they wanted
to control the vote its members had.

The ADC learned very rapidly that my vote is not, and never has
been, for sale. I do not have to explain my vote to anyone, and I am not
going to vote one way solely because a group told me to. The local ADC
found this out when a well-qualified black man, James America, ran for
the state legislature against a white man that the ADC supported named
Skippy White. Before White moved to Brewton, he was a firefighter in
Pensacola. I supported America because his qualifications made him a
more attractive candidate than White.

One incident occurred soon after the election campaign began that
legitimized my decision. Several local blacks informed me that White
made insulting comments concerning blacks at a public event. He was at
his daughter's high school basketball game and had became angry because
of the team's poor play and his child's lack of playing time. He became so
upset that he yelled from the stands, "Get those niggers out of my gym." I
decided after hearing numerous accounts of the incident that my decision
to support America was correct. The ADC became quite upset with me,
and America was eliminated in the primary. However, I still pledged to
not support White until he apologized for his public outburst.

One day he called me to his office at the county courthouse and asked
what he had to do to earn my support once again. I told him to admit
what he said so that we could both move forward. He confessed that he
lost his cool and made the offensive remarks, but apologized and asked
for my support. I asked why it took so long for him to call and he said,
"H. K., I know you. I knew that you would support the African-American candidate because of his qualifications and due to my comments,
despite what the ADC asked you to do. So I decided to talk with you
after our election." Soon after that election, ADC members distanced

themselves from me because I did not jump when told. I, unlike many people in this county, know what it is like to have my vote taken for political reasons, so I refuse to abandon my chosen candidate due to an organization's philosophy.

An NAACP branch existed in Brewton before I arrived in town, but it was not effective nor particularly active. Still, I joined the body because I wanted to keep my finger on the pulse of local affairs. The president of the local chapter was Theodore Dean, and we worked together on a few issues. For example, we investigated the alleged unfair treatment of black workers in local industries and businesses.

The most successful project, though, that I initiated while working with the NAACP and President Dean, was renaming a local road after Dr. Martin Luther King, Jr. I noticed in the early 1980s that many cities were renaming streets for Dr. King, and I believed that Brewton needed to follow suit. I brought the idea to the attention of the local NAACP and they supported the issue. Dean and I went door-to-door to obtain signatures from citizens who welcomed the change, and our work eventually paid off. The Brewton city council renamed Rabb Street after Dr. King. We only faced direct resistance from one black; a Rabb Street resident named Mrs. Mary McCorvey. When I think back on the affair, her struggle to keep the street from being renamed was both sad and humorous. She appeared at city council meetings and fought the proposal with all of her energy. She said that her address just "did not sound right" as MLK Boulevard, that older residents would have to notify Social Security and Medicaid of their address change, that the post office would lose mail, and that people would not be provided fire and police services. Nevertheless, the measure passed with no dissenting votes from the four whites and one black who served on the city council. It meant a lot that we encountered no visible opposition from the city fathers, which I considered progress. My only regret is that we should have picked a more visible street to target for renaming. The NAACP chose Rabb Street because it ran past a predominantly black school. Few residents used the street on a daily basis, which may be one reason that more whites did not oppose it. Despite our success in the street campaign, though, I noticed a discernible difference between my approach and the philosophy of Theodore Dean.

I have always believed in confronting racism directly but peacefully. Dean had another approach. He did not believe in rocking the boat for blacks in Brewton. He would shake it a little, but stopped as soon as he believed his actions could offend the "good white folks" in Brewton. The problem was that many local blacks believed that even Dean's conservative approach was dangerous. They would do nothing that could possibly make their personal situations more uncomfortable than they currently were, so the complacency of Brewton blacks limited what the NAACP could accomplish.

For example, I have questioned the number of blacks who served on the city council since my arrival in Brewton. The city is nearly 40 percent black, but only one black at a time has served on the council during my first quarter-century in town. The same held true for school board membership. Yet the area NAACP continuously refused to support my efforts to change or even question the matters. In fact, several members promised to vote for me when I ran for a city council position in 1984, but the group failed to publicly support my efforts. Consequently, I lost the election to white incumbent John Gleaton by a more than a two-to-one margin. Turnout was only 36 percent of all registered voters, despite the fact that it was the first time a black man had challenged a white incumbent in Brewton's modern history. The low turnout was a shame, because voting patterns demonstrated that I had a respectable amount of white support. Blacks, though, turned their backs on me at the polls. Some even admitted that they voted for my opponent. The Brewton NAACP, then, served as a fund-raising body for the national office and did little to fight injustice on a local level. When the group does come forward to support a cause, their participation is so limited that it matters little. In other words, the Brewton NAACP continues to be weak, quiet, and of no help to blacks who most need assistance. I still renew my NAACP membership when it expires, but it's due to the respect I have for the national organization. The local group is a non-entity when it comes to fighting for racial equality in Escambia County.

The lack of enthusiasm many African-Americans in Brewton had, and still possess, in pursuing their civil rights is often discouraging. One thing that Brewton and Pensacola had in common, though, is the level of resistance upper class blacks demonstrated toward my activities. This is something that will never change. Those who have material or social success often forget that they have it because people like me put our lives on the line for them. They forget that their opportunities were bought with the blood, sweat, and tears of people who sacrificed for them to have more than their parents and grandparents. Yet blacks have become complacent and will not put themselves in uncomfortable situations so that others could later succeed in life. They become scared that they could lose prestige because of associating with me. People who feel that way do not even have to say a word. Their actions reveal their feelings. Many of the so-called "successful African-Americans" in Brewton will not even make eye contact with me when I pass them in public, they refuse to speak even when I speak to them first, and they go out of their way to avoid me when others are present. I encountered the same treatment from similar people in Pensacola. Still, I can not hold bitterness in my heart and I refuse to be angry with those people. What they fail to understand is that their attitudes and non-action makes their lives and their children's lives harder, not easier.

In response to the shortcomings of local organizations to adequately address problems the black community faces, I initiated some grass-roots activities after I moved to Brewton. In 1981, for instance, I created the Brewton Green Ribbon Committee to express communal support for the families of the murdered and missing children in Atlanta. We wore green ribbons on our shirts as a reminder for all citizens to pray for justice in the matter. The committee was not formed for the sole purpose of helping blacks, but to assist all people. Had those children in Atlanta been white, our outrage and response would have been no less, for all of us were created by one God and all of us are answerable to that God. The committee did not limit its activities to Brewton alone. I took our cause to Alabama Governor Fob James, who declared March 22, 1981 an "Official Day of Prayer in Alabama" for those who lost loved ones during the Atlanta crisis.

In 1990, I formed another organization in Brewton on behalf of children. I deemed it Citizens United to Save Our Youth (CUTSOY) and held its initial meeting at the church I pastored, Zion Fountain AME Zion Church. I created CUTSOY to inspire children in our area to rise to greatness. The group was meant to provide a positive force in our community. CUTSOY members aimed to steer children away from crime, gangs, and drugs. Those things lead to social problems and brought jail, often death, to offenders. Furthermore, no one wants to live in a place where they are afraid to sit on their back porch at night. It is useless to live in a community where fear and intimidation exists. I had a young son and understood the troubles local youths faced. I had also worked with young people in Pensacola. In fact, the first position I held in a civil rights organization was as president of the Pensacola NAACP Youth Council. As director of CUTSOY, I met with students and parents to promote positive values to both groups. I did not form the organization for adults, although many supported me. I did it for the kids.

CUTSOY members organized workshops for and brought in inspirational speakers to address the children and their parents. Doctors, attorneys, police officers, business owners, and other professionals encouraged the young people to make something of their lives. It was not a "scared straight" program, but we did discuss the consequences of bad decisions. The pews at Zion Fountain were packed for each assembly. I tried to resign from CUTSOY in March 1992, but the members asked me to retain the position. I had numerous obligations from my church, job, and as a public speaker, but it was an honor to be needed so I returned to the group. Even when I tried to withdrawn from public activity, therefore, people often came to me when they experienced troubles. During the same time, I also fought a personal battle at my new place of employment.

In September 1979, I quit my part-time substitute teaching position when I found full-time work at Jeff Davis State Junior College (JDSJC) in Brewton. President George McCormick hired me as a Financial Aid clerk and I made about seven hundred dollars a month, which was much more than I made as a middle school substitute teacher. My family could live off of my new salary, and that was all that mattered to me. I knew nothing about college financial aid programs at the time, but I learned on the job because it was the only position available and I honestly thought it could be my last opportunity to find meaningful employment in Brewton. After three years, Dr. McCormick promoted me to Financial Aid Officer. I stayed in that position until I was transferred to the JDSJC prison program in 1986. I enjoyed my early years at Jeff Davis tremendously, but things changed when a new president came to the campus.

In 1985, Dr. Sandra McLeod became the new president at Jeff Davis. At the time of her appointment, I was the only black male administrator working at the college. A lot of people, particularly older whites, demonstrated displeasure that a black occupied such an important position. Many then did not appreciate the need for diversity and did not want to work with or answer to a black man. I used this attitude to my advantage, though, and applied for a position as the assistant director of the school's prison program. I wanted the job because I felt restricted as a financial aid officer. I wanted to help more people and wanted the freedom to travel to our various campuses that came with the prison position.

Dr. McLeod granted my request and transferred me from Brewton to the JDSJC campus located in Atmore, Alabama. The campus in Atmore lay about thirty miles west of Brewton and formerly existed as a technical school. It merged with JDSJC during the 1980s and became the headquarters of the college's prison program. I initially split my time between the Brewton and Atmore campuses. I loved the new position for several reasons. It brought a degree of freedom from the main campus, I could travel, and it was a promotion within the school hierarchy. I also liked working with the inmates because I could, to a degree, relate to their predicament. The circumstances of our incarcerations may have differed, but I understood what many inmates went through as wards of the state. Furthermore, I provided the inmates with a service that could improve their lives after they served their time, so I performed my job with great purpose and enthusiasm.

I initially worked under the director of the prison program, Eldred Pritchett. I had to make sure that the students had books, that the classes we offered reached minimum enrollment figures, that the students properly registered for courses that they wanted to take, and that we had enough teachers in the program. I had a good reputation among the inmates because I treated them as I wanted to be treated. The students resisted and acted suspicious towards me at first, but I always tried to make them feel comfortable. I let them know that I was there to help them and treated them as dignified human beings. Besides, prisoner education was mandated by law and I wanted to provide that service to the best of my abilities. As a result, the inmates came to respect and trust me. I enjoyed my work in the prison very much. I dealt with people who were underprivileged, which I had done throughout my entire life. I never asked anyone why they were in prison, because it was not my business. If they told me, that was another issue entirely. But I was in a position to help people who needed to understand that someone cared about them. I have always thought that God loves the underdog because He made so many of us.

I had the opportunity to work at two prisons. I worked at Fountain Correctional Facility, which was a minimum security facility, and the maximum security prison, Holman Correctional Facility. During my work at the latter, I had the chance to meet many condemned inmates because executions were, and still are, legal in Alabama. We offered some classes on death row and I got to see the death chamber numerous times. Despite their predicaments, I treated all inmates as people. It did not matter to me if they had a date with "yellow mama," as prisoners called the electric chair. God loved them just as much as He loved me, and they needed to see that love more than anyone. JDSJC even offered graduation ceremonies at each of the prison facilities. I have had the chance to speak at graduations for prisoners and free citizens in Alabama. The only difference between the two was that instead of caps and gowns, the inmates who graduated wore white uniforms. But they were just as proud of their accomplishments as any other group of students that I have seen. Although my work with the prison program proved reward-

Matthews, with son Chris, in his office at Jefferson Davis Junior College in Brewton, September 30, 1988.

ing, my experiences with the administration at Jeff Davis was a source of constant frustration.

The authorities at JDSJC treated me differently than any other employee they had on any campus. For example, I was the only one who had to give a specific account of my work hours. I had to keep track of my whereabouts by signing in and out when I left campuses, and I had to produce paperwork on a daily basis that tracked my activities at the prisons. I basically had to document every move that I made. Again, I was the only one fortunate enough to be burdened with the responsibility and I voiced my displeasure concerning the situation to Dr. McLeod and Dr. Tommy Booth, the Dean of Instruction at Jeff Davis. Neither individual acted crazy about me personally or with my position as a college professional. Other than me, the only black males on campus were maintenance workers. Furthermore, I was not a "yes man," which did not sit too well with campus administrators. McLeod and Booth learned that I do not grin when tickled or scratch when there was not an itch. No one but God controlled me, and my supervisors did not appreciate my so-called "lack of appreciation" that I had for the job. Neither administrator wanted me on the main campus, so they thought that giving me the position with the prison program was a good way to get rid of me. Even though I loved my job at the prisons, I did not appreciate my special treatment and shared my displeasure with campus administrators.

One afternoon, I met with Dr. Booth concerning what I believed was my unequal treatment. I had to go to Booth because of his position on campus, even though he had problems with me from the time he began working at Jeff Davis. Unsurprisingly, my complaints fell on deaf ears. In fact, Booth took the offensive and accused me of starting trouble at the college. He even blamed me for the low enrollment numbers in the prison program, which was ludicrous. We could not force people to sign up if they did not want to, but, according to Booth, the decline was entirely my fault. He even yelled at me and called me "a no-good nigger." I still feel that he deliberately tried to provoke me into doing or saying something that could have led to my termination, but I calmly walked out of the room and went home. I nearly had to tie Bobbie to the bed when I told her what happened. She was so upset that she was determined to go to the college to confront Booth herself!

Regardless, I met with Dr. McLeod the next day and told her what happened. She dismissed the situation entirely because I had no concrete proof that Booth made the statement that he did. To support what she deemed a "serious allegation," I evidentially needed it on tape. Soon after I discussed my peculiar situation with Booth and McLeod, I was transferred to an office the size of a janitor's closet at Fountain prison and had to run the program from there. I was constrained to the office and was not allowed to work at any of the JDSJC campuses. The freedom to work at different locations, the main reason that I applied for the prison program position, was taken away. In addition, the college cut the resources needed to adequately run the prison classes. The situation with prison program got so bad that Mr. Pritchett retired. I had to run the program myself for a period, but never got paid for the extra responsibilities.

I took my latest tribulations about the case to the Brewton NAACP in the hopes that they would provide assistance. Theodore Dean, however, did nothing to address my situation. In fact, he did not even mention it to branch members. I know this is true because I attended a local meeting some time after the Booth situation, reminded those in attendance of my plight, and asked what they had decided to do about it. Much to my surprise, no one there knew about the harassment and intimidation I dealt with at the college. I asked Dean why he had not discussed it with his organization and he said that my situation had slipped his mind. Yet everyone present knew that he did not mention it because he was afraid to champion what would possibly be an unpopular cause. Instead of handling the situation within the framework of a local organization, I decided to take my case to higher authorities.

In the fall of 1990, I contacted a civil rights attorney from Mobile named Gregory Stein and asked him to file a complaint on my behalf with the Birmingham branch of the Equal Employment Opportunity Commission (EEOC). I met Stein during my work in the Mobile movement and knew that he would do what was necessary to achieve justice. Stein took my grievance to the EEOC and charged Jeff Davis leaders with creating a "racially hostile environment" and following "a pattern of adverse treatment" toward me. I did not want to resort to such drastic actions, but felt that I had to go outside of the college for redress. I loved my position at Jeff Davis but did not appreciate the permanent transfer away from the main campus. I mixed and mingled well with students at the prison, but removal from the sight of administration was demeaning. The interesting thing about my actions is that they were resolved after EEOC intervention. Dr. McLeod brought me back to campus, returned my on-campus office to me, and no longer required me to keep detailed records of my daily activities or work hours. Furthermore, all records of our dispute were purged from my permanent employment file. I received my previous responsibilities back but, most importantly, my dignity was returned. I basically got everything that I wanted except an apology. Campus leaders showed their remorse in an indirect way, but I learned long ago that some folks would rather die and go to Hell than offer an

apology. Several relatives, church members, and close friends wanted me
to pursue financial restitution from JDSJC for all that the administrators
had put me through. But I truly got what I wanted out of the situation,
which was fair treatment. The interesting thing about the entire ordeal
is that soon after the EEOC resolved the conflict, Dr. McLeod became
one of my biggest supporters on campus.

Only weeks after I returned to the Brewton campus, Dr. McLeod
read a *Pensacola News Journal* article in which I spoke out against sexual
harassment in the workplace. She was so impressed with my statements
that she soon thereafter asked me to be the campus compliance officer for
the Americans with Disabilities Act (ADA). I jumped at the opportunity
because it continued my life's work of championing the disenfranchised.
The ADA compliance position gave me a chance to continue speaking
for those with no voice, which is an indispensable part of my life and
identity. It represented an opportunity to continue doing what God
put me on earth to do, so I gladly accepted the job. Soon thereafter, Dr.
McLeod asked me to be the federal compliance officer for all aspects of
discrimination at Jeff Davis. I monitored discrimination in hiring and
admissions due to age, disability, sex, race, or religious beliefs. I enforced
equal access for all groups and met with administrators, faculty members,
staff, and students to answer their questions and address their grievances.
The job was a natural fit for me and I loved it. I retired from full-time
employment in that position in 1996. I worked part-time at Jeff Davis
Community College, as it was renamed, for two more years but retired
permanently in August 1998. Even in victory, therefore, my journey has
not been without constant and exhausting struggle.

The most memorable aspect of my time in Brewton has been the
plethora of awards, honors, and recognition that I have achieved due to my
civil rights work. Literally dozens of community, fraternal, and religious
organizations have recognized my sacrifices and publicly acknowledged
my contributions to the black freedom struggle in Escambia County,
Florida, and the United States as a whole. The first significant honor I
received came in 1978, when I was placed in the initial edition of *Who's
Who Among African-Americans*. Throughout the late 1970s and 1980s, I

earned recognition from the Jackson County, Mississippi branch of the SCLC, the Pensacola NAACP, several African-American fraternal organizations, local black heritage committees, and numerous Escambia County, Florida churches. On November 10, 1989, the Chicago City Council presented me with an honorable distinction. They issued a proclamation that honored my contributions to the national civil rights movement. City Alderman Dorothy Tillman was born in Pensacola and participated in the local struggle as a child. She was a very active member of the SCLC and NAACP, and continued her work after she left northwest Florida. The Chicago award was particularly flabbergasting because it placed me in the esteemed company of Frederick Douglass, Sojourner Truth, Malcolm X, and Dr. King. I have never placed myself in the class of such heroic figures, and it overwhelms me that anyone else would. The day after the Chicago City Council honored me, I became a member of the first class inducted into the Northwest Florida Afro-American Hall of Fame.

The most rewarding of the awards I received came from institutions and individuals from the area that I had sacrificed so much for: northwest Florida. One of the most gratifying distinctions came when Pensacola mayor Vince Whibbs and the city council proclaimed July 12, 1987, "H. K. Matthews Day" in Escambia County. A ceremony was held at the Zion Hope Primitive Baptist Church in downtown Pensacola in my honor. Over one thousand people attended, Rev. R. N. Gooden delivered the keynote address, and I was presented with a key to the city. It was a strange yet exciting experience for the town to recognize and celebrate me for organizing activities that got me exiled a decade earlier. As I stated then, it made me feel good that the same city that locked me out gave me a key to return. At the same ceremony, the Black Heritage Committee of the Fiesta of Five Flags announced the creation of both the "H. K. Matthews Freedom Award" and the "H. K. Matthews College Scholarship." I still remember seeing people in the audience, both black and white, who sided against me at pivotal times during the Pensacola movement. The entire procession was flattering, but I wanted to remind everyone in attendance that the goals I had fought to achieve were still unrealized. In fact, I asked the audience during my acceptance speech, "What are you all doing? You all must not be doing anything, because every time I read the newspapers something has happened to somebody black in this county and nobody is doing anything about it." H. K. Matthews Day was only one honor, though, that came from my adopted hometown.

In the early 1990s, Pensacola radio station WBOP awarded me with an "Appreciation for Civil Rights Leadership" in northwest Florida, while the Escambia County SCLC distinguished my "meritorious service in civil rights." The Escambia-Pensacola Human Relations Commission, which once fired me, gave me a Distinguished Service Award during the same period. In addition, on his cable television program "Pensacola Wants to Know" WHBQ owner Vernon Watson declared me "The Martin Luther King of Pensacola," which is one of the highest compliments I could ever attain. In 1997 *Outfront* magazine, a Pensacola publication that emphasized African-American life and culture on the Gulf Coast, gave me the Lifetime Achievement Award for Civil Rights. A year later the University of West Florida asked me to serve on its Minority Affairs Committee, an invitation that I gladly accepted. I have even lived to see my image preserved as art. In my wildest dreams, I never thought that my pretty face would be duplicated in bronze. In December 1998, though, that very thing happened when the Kwanzaa Committee of Pensacola revealed a sculpture of my bust that it had made the previous month. The honors that I earned even extended into my new home state. Alabama Governor Don Siegelman declared August 29, 1999 "H. K. Matthews Day" in the state, and in July 2001 he made me one of his twelve appointees to the state Tourism Bureau's advisory board. On August 26, 2001 the AME Zion district that I serve held an appreciation service in my honor at Zion Fountain and Governor Siegelman served as the keynote speaker. I still return to Pensacola on a regular basis and speak to community groups and religious assemblies.

The Escambia County SCLC, which still existed in 2004, also brings me back to the area on occasion. In fact, local SCLC president Ellison Bennett makes sure that the group has a car for me to ride in during each Martin Luther King Birthday Parade in Pensacola. Bennett wanted to be sure that the organization acknowledges my contributions to local

Matthews with state representative Buzz Ritchie, the recipient of the "First Annual H. K. Matthews Image Award," June 11, 1996.

history, and I truly feel like a king every time I appear in the downtown celebration. I know that sounds egotistical to a degree, but it shows me that Pensacola residents appreciate what I have endured for them. Every time I return to Escambia County, Florida, the public treats me tremendously. It is always refreshing and rewarding to interact with local blacks when I have the opportunity, because it is then that I clearly see the fruits of my labor.

My activism has touched many different people in numerous ways, and I often forget this. Yet with each public appearance in Pensacola, I am reminded of how important my sacrifices were. The awards and recognition bestowed upon me in the past twenty years have been staggering. I often think that what individuals selflessly do for others is often done in vain. But when your life's work is recognized, it is a marvelous experience and it renews your faith in humankind. But I have never been one

to reflect on what I have done as anything substantial or extraordinary.
I have been blessed by God with the gift of discernment when it came
to recognizing social injustices and a passion for seeing righteousness
prevail. I appreciate all of the honors I have received, but they do not
mean as much to me as long as racism continues to exist. Even when I
try to withdraw from civil rights activism, circumstances and concerned
individuals draw me back into the never-ending fight. This serves true
particularly for my people in Pensacola.

I still have an interest in Pensacola's racial affairs because the city played
an important role in forming my identity. Just like Snow Hill, Evergreen,
and Brewton, then, Pensacola is home. But after I left northwest Florida,

Matthews with his bust, presented in 1998.

the civil rights movement there died. Some organizations remained, like the Pensacola-Escambia County Human Rights Commission and the local NAACP and SCLC, but they were very passive when it came to confronting racism in the area.

In January 1998, a new group named Movement for Change (MFC) formed and tried to shake Pensacola citizens out of their complacency. The organization was a coalition of several small factions that believed existing groups did little to promote racial equality in the area. MFC planned to actively confront white supremacy in and around Escambia County, and its president was a man named LeRoy Boyd. I have known LeRoy for some time; he was one of my earliest supporters and belonged to the local NAACP Youth Council. He was arrested with our group once during an integration attempt at a Pensacola pool hall, the Hall Family Recreation Center, during the early 1970s. LeRoy, therefore, grew up as and remains a strong advocate for civil rights. Because his social consciousness matured in my shadows, he understands how important it is to advocate justice for all people, regardless of sex, race, or age. He also picked up my dogmatic characteristics. LeRoy does not settle for anything less than what he believes is just and fair. Some people have misunderstood him, but I know exactly where he is coming from on topics that he feels strongly about. He probably does become attached to causes without researching them thoroughly and sometimes acts more hurriedly than I would like, but his intentions are always noble. I support the organization because its leader is concerned with achieving justice and not with glorifying himself. I hope this is what people saw in me, but I can not take any credit for what LeRoy has become. In short, Movement for Change is an organization that supports their leader and is completely focused on achieving justice. It seems that LeRoy and I have switched roles over the past two decades. He once followed me, now I follow him!

Their first goal of MFC was to have the name of Alcaniz Street in downtown Pensacola changed to Martin Luther King Boulevard. LeRoy contacted me and asked if I would help his group achieve their goal. I naturally agreed to assist in any way possible, and MFC began to gather

Above left, Matthews with Chris on JDJC campus, 1988. Above right, with Chris, August 2002. Right, with granddaughter, Taylor Stewart, August 2004.

petitions signed by those who supported the change. We brought the issue before the city council, but they staunchly opposed renaming any street to honor Dr. King. I discovered rapidly that the attitudes concerning blacks that white leaders possessed had changed very little since I left Pensacola. On February 11, 1998, MFC began a boycott of two hundred and fifty downtown stores because they would not support our efforts, despite the fact that blacks provided a majority of their customers. It seemed that the old saying that "the more things change, the more they remain the same," was an accurate depiction of race relations in Escambia County. MFC and LeRoy Boyd applied tactics to bring about racial changes similar to those that I had used in the 1960s and 1970s. The Pensacola Chamber of Commerce endorsed the MFC effort later the next month, but the city council continued to reject the change. Finally, city leaders agreed to change the name of a downtown street to Martin Luther King Drive. The street project was not the last time MFC asked for my assistance with a local situation.

As a new century began, the biggest problem facing the Pensacola black community continued to be the shooting of unarmed residents by members of the county sheriff's department. From 1991 through 2000, deputies shot and killed fourteen residents. More than half of the victims were unarmed blacks. In February 2000, MFC sponsored marches and demonstrations that protested the latest killing. The rallies reminded me of past times. We marched through downtown areas, carried signs that criticized the sheriff's department, and held rallies in public areas. Hundreds of people attended the protests, and the black community seemed interested once again in area racial injustice. MFC activities peaked in June 2000, when the group announced that it would hold a massive demonstration on the Pensacola Bay Bridge during the July 4 holiday to protest deputy violence against black citizens. The "Countdown to Shutdown" campaign was an important idea because it would block tourist access to local beaches during the summer's busiest weekend. LeRoy hoped the boycott would encourage department leaders to sit down with local blacks and discuss their grievances. We even threatened to bring the Justice Department to the area to conduct their own investigation of the fatal shootings, but I am still apprehensive concerning their willingness to help blacks due to my past experiences with the federal government. Only days before the holiday began, a federal mediator came to Pensacola and organized meetings between community leaders and residents at the county sheriff's department. MFC suspended the planned demonstration because the department agreed to meet with their officials.[153] In June 2001, Movement for Change gave me a certificate of appreciation for my civil rights work before and with their organization.

The racial situation in Pensacola may finally be improving. The willingness of local leaders to meet with a black organization, even when encouraged by federal intervention, is one thing that has changed since my ordeal. Another thing that differs now in the area is that Escambia County elected a sheriff who promised to treat black citizens with dignity. In November 2000, Ron McNesby won his campaign for the position. McNesby was a deputy who was present during our downtown activities in 1975. He was one, if not the only, officer who treated us humanely at the time. Activists recognized McNesby for not displaying outright hatred toward us or frequently calling us insulting names, so his election as the new sheriff was definitely a step in the right direction for racial reconciliation in the county. Now, public leaders in Escambia County at least have the appearance of being dedicated to fair play.

Yet not everyone has welcomed my occasional involvement in Pensacola's racial affairs. Some of the younger, middle class black leaders disdain my presence. The city's Martin Luther King Commemorative Committee, for example, has totally ignored me. They have never invited me to appear at their functions or have publicly acknowledged what I have done on behalf of blacks in their area. Every time I have participated in local events, even ones that involved the Pensacola NAACP, I came because individual members invited me. That is a sad commentary, but not because the MLK Commemorative Committee consciously excludes me from their affairs. I chalk up much of their resentment to professional jealously. Their actions are regrettable because our young people do not know about the local freedom struggle or those who participated in it. Some blacks believe that I take the spotlight off of them and they say that my time as a civil rights leader has passed. They treat old folks who belong to local organizations like they should stay out of the way, and they fail to understand that those people are the reason that their organization exists. In short, people do not understand or appreciate how they got where they are, yet they want to reap the benefits of what I fought for them to have. But I have no regrets about leaving Pensacola when I did. In fact, since my departure, many things happened to those who conspired against me during the movement that revealed their true characters.

There is no room in my heart for hate, but I certainly had little affec-

In recent years, Matthews's role in the movement has been recognized by a variety of black leaders. Here he is pictured with, clockwise from top left, Dick Gregory; Al Sharpton; former Alabama Supreme Court Justice Oscar Adams; and Fred Shuttlesworth and Greg Mathis.

tion for the people who were responsible for my demise in Pensacola such as Royal Untreiner, Jim Edson, and Doug Raines. Interestingly enough, after I was chased out of Escambia County by those criminals they all eventually encountered public humiliation. This was especially true for the sheriff's department. Royal Untreiner's office was literally shaken by one scandal after another in the late 1970s. The county grand jury investigated the office numerous times for corruption before Untreiner's tenure expired. For instance, Captain W. E. Ambrose, the chief deputy who greeted my numerous arrivals to the county jail with a devious smile on his face, was indicted for larceny and perjury. A county grand jury even indicted Untreiner's secretary for committing perjury on the behalf of her boss. Scandal so plagued the sheriff's administration that WEAR and the *Pensacola News Journal* released editorials that urged both Untreiner and Jim Edson to resign because the two had caused the community to lose confidence in the department. That was the same thing African-Americans had been saying for years, but it took criminal acts against white citizens for anyone to pay attention to our earlier claims. The disgrace Untreiner encountered legitimized my years of complaint concerning his attitude toward common citizens and reflected the dubious quality of his leadership. He finally retired in 1982 with little dignity intact. But Untreiner was not alone in his fall from power.

Douglas Raines and Jim Edson, the officer who killed Wendel Blackwell and the sheriff department's riot squad commander, respectively, each committed crimes that led to their dismissals from the law enforcement profession. Raines's true colors resurfaced approximately one year after I was sentenced to prison for the extortion charge. In July 1976, Raines beat a prisoner unconscious because he did not get off of the jailhouse phone fast enough to suit the deputy. Once again, Raines experienced no punishment for the deed. In 1981, though, no one could ignore Raines's illegal actions. On March 11, 1982, the county Civil Service Board found Raines guilty of showing pornographic movies to, taking nude photographs of, and having sex with a juvenile. While he served a prior suspension for breaking a man's arm while removing him from a Pensacola nightclub, the county agency finally dismissed Raines from the sheriff's department permanently.[154]

Jim Edson's career also ended because of his own corruption. Of all the officers whom I consider responsible for my conviction and incarceration, Sgt. Jim Edson heads the list. He consciously and purposely lied at my trial. He also controlled the other deputies and directed their testimonies. Edson was the state's chief witness and it was on the basis of his numerous lies that I was sent to prison. Despite several testimonies and abundant evidence that proved Edson had perjured himself repeatedly during my trial, no one within the sheriff's department or in a position of local leadership did anything about it. It came as no surprise to me, therefore, that later evidence further revealed Edson as the thief and liar that he was. In 1978, a department investigation discovered that Edson falsified documents to receive his 1973 promotion to crowd control supervisor. He had obtained a copy of his son's college transcript, changed the name, notarized the copy, and turned it in as his own in order to achieve the promotion. In other words, he should not have even been in a position to arrest me in 1975 because he did not meet the minimum educational requirements needed to be a departmental supervisor. Despite the blatant forgery, the Civil Service Board only gave him a thirty-day suspension. Yet during their investigation of Edson's qualifications, the board uncovered further evidence of wrongdoing and turned it over to the county grand jury for investigation. The grand jury discovered that Edson had stolen several vehicles from his division's "boneyard," which is where the sheriff's department kept stolen and abandoned vehicles. I suggested the department rename the impound lot "the Milk-Bone yard," in honor of the comments Edson made about his dogs preferring blacks to the treats. Regardless, the county grand jury charged Edson with twelve counts of grand larceny and one count of petty larceny for stealing "boneyard" vehicles and selling them, giving them away as gifts, and using them for his personal pleasure. Edson resigned from the department before he faced trial for the thefts, but he did not escape justice. A jury later found him guilty on eight of the felony counts and sentenced him to three years in state prison and twenty years of probation.

The conviction of Jim Edson aroused mixed feelings inside of me. I was glad that the general public finally recognized what kind of person led their sheriff's deputies. The conviction also validated my claims that Edson and the rest of the department leaders lied about my activities to put me away. The *St. Petersburg Times*, for example, asked the question in a headline, "The Deputy lied about his record; did he lie about Rev. Matthews?" The paper's editor asked rhetorically that if Edson stole from his department and lied about it repeatedly while under oath, "Then is it not also reasonable to assume that his testimony in the Matthews case might likewise be false?" Yet Edson had always been of questionable character and I had maintained as much for years, but no one listened because I was the person who levied the accusations. It hurt that no one considered my claims to be true, despite the fact that a person's very life rested in the balance.

I remember the night of Jim Edson's trial very clearly. I was in Pensacola's Sacred Heart hospital recovering from a minor surgery with my wife at my side. I heard about the verdict on the evening news, but a deputy who was on duty in the area and knew about the role Edson played in my conviction came to my room to relay the information. He asked if I had heard the verdict, and I told him I had. He said, "Well, I figured that ought to make you feel a little bit better." But it did not. I could not take much joy in the verdict because I wondered if he could be found guilty of stealing vehicles from a county boneyard, than why was he not found guilty of trying to steal a human's life? He had committed perjury against me and his lies put me behind bars in the state prison system, but the message I got was that those actions were not as important as falsifying records or stealing vehicles from the county. I was glad Edson was being taken off of the streets because he was nothing but a criminal—always had been—but I was not overjoyed because it came long after the conspiracy against me succeeded.

Another staunch adversary from my struggles in Pensacola was the "Banty Rooster" himself, state representative W. D. Childers. While the sheriff's department resisted our activities to bring justice in the Wendel Blackwell case, Childers zealously opposed black efforts to remove the offensive Confederate images at Escambia High School. Yet much like law enforcement officials experienced before him, Childers also endured a very public downfall that his own greed caused. In the fall of 2002, Childers was accused of extorting almost one hundred thousand dollars from the Escambia County Commission, which he chaired. Childers was elected to the County Commission in 2000 after he served in the Florida Senate for thirty years. State prosecutors officially charged Childers with money-laundering, bribery and unlawful compensation for an official act. The person implicated as the recipient of the commission chairman's alleged bribes was Willie Junior. Junior, a member of the county commission since 1985, fired me from my $2.50 an hour job with the Escambia-Pensacola Human Relations Commission in 1978 to please local politicians. He claimed that Childers paid the bribes to attain his vote on a property issue. The Escambia County Commission grew so corrupt with Childers as its chairman that the governor had to restructure the entire body. The whole incident resembled a soap opera. Junior once denied the allegations of accepting bribes, but turned on Childers after he was caught in thievery that could have earned him up to one hundred and twenty-five years in prison. Junior cut a deal with prosecutors in which he pleaded no contest to eleven charges, agreed to testify against Childers, and was guaranteed a prison sentence of no more than eighteen months. I have always thought it fitting that those who sided against me during the struggles for human dignity in the 1970s have had a very public falling from grace, while my dignity remains intact.

When I was in prison, my prayers almost always ended the same way: "Lord, please deal with those responsible for my being here." I fully believe that God played an active role in the public demise of those who conspired against me. As Romans 12:19 says, "Avenge not yourselves, but rather give place unto wrath: for it is written, Vengeance is mine; I will repay, saith the Lord." I want to make clear, however, that I have never tried to "sic" God on anyone. I did not want to see anyone killed with lightning bolts from the sky, or anything of that nature. A lust for revenge through God is not Christian. But I did pray that God's will be done and I wanted Him to deliver justice for those who tried to destroy my life. I fully believe that it was His will that their downfalls all happened

in a public forum and that I got to witness it all transpire. I did not feel
vindicated by the ordeals of Royal Untreiner, Doug Raines, Jim Edson,
W. D. Childers, and Willie Junior. Governor Askew's commutation of my
sentence and Governor Graham's pardon vindicated me. I did not believe
that their trials cleared me in the public's eyes, either. Those who believed
I was guilty have always felt that way, and nothing will ever change their
minds. On the other hand, those who knew that I was a political prisoner also felt that way since my 1975 arrest and nothing would change
their minds. But it did reinforce my belief that our God is a just God.
The ordeals that each of my past antagonists went through confirmed
that humans will answer for their transgressions. As Galatians 6:7 says,
"For whatsoever a man soweth, that shall he also reap." Despite the fact
that many of the individuals who persecuted me during the Pensacola
civil rights struggle encountered turmoil and disgrace in their personal
and professional lives, I never took pleasure in their suffering. I knew if
I rejoiced in their troubles that I would sink to their level. Besides, I am
too busy to waste time on such selfish pursuits because the struggle for
black equality in the United States still continues.

Many things trouble me about American race relations as the
twenty-first century begins. The problems African-Americans face have
diminished, but have by no means disappeared. There are forces at work
in this country that want to turn the clock back to a time that should
have never been, and the nation's citizens must know about it and fight
the disturbing trend. We are living in a society where some national
politicians are doing all they can to put out the torches of nonviolence,
of equal treatment, of equal protection, and affirmative action.

Racism, in other words, is running rampant in the United States,
but it is much more indirect than the days when blacks rode in the back
of the bus and used segregated restrooms. The new racism is much more
intellectual and intelligent. It takes place on the job when small errors are
magnified, employees are passed over for promotions, or dismissed for
no apparent reason. Blacks are still the last hired and first fired. If black
applicants are not labeled underqualified, they are deemed overqualified.
We are often still denied dignified treatment in places of public accom-

modation. Sometimes blacks are simply ignored, which is often worse than facing open hostility. I speak to these situations because they still happen. African-Americans are still not satisfied with and will never accept being treated as second-class citizens. Black churches are still being burned down. Young black kids are still being shot down by white police for the smallest offenses. We have been manacled with invisible chains; chains that do not bind us physically but bind us in spirit. As I have always said, those in power took the shackles off our behinds and put them on our minds. Laws have changed, but many attitudes toward those of the opposite race have not. Blacks are still reminded of our color, albeit in subtle ways.

For instance, there are still many racist parents who raise their children to be racists. I remember going into a grocery store in Pensacola some years ago when two children seated in a parked car called me a nigger. I asked where their parents were, and they said their father was in the store and described him. I went into the store, found the father, and told him what his children had said. He acted angry and said he was going to beat them when he got home. I told him, "There is no need to do that; just don't let them hear that word at home anymore." The man just turned and walked away after hearing my comments. For racial equality to become a reality in this nation, attitudes must change. But, sadly enough, the only way that is going to happen is through a massive dying-out of some adults. Kids are not born hating. They learn it.

Some giant steps and tremendous progress has been made in the area of race relations since the 1950s and 1960s, but that is not saying much. The civil rights gains of the past can be compared to Ernest Hemingway's *The Old Man and the Sea*. The fisherman was so proud of his catch that he had completely forgotten about the sharks when he strapped the huge fish to the side of his boat as he turned toward shore. As he traveled through the waters, he did not realize that sharks continuously nibbled at his catch. When he got home, all the fisherman had left was a carcass. Blacks have lulled themselves to sleep because they believe that after lunch counters and schools integrated, they had caught the big fish. But we forgot about sharks that are still in the water and strike at the modest gains blacks have made. In some cases, all blacks have left is the carcass of past victories. We still have a long way to go in having a truly equal society, but blacks must also work together to achieve this goal. Too many African-Americans still have a "plantation mentality" where they accept their fate and do not question the status quo out of fear of white reprisals. Blacks must reach the point where they do not only blame those who push them back or try to keep them "in their place." We have to share much of the blame ourselves. A disturbingly high number of blacks tend to sit passively by and say, "Somebody ought to do something to fight racism" and do nothing to change conditions on their own. All Americans should continue to demand equal treatment for their brothers and sisters, but many do not out of fear that they may experience a little inconvenience or lose some comforts they have. This particularly applies to many wealthy blacks.

Too many African-Americans retard the continuing struggle for racial justice because they are complacent. They have the nerve to say that the time for activism has passed. They say a need for demonstrations, boycotts, and marches in times of crisis are over. Some blacks even castigate activists who "start all of that civil rights mess" and treat civil rights activists with contempt. I tell them that they do not know what they are talking about. They need to understand how they got to where they are. It bothers me that many African-Americans know nothing about or attach very little significance to the struggle of the 1960s and 1970s. This is more understandable coming from some sections of the white community, but blacks are often just as ignorant. They have selective amnesia about what past struggles have done for them. Often those who were the direct beneficiaries of the movement grew content in their privileged positions and forgot about the sacrifices made to improve their lives. When Kunta Kinte was in the bottom of the ship that brought him from Africa to the New World, he expressed pain and dissatisfaction with his plight by rattling his chains. Many contemporary blacks have simply quit rattling the chains, and their crisis is ignored. It is disturbing that they seem to take for granted the fight that we went through to get where we are today. For instance, it enrages me to see any African-American of voting age who does not go to the polls on election day after what we endured at Selma to gain that right for them. The nation is not as fired up as it should be concerning civil liberties, particularly the black community, but I am still fired up. Young people say that the torch needs to be passed, but they need to realize that older people bought that torch with their blood.

Sometimes I feel discouraged and believe that my work was done in vain. I have even thought from time to time that I should put my interests first for a change. I have contributed more than my share to the movement. I have lost family members, money, and my very freedom because of my commitment to human equality. My track record is established. I and countless others know what I have done for humanity during my time on earth. Yet each time I feel that my time has passed and I should cease my activities, the Holy Spirit revives my soul again. As a child growing up in Snow Hill, I remember going to Rev. Dan House's Holiness Church and hearing a lady named Mrs. Brown singing, "The Lord is on our side, Emmanuel." The words did not register at the time because her voice was shrill and unpleasant. However, after I experienced some of the horrors which come with being black in this country, the words have taken on new meaning for me, so I will continue my fight.

I focus particularly on black voter registration and encourage them to go to the polls on election days. I investigate minority hiring patterns, particularly where blacks tend to spend their money, and also believe that combating illiteracy will bring greater opportunity for young African-Americans. Furthermore, I still vocally oppose blatant signs of hatred like the presence of Confederate flags, especially on government property. My argument against it at Escambia High School in the mid-1970s still holds true; the flag is a symbol of defiance to black equality and represents oppression. I do not want to be reminded on a daily basis of a time when black people were bought and sold like cattle. The issue is not meant to bring division or separate blacks from the white community. We ought to work together with the issue because its resolution could help bring understanding and will open dialogue between whites and blacks. Yet the Confederate battle flag and Civil War-era Rebel mascots still exist in far too many schools, which isolates blacks students. Its presence on state property is detrimental because tourists and business owners refuse to come to places that still honor the Confederate ideal. So it not only hurts me and other African-Americans in a very personal way, but it can also hurt local economies. The way that I thought the Confederate flag issue should be handled is simple. All blacks should put a Confederate flag license plate on their vehicle. It would not take a week before whites distanced themselves from the symbol.

In spite of my perpetual fight for righteousness in all contemporary society, I consider myself semi-retired from public affairs. People still come to me in time of need and I listen to their concerns. I remain everybody's pastor in Brewton when they need help. However, I do not always act according to their wishes. My current life has made me more judicious. Some of the restraint comes from past experiences, some of it comes from my responsibilities as a husband, and some of it comes from the fact that I am growing older. The leadership torch really must be passed. It is time that younger generations take up the fight for justice in our society. That is one reason that they should embrace freedom fighters from the past, not neglect them. We know what it takes to obtain justice, and they do not. We have been beaten, imprisoned, spat upon, sent to jail, and lost material possessions. We understand that public service is hard work that takes both courage and commitment, neither of which come easily for most people. We did not do what we did in the 1960s and 1970s for the publicity. The attention was a consequence of our struggle. Today, however, it seems that many seek the publicity and focus their activities upon whatever will bring the most attention to themselves. It seems that the dedication and commitment individuals must have to achieve their goals is missing. My gradual withdrawal from public life does not mean that my commitment to fair play has weakened; on the contrary. But it is no longer my era. I still possess hope, though, that the younger generation will learn from the past and continue to fight the good fight.

When I look back over my life, I am overwhelmed that God has used me in such a powerful way for so great a purpose. Racial reconciliation is one of the most important needs of the United States, but I never viewed my struggle as one of black against white; it was one of right against wrong. God is always right, regardless of the color of those involved in the issue. We are all created in His image and should treat each other the same way. Equal treatment is mandated by God and guaranteed by the American Constitution. No one, therefore, has a right to deny equality to any citizen for any reason. Interracial cooperation is still necessary and would only make our nation stronger. I use a piano reference to illustrate this point. If a musician only plays the black or white keys on a piano, they do not get the beautiful music they will when all keys are played together in harmony. Yet we remain out of tune as a nation. Racially-based prejudice continues to be one of the biggest problems facing contemporary America. We must come together as brothers and sisters, or we will die separated as fools. Short of dying, I believe I have done all that a person could to bring people closer together, and I do not regret anything I did or experienced during my fight for racial justice.

My personal satisfaction in the suffering and pain that I have endured has come in the relationship I have forged with my Lord. My faith is inseparable from my experiences as a civil rights leader. I have seen pure hatred and endured much undue suffering, but still prevailed because of my faith in God. It is because of the example set by Christ himself that I worked for the causes I have, and God protected me in times of extreme peril. If not for God, I would not have lived to recall my story. Yet I would not exchange my experiences for anyone's. My struggles, disappointments, trials, and tribulations have made me a better person. I am stronger, more tolerant, and have a heightened sense of compassion for my fellow man because of what I have been through. The crown jewel of my life, however, is that I have grown closer to God. I do know, from first-hand knowledge, that God answers prayers, provides strength at our weakest moments, dries our tears, and is not untouchable from any place at any time. I am a living testimony that it is God, and God alone, who can provide us with victory after the fall.

Notes

Introduction
1. *Pensacola Journal*, January 23, 1975.
2. *Pensacola Journal*, June 10, 1975; *Pensacola News*, July 17, 1975.
3. Aldon Morris, *Origin of the Civil Rights Movement: Black Communities Organizing for Change* (New York: Collier McMillan, 1984), 4. For the more recent studies of the African-American church, see C. Eric Lincoln and Lawrence Mamiya, *The Black Church in the African-American Experience* (Durham: Duke University Press, 1990); James Melvin Washington, *Frustrated Fellowship: The Baptist Quest for Social Power* (Macon: Mercer University Press, 1986); Paul Harvey, *Redeeming the South: Religious Cultures and Racial Identities Among Southern Baptists, 1865–1925* (Chapel Hill: University of North Carolina Press, 1997).
4. "The Administration of Justice in Pensacola and Escambia County: A Report Prepared by the Florida Advisory Committee to the U. S. Commission on Civil Rights," Florida Advisory Committee, Ted Nichols, Chairperson, April, 1981, 4–5.

1. Origins and Inspirations
5. Florida v. H. K. Matthews and B. J. Brooks, #75-2715, "Presentence Investigation," p. A–37, Florida Department of Archives and History, Tallahassee, Florida.
6. Florida v. H. K. Matthews and B. J. Brooks, #75-2715, "Presentence Investigation," p. A–37.
7. The word "nigger" is one of the most insulting, dehumanizing, and offensive in American history. However, I will use the term at points in this work when appropriate. To remove the term completely would present an inaccurate and misleading account of the past, but it is there where the word should remain.

2. Awaking A Sleeping Giant
8. *Pensacola News Journal*, April 1, 1960; *Pensacola News*, April 5, 1960; *Montgomery Advertiser*, April 6, 1960; *St. Petersburg Times*, April 7, 1960.
9. Advertisement, *Pensacola News Journal*, no date, author's collection.

3. Building Momentum
10. *Baltimore Afro-American*, December 30, 1961; *Montgomery Advertiser*, February 23, 1962; *Baltimore Afro-American*, October 13, 1962.
11. David Garrow, *Bearing the Cross: Martin Luther King, Jr., and the Southern Christian Leadership Conference* (New York: William Morrow, 1986), 396.
12. Dreamland Skating Rink announcement, May 20, 1968, author's collection.
13. The wash-in was covered by the *Pensacola Call and Post*, June 21, 1969.

4. The SCLC Comes to Northwest Florida
14. *Jet*, no month or page number, 1969, author's collection.
15. *Pensacola News*, August 27, 1969.

16. *Pensacola Journal*, October 5, 1969; *Pensacola Journal*, October 6, 1969.

17. Florida v. H. K. Matthews and B. J. Brooks, #75-2715, "Presentence Investigation," p. A–36.

18. *Pensacola News Journal*, March 16, 1969. For early local coverage of the SCLC in Escambia County, see *Broadview Magazine*, August, 1971, p. 12, 13, 16.

19. *Pensacola Call and Post*, June 7, 1969.

20. *Pensacola Call and Post*, June 14, 1969.

21. Letter, H. K. Matthews to Leighton H. Pearce, Florida State Employment Service Manager, April 14, 1969; Letter, L. F. Shebel, Florida State Employment Director to H. K. Matthews, April 30, 1969. Both in author's possession.

22. I taped a short meeting between myself and other SCLC members from across the state when we planned this rally. The recording that survives documented our plans to bring in a notable personality to lead the organizational rally, and details where we decided to have the meeting. See "Matthews Tapes," Vol. VIII, author's collection.

23. See "Matthews Tapes," Vol. VIII, author's collection.

24. Glover and Huff Drowning Report and Recommendations, August, 1970, in author's possession.

5. "Rebels," Riots, and Freedom Schools

25. "Matthews Tapes," Vol. XIII, author's collection.

26. *Pensacola News*, November 17, 1972; *Pensacola News*, November 18, 1972; *Pensacola Journal*, November 28, 1972.

27. *Pensacola News*, December 12, 1972; *Pensacola News*, December 13, 1972.

28. *Pensacola Journal*, December 14, 1972; *Pensacola News*, December 14, 1972; *Pensacola Journal*, December 15, 1972; *Pensacola Journal*, December 19, 1972; *Pensacola News Journal*, December 31, 1972.

29. *Pensacola Journal*, December 21, 1972; *Pensacola Journal*, December 22, 1972.

30. *Pensacola Journal*, December 23, 1972; *Pensacola Journal*, December 29, 1972; *Pensacola Journal*, December 30, 1972.

31. *Pensacola Journal*, January 2, 1973; *Pensacola News*, January 2, 1973; *Pensacola Journal*, January 3, 1973; *Pensacola News*, January 3, 1973.

32. *Pensacola Journal*, January 4, 1973; *Pensacola News*, January 4, 1973.

33. *Pensacola News*, January 5, 1973; *Pensacola Journal*, January 6, 1973.

34. *Atlanta World*, January 9, 1973; *Pensacola News*, January 10, 1973; *Pensacola Journal*, January 11, 1973; *Pensacola News*, January 11, 1973; *Pensacola Journal*, January 12, 1973.

35. *Pensacola Journal*, January 17, 1973.

36. *Pensacola Journal*, January 20, 1973.

37. *Pensacola Journal*, January 25, 1973; *Pensacola News*, January 25, 1973.

38. *Pensacola Journal*, February 1, 1973; *Pensacola News*, February 1, 1973.

39. *Pensacola Journal*, March 22, 1973; Florida v. H. K. Matthews, #73-911B, Escambia County Court Archives, Pensacola, Florida.

40. *Pensacola News*, July 10, 1973; *Pensacola News*, July 11, 1973; *Pensacola Journal*, July

12, 1973; *Pensacola Journal*, July 24, 1973; *Pensacola News*, July 24, 1973.

41. *Pensacola News*, July 24, 1973; *Pensacola Journal*, July 25, 1973; Augustus v. Board, July 24, 1973, 361 F.Supp.383.

42. Augustus v. Board, 361 F.Supp.383, "Order," July 24, 1973, case file; *Pensacola News*, July 26, 1973; *Pensacola Journal*, August 10, 1973; *Pensacola Journal*, October 10, 1973; *Pensacola Journal*, October 25, 1973.

6. December 1974: The Showdown Begins

43. *Pensacola News Journal*, December 1, 1974; *Pensacola Journal*, December 2, 1974; *Pensacola Journal*, December 4, 1974.

44. *Pensacola Journal*, December 2, 1974; *Pensacola News*, December 2, 1974; *Pensacola News Journal*, January 19, 1975.

45. *Pensacola Journal*, December 12, 1974.

46. *Pensacola Journal*, December 13, 1974; *Pensacola News Journal*, January 19, 1975.

47. *Pensacola Journal*, December 13, 1974; *Pensacola News Journal*, January 19, 1975.

48. *Pensacola Journal*, December 10, 1974; *Pensacola News*, December 12, 1974.

49. *Pensacola Journal*, December 10, 1974; *Pensacola Journal*, December 12, 1974; *Pensacola Journal*, December 13, 1974.

50. *Pensacola Journal*, December 12, 1974; *Pensacola Journal*, December 13, 1974.

51. *Pensacola Journal*, December 13, 1974.

52. *Pensacola Journal*, December 14, 1974; *Pensacola News Journal*, December 15, 1974.

53. *Pensacola Journal*, December 17, 1974; *Pensacola Journal*, December 28, 1974.

54. *Pensacola Journal*, December 13, 1974.

55. *Pensacola News Journal*, December 22, 1974; *Pensacola News Journal*, January 12, 1975.

56. *Pensacola Journal*, December 27, 1974.

57. *Pensacola News*, December 27, 1974; *Pensacola Journal*, December 28, 1974.

58. *Pensacola News*, December 27, 1974; *Pensacola Journal*, December 28, 1974.

59. "Matthews Tapes," Vol. IX, January, 1975, author's collection.

60. "Matthews Tapes," Vol. IX, January, 1975, author's collection.

61. *Pensacola News Journal*, no date, author's collection.

62. *Pensacola Journal*, January 9, 1975.

63. *Pensacola News Journal*, January 19, 1975; *Pensacola Journal*, January 22, 1975.

64. *Pensacola Journal*, January 23, 1975.

65. *Pensacola Journal*, January 23, 1975.

66. *Pensacola Journal*, February 1, 1975.

67. *Pensacola Journal*, January 25, 1975.

7. The Arrests and Their Effects

68. Sgt. Jim Edson, "Deputy Field Report," complaint number 343709, February 6, 1975; Edson, "Deputy Field Report," complaint number 343710, February 7, 1975;

NOTES

Edson, "Deputy Field Report," complaint number 342763, February 11, 1975; Edson, "Deputy Field Report," complaint number 343719, February 14, 1975; Edson, "Deputy Field Report," complaint number 344815, February 18, 1975.

69. Edson, "Deputy Field Report," complaint number 343709, February 6, 1975; Edson, "Deputy Field Report," complaint number 343712, February 8, 1975; Edson, "Deputy Field Report," complaint number 342763, February 11, 1975; Edson, "Deputy Field Report," complaint number 343719, February 14, 1975; Edson, "Deputy Field Report," complaint number 344813, February 19, 1975; Edson, "Deputy Field Report," complaint number 394814, February 20, 1975.

70. *Pensacola Journal*, February 22, 1975; Edson, "Deputy Field Report," complaint number 345574, February 21, 1975.

71. Edson, "Deputy Field Report," complaint number 345575, February 23, 1975; Richard Nix, "Deputy Field Report," complaint number 345576, February 23, 1975.

72. *Pensacola Journal*, February 25, 1975; *St. Petersburg Times*, March 2, 1975; Matthews v. Florida, #50350, Florida Supreme Court, July 27, 1978, 363 So.2d 1066; Florida v. Brooks, Billie Joe Sr., and Matthews, Hawthorne Konrade, #75-390, June 10, 1975, trial transcript, p. 13, case file, Florida State Department of Archives and History, Tallahassee, Florida.

73. *Pensacola News Journal*, March 2, 1975; *Pensacola News*, March 5, 1975; *Pensacola Journal*, March 3, 1975; *Pensacola News Journal*, March 9, 1975; *Pensacola News*, March 10, 1975; *Pensacola News*, March 15, 1975.

74. Edson, "Deputy Field Report," complaint number 344647, February 24, 1975.

75. Florida v. Brooks, Billie Joe Sr., and Matthews, Hawthorne Konrade, #75-390, July 26, 1976, First District Court of Appeals opinion, case file, Escambia County Courthouse; Edson, "Deputy Field Report," complaint number 344647, February 24, 1975; State v. Sylvester Gaines, et al., #75-2715-Z-MM, Officer W. K. Sandifer, "Affidavit of Complaint," February 24, 1975, case file, Escambia County Courthouse; *Pensacola News*, February 25, 1975; *Pensacola News*, June 10, 1975; *St. Petersburg Times*, March 2, 1975; State v. Robert T. Malden, #75-2715-AA, Arrest report, February 24, 1975, case file, Escambia County Courthouse; State v. Etta Hall Davis, #75-2715-DD, Arrest report, February 24, 1975, case file, Escambia County Courthouse; State v. James Leon Davis, #75-2715-BB, Arrest report, February 24, 1975, case file, Escambia County Courthouse; State v. Bertha Rene Bradley Jackson, #75-2715-CC, Arrest report, February 24, 1975, case file, Escambia County Courthouse; Florida v. Brooks, Billie Joe Sr., and Matthews, Hawthorne Konrade, #75-390, June 10, 1975, trial transcript, p. 2–3, 10–17, 22, case file, Escambia County Courthouse; Florida v. Brooks, Billie Joe Sr., and Matthews, Hawthorne Konrade, #75-390, June 27, 1975, "Extortion Complaints" and "Bond motion," case file, Escambia County Courthouse; *Pensacola Journal*, February 25, 1975, *Pensacola News*, February 25, 1975; *Pensacola Journal*, February 26, 1975; *Pensacola News Journal*, March 2, 1975; *Pensacola Journal*, September 10, 1975.

76. *Pensacola Journal*, February 25, 1975.

77. *Pensacola Journal*, February 26, 1975.

78. Edson, "Deputy Field Report," complaint number 345576, February 25, 1975; *St.*

Petersburg Times, March 2, 1975; *Pensacola Journal*, February 27, 1975; *Pensacola Journal*, February 26, 1975; *Pensacola News*, February 26, 1975; *Pensacola News*, February 27, 1975; Edson, "Deputy Field Report," complaint number 345577, February 26, 1975.

79. *Pensacola News*, February 27, 1975; *Pensacola Journal*, February 27, 1975; *Pensacola News*, February 28, 1975; *St. Petersburg Times*, March 2, 1975; Edson, "Deputy Field Report," complaint number 345579, February 27, 1975.

80. *St. Petersburg Times*, March 2, 1975.

81. *St. Petersburg Times*, March 2, 1975.

82. *Pensacola News*, March 17, 1975; *Pensacola News*, March 18, 1975; *Pensacola Journal*, March 18, 1975; *New York Times*, March 18, 1975; *Pensacola Journal*, March 21, 1975; James Edson Personnel File, Escambia County Civil Service Department, Pensacola, Florida.

83. *Pensacola Journal*, March 18, 1975.

84. *Pensacola News*, February 26, 1975; *Pensacola Journal*, March 15, 1975.

85. *New York Times*, March 18, 1975.

86. *Pensacola News*, May 3, 1975; *Pensacola Journal*, May 24, 1975; *Pensacola News*, May 26, 1975.

87. *Pensacola Journal*, May 24, 1975; *Pensacola News Journal*, May 25, 1975; *Pensacola News*, May 26, 1975.

88. Ronnie Nixon, "Deputy Field Report," complaint number 345126, March 3, 1975; *Pensacola Journal*, March 3, 1975; *Pensacola Journal*, March 4, 1975; *Pensacola Journal*, March 5, 1975; *Pensacola News*, March 5, 1975; *Pensacola Journal*, March 7, 1975; *Pensacola News*, March 10, 1975.

89. *Pensacola News Journal*, March 2, 1975; *Pensacola News*, March 5, 1975; *Pensacola Journal*, March 3, 1975; *Pensacola News Journal*, March 9, 1975; *Pensacola News*, March 10, 1975; *Pensacola News*, March 15, 1975.

90. *Pensacola News Journal*, March 2, 1975; *Pensacola Journal*, March 4, 1975; *Pensacola News*, March 5, 1975; Edson, "Deputy Field Report," complaint number 345581, February 28, 1975; H. K. Matthews interview with author, Brewton, Alabama, October 27, 2000.

8. A Legal Lynching

91. *Pensacola Journal*, March 27, 1975; *Pensacola Journal*, March 28, 1975; *Pensacola Journal*, April 26, 1975; B. J. Brooks v. Department of Transportation, Florida, #77-2163, case file, Escambia County Court, Archives and Records, "Career Service Commission" hearing, Pensacola, Florida, January 12, 1976.

92. *Pensacola Journal*, April 11, 1975; *Pensacola News*, April 17, 1975; *Pensacola Journal*, April 24, 1975; *Pensacola Journal*, April 26, 1975.

93. *Pensacola Journal*, March 27, 1975.

94. *Pensacola Journal*, March 20, 1975; *Pensacola Journal*, March 25, 1975; *Pensacola Journal*, March 26, 1975.

95. *Pensacola News*, March 20, 1975; *Pensacola Journal*, March 29, 1975; Radio report.

96. *Pensacola Journal*, March 29, 1975; *Pensacola News*, April 2, 1975; *Pensacola Journal*, April 3, 1975; *Pensacola Journal*, April 5, 1975.

97. *Pensacola Journal*, April 11, 1975; *Pensacola Journal*, April 17, 1975; *Pensacola Journal*, April 24, 1975.

98. *Pensacola Journal*, March 5, 1975; *Pensacola Journal*, May 1, 1975; *Pensacola Journal*, April 30, 1975; State v. Leverette, Matthews, Brooks, et al., #75-2716-MM, case file, Escambia County Courthouse; State v. Sylvester Gaines, et al., #75-2715-Y-MM, case file, Escambia County Courthouse; State v. Sylvester Gaines, et al., #75-2715-Z-MM, case file, Escambia County Courthouse; State v. Robert T. Malden, #75-2715-AA, case file, Escambia County Courthouse; State v. Etta Hall Davis, #75-2715-DD, case file, Escambia County Courthouse; State v. James Leon Davis, #75-2715-BB, case file, Escambia County Courthouse; State v. Berth Rene Bradley Jackson, #75-2715-CC, case file, Escambia County Courthouse.

99. *Pensacola Journal*, May 2, 1975; H. K. Matthews interview with author, Brewton, Alabama, October 27, 2000.

100. *Pensacola Journal*, May 7, 1975; *Pensacola Journal*, May 8, 1975.

101. *Pensacola News*, June 9, 1975.

102. *Pensacola News*, June 9, 1975; The State of Florida v. Hawthorne Konrad Matthews and Billie Joe Brooks, #75-390, June 9, 1975, trial transcript, Florida Department of Archives and Florida, Tallahassee, Florida, p. 82, 32–33, 36–37.

103. Florida v. Matthews and Brooks, #75-390, June 9 trial transcript, 4, 11, 30–31, 51.

104. Florida v. Matthews and Brooks, #75-390, June 9 trial transcript, 78, 87, 80, 89.

105. *Pensacola News*, June 9, 1975; *Pensacola Journal*, June 10, 1975; *Pensacola News*, June 10, 1975; Florida v. Brooks and Matthews, #75-390, May 25, 1975, "Request for Change of Venue," case file; Florida v. Brooks and Matthews, #75-390, "Affidavit: K. C. Bass," June 9, 1975, case file; Florida v. Brooks and Matthews, #75-390, "Affidavit: Elouise D. Savage," June 9, 1975, case file; Florida v. Brooks and Matthews, #75-390, "Motion For New Trial," June 18, 1975, case file.

106. Florida v. Matthews and Brooks, #75-390, June 9 trial transcript, 98, 104, 103, 106.

107. Florida v. Matthews and Brooks, #75-390, June 9 trial transcript, 104.

108. Florida v. Matthews and Brooks, #75-390, June 9 trial transcript, 130, 149, 133.

109. Florida v. Matthews and Brooks, #75-390, June 9 trial transcript, 135.

110. Florida v. Matthews and Brooks, #75-390, June 9 trial transcript, 143, 170.

111. Florida v. Matthews and Brooks, #75-390, June 9 trial transcript, 153-53.

112. Florida v. Matthews and Brooks, #75-390, June 9 trial transcript, 165, 167–68 and June 10, 1975, 22, 24.

113. Florida v. Matthews and Brooks, #75-390, June 10 trial transcript, 59.

114. Florida v. Matthews and Brooks, #75-390, June 10 trial transcript, 118–124; *Pensacola News*, June 10, 1975.

115. Florida v. Matthews and Brooks, #75-390, June 10 trial transcript, 62–71.

116. Florida v. Matthews and Brooks, #75-390, June 10 trial transcript, 99, 100.

117. Florida v. Matthews and Brooks, #75-390, June 10 trial transcript, 120–28.

118. Florida v. Matthews and Brooks, #75-390, June 10 trial transcript, 149, 164.

119. Florida v. Matthews and Brooks, #75-390, June 10 trial transcript, 176.

120. *Pensacola News*, June 11, 1975; *Pensacola News Journal*, July 13, 1975.

121. *Pensacola News*, June 11, 1975; *Pensacola Journal*, June 13, 1975; B. J. Brooks v. Department of Transportation, Florida, #77-2163, case file, Escambia County Court, Archives and Records, "Career Service Commission" hearing, Pensacola, Florida, January 12, 1976.

122. *Pensacola Journal*, June 19, 1975; *Pensacola Journal*, July 9, 1975.

123. *Pensacola News*, July 9, 1975; *Pensacola News*, July 10,1975.

124. *Pensacola News*, July 10, 1975; *Pensacola Journal*, July 11, 1975; *Pensacola News*, July 11, 1975; *Pensacola News Journal*, July 13, 1975.

9. The Fall

125. *Pensacola News*, July 17, 1975; "Copy of Presentence Investigation Report Concerning Hawthorne Konrad Matthews," July 16, 1975, Florida State Archives, Tallahassee, Florida.

126. *Pensacola Journal*, July 18, 1975; For more on the B. J. Brooks employment situation, see B. J. Brooks v. Department of Transportation, Florida, #77-2163, case file, Escambia County Court, Archives and Records, Pensacola, Florida.

127. *Pensacola Journal*, July 29, 1975; *Pensacola Journal*, August 2, 1975.

128. *Pensacola Journal*, July 25, 1975; *Pensacola Journal*, September 13, 1975.

129. *Pensacola Journal*, December 10, 1975.

130. *Pensacola Journal*, August 18, 1978; Letter, Reverend Joseph Lowery to SCLC Supporters, October/November 1978, author's collection.

131. Elaine R. Blackwell v. Royal Untreiner, Douglas Raines, and U. S. Fidelity and Guaranty Company, February 20, 1976, #76-651, Escambia County Circuit Court, Pensacola, Florida; Case File, Escambia County Court House Archives, Elaine R. Blackwell v. Royal Untreiner, Douglas Raines, and U. S. Fidelity and Guaranty Company, "Summary Judgement," November 14, 1977, "Denial for Rehearing," November 23, 1977, #76-651.

132. *Pensacola Journal*, August 4, 1975.

133. *Pensacola News*, August 5, 1975; *Pensacola News*, August 11, 1975; *Pensacola News*, August 12, 1975.

134. Florida v. Brooks and Matthews, #75-390, "Order," December 11, 1975, case file; Florida v. Brooks and Matthews, #75-390, "Petition to Reduce Sentence," December 22, 1975, case file; Florida v. Brooks and Matthews, #75-390, December 24, 1975; *Pensacola Journal*, December 23, 1975.

135. Florida v. Brooks and Matthews, #75-390, "Affidavit of Vincent Ponciano," December 12, 1975, case file; Florida v. Brooks and Matthews, #75-390, "Motion for New Trial," January 20, 1976, case file; Florida v. Brooks and Matthews, #75-390, "Order Denying Amended Motion for New Trial on Basis of Newly Discovered Evidence," March 1, 1976, case file.

136. *Pensacola Journal*, March 13, 1976.

137. *Pensacola Journal*, March 13, 1976; Matthews tapes, Vol. V.

138. *Pensacola News Journal*, March 7, 1976.

139. Florida v. Brooks and Matthews, #75-390, "Order Denying Amended Motion for New Trial on Basis of Newly Discovered Evidence," April 26, 1976, case file.

140. Florida v. Brooks and Matthews, #75-390, July 26, 1976, First District Court of Appeals opinion, case file; *Pensacola News*, July 26, 1976; *Pensacola News*, August 10, 1976; *Pensacola Journal*, August 12, 1976.

141. *Pensacola Journal*, August 5, 1976; *Pensacola News Journal*, August 15, 1976.

142. H. K. Matthews v. Florida, case file. *Pensacola Journal*, September 20, 1976; *Pensacola Journal*, September 22, 1976.

143. *Pensacola News*, September 20, 1976; *Pensacola Journal*, September 21, 1976; *Pensacola News Journal*, October 2, 1988.

144. *Pensacola News*, October 22, 1976; *Pensacola News*, February 9, 1977; *Pensacola News*, February 10, 1977; *Pensacola News*, February 14, 1977.

145. *Pensacola Journal*, March 13, 1976; Author's collection.

146. *Pensacola Journal*, May 31, 1975; *Pensacola Journal*, July 8, 1975; *Pensacola News*, July 10, 1975; *Pensacola Journal*, February 5, 1976; *Pensacola News*, February 5, 1976; *Pensacola Journal*, February 6, 1976.

147. *Pensacola Journal*, March 18, 1976; *Pensacola Journal*, April 22, 1976; *Pensacola Journal*, April 24, 1976; *Pensacola News*, April 26, 1976; *Pensacola News*, April 28, 1976; *Pensacola News*, April 29, 1976; *Pensacola Journal*, August 11, 1977; *Pensacola Journal*, August 15, 1977; *Pensacola Journal*, September 2, 1977; *Pensacola Journal*, September 8, 1977; *Pensacola Journal*, September 15, 1977.

148. *Pensacola News Journal*, July 10, 1977; *Pensacola Journal*, July 12, 1977; *Pensacola Journal*, July 13, 1977; *Pensacola Journal*, July 14, 1977; *Pensacola Journal*, July 16, 1977; *Pensacola Journal*, August 10, 1977; *Pensacola News Journal*, September 12, 1976.

149. H. K. Matthews v. Florida, "Brief of Appellant," March 2, 1977, case file; H. K. Matthews v. Florida, "Reply Brief of Appellant," April 7, 1977, case file.

150. *Pensacola News*, July 28, 1978; Matthews v. Florida, #50350, Florida Supreme Court, July 27, 1978, 363 So.2d 1066.

151. *Pensacola Journal*, July 28, 1978; *Pensacola Journal*, July 29, 1978; *Pensacola Voice*, July 15, 1978.

152. *Pensacola News*, December 13, 1978; *Pensacola Journal*, December 14, 1978; *Pensacola Journal*, December 15, 1978; *Pensacola Journal*, December 26, 1978, *St. Petersburg Times*, December 12, 1978.

10. Victory

153. *Pensacola News Journal*, June 11, 2000; *Pensacola News Journal*, June 29, 2000; *Pensacola News Journal*, July 1, 2000; *Pensacola News Journal*, July 17, 2000.

154. *Pensacola News*, July 28, 1975; "Notice of Disciplinary Action," August 10, 1981, Douglas Raines Personnel File, Escambia County Civil Service Department, Pensacola, Florida; "Order," March 25, 1982, Douglas Raines Personnel File, Escambia County Civil Service Department.

ADDITIONAL READINGS

V*ictory After the Fall* complements the growing scholarship concerning the Florida civil rights movement. For more on racial struggle in the Sunshine State, see Abel Bartley, *Keeping the Faith: Race, Politics, and Social Development in Jacksonville, Florida, 1940-1970* (Greenwood Press: 2000), David R. Colburn, *Racial Change and Community Crisis: St. Augustine, Florida, 1877-1980* (Columbia University Press: 1985), Edward D. Davis, *A Half Century of Struggle for Freedom in Florida* (Drake's Publishing: 1981), David Garrow, *St. Augustine, Florida, 1963-1964: Mass Protest and Racial Violence* (Carlson Publishing Inc.: 1989), Ben Green, *Before His Time: The Untold Story of Harry T. Moore, American's First Civil Rights Martyr* (University Press of Florida: 2005), Raymond Mohl, *South of the South: Jewish Activists and the Civil Rights Movement in Miami, 1945-1960* (University Press of Florida: 2004), Glenda A. Rabby, *The Pain and the Promise: The Struggle for Civil Rights in Tallahassee, Florida* (University of Georgia Press: 1999), Robert W. Saunders, *Bridging the Gap: Continuing the Florida NAACP Legacy of Harry T. Moore, 1952-1966* (University of Tampa Press: 2000), Charles Smith, ed., *The Civil Rights Movement in Florida and the United States: Historical and Contemporary Perspective* (Father and Son Publishing, Inc.: 1989). To verify certain dates and events that occurred outside of Escambia County during the civil rights movement, the authors used Taylor Branch's magnificent trilogy for reference. See *Parting the Waters: America in the King Years, 1954-63* (Simon & Schuster: 1988), *Pillar of Fire: America in the King Years, 1963-65* (Simon & Schuster: 1998), and *At Canaan's Edge: America in the King Years, 1965-68* (Simon & Schuster: 2006).

Index

Kendrix, Rev. J. H. 79
Kennedy, John F. 168
Kennedy, Robert 168
Key, Eugene 279
King, Coretta Scott 210
King, Martin Luther, 18-20, 22, 67, 72,
    85, 92, 105, 125, 139, 168, 171, 191,
    203, 254-255, 268, 289, 301, 303-305
    Commemorative Committee, Pensacola
    See Pensacola Martin Luther King
    Commemorative Committee
    Matthews compared to 11, 28, 282,
    299-300
    1965 Selma march 86, 89-90
King, Wayne 198
Kinte, Kunta 314
Korean War 21, 48-50, 61
Kress Department Store (Pensacola) 61,
    65, 70
Ku Klux Klan 19, 90, 118-120, 197, 199-
    200, 256-257, 276, 283. See also Gulf
    Coast Knights of the Ku Klux Klan;
    Pensacola, Ku Klux Klan; United Klans
    of America (UKA)
Kwanzaa Committee of Pensacola See Pen-
    sacola, Kwanzaa Committee of
Kyle, Merenda 143

L

Lake Butler Processing Center 242-243,
    245-247, 249, 252-253, 263, 270-273,
    281
Langergren, Walter 221-222, 239, 260,
    262-263
Lanier, Eddie 167
Lee, Bernard 157
Lee Square, Robert E. (Pensacola) 177
Lee, Spike 39
Leeper, Richard 130, 133-134
Leroy, Admiral 123
Leverette, Rev. Otha 108, 130-131, 135,
    141, 145, 157, 160, 166-167, 170, 175,
    180, 184-186, 191, 193, 214, 219-220,
    236, 239, 242, 250, 259-260, 265, 270-
    271, 277
Lewis, John 86-88
Liberty Lanes Bowling Alley 94-95
Little Rock, Arkansas 48
Liuzzo, Violet 90
Live Oak, Florida 117
London, England 226

Lott, Isadore 39-40
Lowery, Joseph 254
Lowndes County, Alabama 90

M

McDougal See Matthews, attempted assas-
    sination
Magnolia Nursing Home 263-264
Malcolm X 299
Marion, Alabama 85
Marshall, Rev. William 13, 263-264
Marshall, Thurgood 203
Mason, Doris 155-156
Mathis, Greg 307
Matthews, Bobbie Ann Avant 12, 285-287,
    296
Matthews, Charlie 36
Matthews, Christopher Jonathan 12, 285,
    295, 304
Matthews, John Henry 35
Matthews, Louveenia Johnson 35
Matthews, Rev. Hawthorne Konrad. See
    also Escambia County Jail, demonstra-
    tions at
alleged "assassination" chant 16, 26, 181,
    189-190, 192, 226, 228-233, 237, 263
    arrests 104, 114, 149, 187-188
    attempted assassination 119-120
    awards and honors 298-302, 305
    and black employment campaigns See
        Pensacola, black employment in and
        black voter registration See NAACP,
        Voting Program
    departure from Pensacola 30, 114
    February 24, 1976 arrest 15-16, 19
    felony trial 211, 219, 222-238
    felony sentence 248-249
    first experience with racism 40-41
    imprisonments 241-243, 244-248,
        271-273
    and J. Michael Butler 10-12, 29-31
    labor activities See Pensacola Baptist
        Hospital, employee strike of; Sacred
        Heart Hospital, employee strike of
    military service 48-51
    and NAACP Adult Branch 92, 101-
        104, 107, 151-152
    and NAACP Youth Council 64-65, 85,
        92, 94-98, 101, 127, 152
    and participation in 1965 Selma dem-
        onstrationSee "Selma to Montgomery

O

Okaloosa County 116, 122
Old Field AME Zion Church 267
Old Man and the Sea, The 313
Orange, James 255
Outfront Magazine "Lifetime Achievement Award for Civil Rights" 300

P

Pak-A-Sak store 123
Palafox Street 61, 74, 83-84, 92, 94
Parks, Rosa 203
Pascagoula, Mississippi 256-257
Paul Robeson Award 13
Peaden, R. W. "Smokey" 129, 131-133, 136-139, 145-147, 151, 278
Pensacola 9-15, 21-22, 36, 45, 51-55, 58-60, 81, 89, 101, 108, 115-118, 121, 130, 135-136, 141-143, 149, 152-153, 155-163, 166-170, 172-181, 184-185, 191-200, 202-203, 205, 207-213, 215-221, 223-226, 233, 238, 240, 243-244, 246, 250-261, 263-264, 266-271, 273-277, 279-280, 284-288, 291-292, 299-306, 308-310, 312-313
    black employment in, 74-77, 82-84, 92-93, 98-99, 109,113, 120-124. *See also* Pensacola Baptist Hospital, employee strike of; Sacred Heart Hospital, employee strike of
    black voter registration in *See* NAACP, Voting Program
    Civil rights movement in, 17-19, 24-28, 126. *See also* Escambia County, Florida, civil rights movement in
    black resistance to 202-208, 211-212, 258-259, 265-266, 291
    white support of 73-74,145
    Ku Klux Klan 65, 72. *See also* United Klans of America (UKA)
    NAACP *See* National Association for the Advancement of Colored People, Pensacola chapter
    race relations in, 61-67, 85, 99, 147, 227, 234
    sit-ins *See* Sit-ins, downtown Pensacola
Pensacola Baptist Hospital of, 59-60
    employee strike of, 101-105
Pensacola Bay Bridge 305
Pensacola Beach 61, 123
Pensacola Call and Post 112

Pensacola City Council 99
Pensacola Chamber of Commerce 218, 305
Pensacola Community Action Program (CAP) 274-275
Pensacola Council of Ministers (PCM) 22-23, 62-67, 79, 81
    and sit-ins *See* Sit-ins, downtown Pensacola
Pensacola Fire Department 98
Pensacola First Baptist Church, 73
Pensacola First Methodist Church 73
Pensacola First Presbyterian Church 182
Pensacola Hardware 183
Pensacola High School 96-98, 126
Pensacola Human Relations Commission *See* Escambia-Pensacola Human Relations Commission
Pensacola Journal See Pensacola News Journal
Pensacola Junior College 13
Pensacola, Kwanzaa Committee of, 14, 28, 300
Pensacola Martin Luther King Commemorative Committee 306
Pensacola Municipal Auditorium 139
Pensacola Naval Air Station 83, 97
Pensacola News See Pensacola News Journal
Pensacola News Journal 13, 65, 67, 75, 77, 79, 99-100, 128, 132-133, 135-136, 139, 151, 153-155, 157, 160-161, 165, 170, 176, 182-184, 188, 195-199, 213-215, 218-219, 222, 225, 233, 236, 238, 241, 243, 248-249, 269, 271, 283, 298, 308
Pensacola Police Department 98
Pensacola Speedway 198
Pensacola Voice 281
Pensacola YMCA 92
Philadelphia, Pennsylvania 264
Pierce, Leighton 91
Pleezing's Supermarket 96
Plights, Rev. Jim 73
Ponciano, Vince 263
Posey, Joseph 54
Posey, Josephine 54
Posey, Mary Lee 54
Potter, Deputy 120
Presley, Elvis 51
Pritchett, Eldred 294, 296

Q

Quincy, Florida 107, 115

Printed in the United States
107457LV00002B/286-333/A

9 781603 060004